Literature, Integration and Harmony in Northern Nigeria

Edited by

Hamzat I. Abdulraheem
Saeedat B. Aliyu
Ruben K. Akano

KWARA STATE UNIVERSITY PRESS

© Northern Nigerian Literature Conference, 2017

Published by
Kwara State University Press
Kwara State University Press, Malete
PMB 1530 ILORIN
Kwara State, Nigeria
Email: kwasupress.edu.ng, kwasupress@gmail.com

ISBN: 978-978-54870-2-2
First Published 2017

All rights reserved:
No part of this book may be reproduced ortransmitted in any form or by any means without prior writtenpermission of Kwara State University Press.

Contents

Foreword ix

Editors' Note xiii

Chapter 1: Integrating the North Through Sustenance of Its Literature
Olu Obafemi 1

Chapter 2: Dramatic Theatre: A Nexus for Resurgence in the Twenty-First Century Northern Nigeria
Abdullahi Salih Abubakar 11

Chapter 3: Northernism in Northern Nigerian Literature: A Study of al-Yāqūtī's *'Abarātul-Amal*
Abdulrazaq M. Katibi & Aliyu O. Ahmad 27

Chapter 4: Traditional Songs as Catalysts for Integration: A Study of Selected Ìlọrin Traditional Songs
Hakeem Ọláwálé 43

Chapter 5: Language and Ideology in Tuface Idibia's Music
Oluwatomi Adeoti & Moshood Zakariyah 57

Chapter 6: Sunnie Ododo's *Broken Pitchers* and *the (Im)possibilities* of National Resurgence

Kayode Niyi Afolayan 71

Chapter 7: Originality in Absentia: A Study of Selected Kannywood Films

Muhammad Muhsin Ibrahim 85

Chapter 8: Odolaye Aremu's Multifunctional Genre and Songs of Exorcism

Kehinde Akano, Abbibah Zaka & Garuba Giwa 99

Chapter 9: Religious Interpretations and Their Implications on the Society in Abubakar Gimba's *Sacred Apples* and Elnathan John's *Born on a Tuesday*

Sarat Adenike Salihu 111

Chapter 10: The Didactic Dimension of Proverbs: A Study of Aliyu Kamal's *Hausa Girl*

Sani Abubakar 127

Chapter 11: The True Images of Northern Nigeria in Kamal's *Hausaland*

Hasheem Abdullahi Tanko 141

Chapter 12: Transforming the Society Through Indigenous Practices: The "Iyawo-Ile" Institution in Okunland as a Case Study

Olushola Ayodeji Akanmode 151

Chapter 13: National Integration in Jamil Abdullahi's *Idfa' Billati Hiya Ahsan*

Abdulrazaq M. Katibi 171

Chapter 14: Ideologies in Conflict: A Critical Discourse Analysis of Auwalu Yusufu Hamza's "Cheating Destiny"
Rabi Abdulsalam Ibrahim..................................... 183

Chapter 15: Re-Thinking the Woman in Northern Nigerian Literature
Abubakar Othman & Razinat Mohammed............ 197

Chapter 16: Theatre for Development and Women Empowerment in Northern Nigeria: A Study of 2015 *Kuyambana* Development Communication Field Experience
Jubril Abdullahi & Habeeb Adebayo Salaudeen... 213

Chapter 17: Language and Cultural Values: The African Socio-Perception to Greetings
Anne Omotayo Alaiyemola 229

Chapter 18: الحرب ضد الإرهاب: دراسة تحليلية لقصيدة عيسى ألَّي أبوبكر

تاج الدين يوسف................................... 243

Chapter 19: مظاهر التآلف في قصة "مأساة الحب" لحامد إبراهيم الهجري

يونس محمّد جامع................................... 253

Notes on Contributors 269

Index.. 271

Foreword

This, yet again, is a harvest of Literature scholarship on Northern Nigeria, ever growing and ever so penetrating, ever so rich! The theme of this year's publication reflects the search-lights adopted by scholars during the last Conference to examine how the literatures of Northern Nigerian peoples have immensely contributed to community integration and community harmony. Evidence of the extraordinary diversity of Northern Nigeria is in the fact that every state of the region - Borno, Kebbi, Plateau, Kwara, Niger, and so on, are pluralistic in language and ethnicity. In fact, there is no part of Nigeria that has the level of ethnic plurality as that of the North, and yet, the popular image that comes through to Nigerians is the homogeneity of the peoples of the North. This is not so much of a negative concept and I will elucidate.

In the face of so large a diversity in a community, the rhetoric of similarity, rather than the rhetoric of difference, took over as the dominating force. This was to promote community regeneration and reinforce commonality among the diverse groups that belong to this region. Much of the early politicians from the North, such as Sir Ahmadu Bello and Sir Tafawa Balewa, among others, promoted this and they deserve to take some credit for this. Importantly too, accolade must be given to cultural producers throughout the North for encouraging this perception. To give dominance to the rhetoric of difference in such circumstance would create tensions that could lead to total and complete disaster. I believe that what the founding politicians of the North mastered before Independence was to mobilise cultural producers such as oral singers to generate songs of unity. Many songs by Mamman Shata Kastina, Dan Maraya Jos, Sanni Dandawo Yauri, Jaigbade Alao Ilorin and others, were messages from politicians to the people, messages promoting unity amongst the people.

I remember one of such lyrics, that of Ilorin's traditional oral partisan poet, the legendary Odòlayé Àrẹ̀mú (1990) who metaphorically calls himself the "Dog of Kwara State that barks with a purpose". He sings that:

Odòlayé Àrẹ̀mú,	Odòlayé Àrẹ̀mú
Ajá Kùárà tí kìí gbó lásán	The dog of Kúárà who doesn't bark without a cause
Bí ò bá rẹran	If he hasn't seen a goat
A sì réèyàn!	He must have seen a human being!
Béèyàn ọ̀ dáa	If a person isn't good
A à ní pọ́ dáa	We won't say he is good
Béèyàn ọ̀ sunhàn	If a person is not decent,
A à ní pó sunhàn,	We won't say he is decent
Àwa náà ọ̀ mà ní figbá kan bọ̀kan ńnú!	We too would never put one calabash into another!

I doubt if any other Nigerian oral poet ever even came close to achieving the feat that Odòlayé performed in the Second Republic, through singing and mobilising for the Unity of Nigeria. His "One Nigeria" song, would say, "from Sokoto, to Kaduna, to everywhere, there should be one Nigeria"! He sang for Shagari, he sang for Saraki, and he sang for the Hausa, the Fulani, the Yoruba, and the Ibo. He explored their commonalities and asked for all to unite.

The thrust of this scholarly book is to find such common threads for unity in cultural productions in Northern Nigeria. From the films, to the kalangu music, to the written literatures, to all sorts of artistic creations, scholars' attention is on how contemporary writers of Northern Nigeria have taken a clue from their literature-producing ancestors. I recommend this fine collection to all who love to read very rich critical and analytical thoughts on Northern Nigerian literature and culture. Even in the face of the murderous Boko Haram, and the persistent agitation for secession from certain Nigerian quarters, cultural products coming from Northern Nigeria, have been vehement about integration and harmony and this book is dedicated to showing how. From works of Kannywood to other forms of dramatic literature, to novels, to poetry and all forms of oral traditions, and to different kinds of cultural and ideological practices, and to literature written in Arabic, Hausa and many other numerous languages spoken in Northern Nigeria, the book promises to be a great companion to students and scholars interested in Northern Nigerian literature and culture.

Finally, this project is also a demonstration of the unity of purpose of the great Bayero University, Kano (BUK) and the Kwara State University (KWASU), to ensure that Northern Nigerian literature continues to earn vigorous readings, purposeful criticisms and analyses, and forever record continued growth as these two universities combine forces to keep the flag of the annual Conference on Literature in Northern Nigerian flying, ensuring that similar publication comes out every year.

Reference:

Odòlayé Àrẹ̀mú. (1990). Olowe Mowe. NEMI 0654B.

Abdul-Rasheed Na'Allah
Vice-Chancellor, Kwara State University

KWARA STATE UNIVERSITY, MALETE

The University For Community Development

The First (1st) Inaugural Lecture

Title

Aeronautics and Astronautics: The Paradigm Shift in Nigeria's Future Space Exploration and Development

By

Professor Leonard F. Daniel

B.Sc./M.Sc. (Soviet Academy of Sciences, NTU), Ph.D. (London), COREN, C.Eng., C.Sci., EUR Ing, AFAIAA, FIM3, FRAeS

Professor of Aeronautics and Astronautics,
Department of Aeronautics and Astronautics
and
Provost College of Engineering and Technology,
Kwara State University, Malete, Nigeria

Date: May 03, 2017

ISBN 978-978-54870-1-5

To obtain your copy, please contact:

Kwara State University Press
Kwara State University, Malete
PMB 1530, Ilorin, Kwara State, Nigeria
Email: kwasupress@kwasu.edu.ng; kwasupress@gmail.com

Editors' Note

The northern part of Nigeria has been disadvantaged in many aspects of development compared to other parts of the country. Leaders of thought in the area, academics and politician try to find lasting solutions to the backwardness and poverty in the region. Literary artists on their part, having seen literature as an important tool to combat societal ills confronting the North, have decided to organise conferences to address various issues affecting the North. Two of such conferences were held at the Kwara State University in 2015 and 2016 where scholarly papers were presented, the product of which is this book titled *Literature, Integration and Harmony in Northern Nigeria*.

Readers will, in this book, be opportuned to read about insurgence that has ravaged the North as well as issues relating to the efforts being made through literature to bring about integration and harmony. Olu Obafemi advocated for the sustenance of literary activities as a way of integrating the geopolities that constitute Northern Nigeria, while Hakeem Ọláwálé considered traditional songs as catalyst for integration in the area. In his contribution, Abdullah Abubakar discussed the role of dramatic theatre in passing coordinated thoughts to larger audience irrespective of the level of education.

In their view, Katibi and Ahmad examined an Arabic work by an Ilorin writer where Northern values and norms were enumerated and discussed with the purpose of getting the concept of Northernism and literary expression. Another important issue in this discourse is the misinterpretation of religious texts which has created misunderstanding among people and has led to religious bigotry and fanaticism as Sarat Salihu discussed in her paper and condemned the use of religious sentiments for selfish purpose. She therefore advocated peaceful co-existence based on fairness and justice among various sections in the society.

In the same vein, Saarat Salihu discussed misinterpretation of religion texts and religious misunderstanding as major factors for religious fanatical as bigotry and called for proper religion understanding for proper integration.

The joint contribution of Katibi and Ahmad examined certain northern values that unite the region which should be encouraged to drive the thinking and actions of the people of the area.

In their joint submission, Adeoti and Zakariyah considered music as an important tool of reshaping the society using Tuface Idibia's music as an example. Akano, Zaka and Giwa also examined popular music with special reference to Odolaye Aremu's music and showed the potency of music in instilling self discipline and standard moral behaviour all of which have bearing on mutual understanding and harmony. Also looking at the importance of proverbs in inculcating moral lessons, Sani Abubakar examined didactic dimensions of proverbs as contained in Aliyu Kamal's *Hausa Girl* and posits that despite the impact of foreign cultures, the indigenous system of moral pedagogy is still relevant. The position of Akanmode also pointed to the need for the North to transform the society for better understanding through indigenous practices.

The concern of these literary scholars about national integration was not limited to the writers in English or Hausa, writers in Arabic have also shown similar concern for integration as a prerequisite for development. This is what Abdulrazaq Katibi discussed in Jamil Abdallah's Arabic novel, *Idfa billati hiya ahsan,* and advocated for social, political and cultural integration irrespective of linguistic and religious backgrounds. Abdullahi and Adebayo explored women empowerment in Northern Nigeria and considered it critical in fostering development in the North.

The last two articles written in Arabic are by Tajudeen Yusuf and Yunusa Jamiu. The first one discussed terrorism as contained in a poem by Issa Abubakar while the second one examined aspect of integration in a novel by al-Hijry. Both called for integration and harmony in the North and condemned terrorism of all kinds.

Altogether, the contributions in this book give the readers the opportunity to be abreast of such important issues concerning integration and harmony in Northern Nigeria.

Hamzat I. AbdulRaheem
Saeedat B. Aliyu
Reuben K. Akano

Chapter 1

Integrating the North Through Sustenance of Its Literature

Olu Obafemi

Preamble

It is a matter of great delight for me to be invited to participate in this year's edition of Northern Nigerian Literature Summit (or what I have always preferred to call it, Literature in the Northern States, now broken into geo-political zones as North West, North East and North Central) taking place in Ilorin but co-hosted by Kwara State University and Bayero University, Kano. I have been actively involved in the Northern Nigerian Literature Conferences. In an early edition of the series of Conferences, I had raised all the rhetorical, definitional and conceptual issues on the whys and wherefores of Northern Nigeria or its Literature, its essential features and character; its informing ideologies and politics—even its production sociology. I shall therefore address simpler issues, which I consider still critical and relevant to ethno-national, national and inter-national discourses, which I insist, this Summit must embrace.

In this paper, purely on account of time constraint, I shall merely raise issues on the all-important question of sustaining literary creativity in Northern Nigeria, as the only way that literature, as a reflector and refractor of society, and society for that matter, can participate in any conception of socio-political integration of the geo-polities that constitute Northern Nigeria or the zones in the old Northern Nigeria formation. I shall also take for granted that the question of developing and nurturing this literature is implied as an underlining perception and conception. I shall also assume that writing in indigenous languages is already accepted as imperative and inviolable in any attempt to find authentic roads to the communal minds and spirit of the diverse people strung together, quite haphazardly, in the unhealthy process described as forming the Northern Protectorate that was amalgamated with the Southern Protectorate in 1914.

Since the dismantling of the regions and the creation of states in 1967 and the subsequent exercises that followed which brought Nigeria to 36 uneven states, the whole essence of Northern Nigeria as a region, and the other two or three regions, has, for all concrete, material and practical purposes, diminished. The heroes, who symbolised the idealism of regionalism achieved through development and inclusiveness in a very competitive fashion, have become sources of national nostalgia. Why is it that the few symbols of our heroic ideals are the personages from the distant past – Chief Awolowo is a beacon of illumination and icon of development for the South West, nay the President that the nation threw away. Sir Ahmadu Bello is the only reminder of the ideal North, different from the myth of the core North that is played up today. The Zik of Africa gave inspiration to the formation of the radical Zikist Movement though he did not swim with it. Aminu Kano inspired the first robust mass-centred Talakawa Movement leading the opposition to the NPC as political definers of the old North, and so on.

As we all know and have lamented in the past two decades, the literary enterprise, like the whole question of literacy in Western education, is under-developed in the Northern states—a defining concept that I have always preferred to Northern Nigeria for many reasons which lie outside of the purview of this present exercise. This is even more glaring when a comparatist approach is adopted—comparing the literary enterprise in the North with its Southern counterpart. The gap has narrowed, considerably, in recent times. But there is certainly still a lacuna to fill—if indeed there is an unwitting competition—in the spirit of positive and healthy rivalry—not in this spirit of a lament or an escape into a certain kind of unedifying insularity.

In a rather sketchy fashion, I shall take a brief look at the history (profile) of creative production in the region, the vital situation of publishing, and a proposal for nurturing, enhancing and sustaining creative writing in the 'Region'.

History

In 1982, The American Africanist and African literary historian and critic, Bernth Lindfors, drew a table of Nigerian Literary Works published between 1952 and 1967. He came up with 32 novels, 28 plays, and 10 books of poetry— a total of 70 published literary works. Note, of course, that works in Nigerian languages were not listed nor counted. There was hardly any mention of any author of Northern Nigerian descent. By 1985, however, a booklist, on stock and price basis, was made by the most notable publisher of literary works in the North, the Northern Nigerian Publishing Company (NNPC). It came up with 68 titles, mostly male authors, if I may add—and this is in spite of the covetable legacy and inspirational source provided by Nana Asmau, the prolific daughter of Shehu Usman dan Fodiyo, the great Islamic reformist, who had pioneered the composition of poems in Arabic and Fulfulde since the second half of the Nineteen century. No need to draw an equivalent from the South, where, as a result of the early incursion of western imperialists and a conscious emergence of multi-national publishing houses - Macmillan, Heinemann, Longman, University Press Limited and so on - based exclusively in the South and with no branches at all in the North, published creative products were in opulent ferment. Happily, today, the creative writing culture has blossomed in the Northern States.

In 2004, I embarked upon and published, on behalf of *The Sun Newspapers*, 21 Nigerian female writers, quite randomly. As it turned out, eight of them were women writers of northern origin—and nearly half of the writers/critics who wrote on them were writers from the North. Northern literature is on the high rise, thanks to the inspiration derived from the award-winning feats attained by the middle and young generations of Northern writers like Zaynab Alkali, Abubakar

Gimba, Yahaya Dangana, the current literary phenomenon – Helon Habila, and the flourish of Creative Writing Associations like the Samaru Writers' Club, the Association of Nigerian Authors (ANA) which is currently receiving its greatest boom from the Northern Chapters in Minna, Kano, Abuja, Maiduguri, Makurdi, Sokoto, Lokoja and so on.

We must not forget the import of the explosive creative burst of the popular literary tradition (famously called *Soyaya*) beginning from the nineties, i.e. the Kano Market Literature, which echoes, quite significantly, the Onitsha Market Literature. This has produced and circulated over 3000 love and romance novels from numerous competing writing clubs. Its emergence and growth are largely attributable to the impact and influence of the electronic media, particularly the Federal Radio Corporation of Nigeria (FRCN), with its multi-million audience capacity. It features readings and has been deployed by writers to enhance and popularise their creative works. Talking about nurturing a literary culture in the North, the electronic and print media will need to be more consciously recoursed and the creative writer in the north and anywhere in our country and continent today must extend his or her scripted story to Nollywood, through which our nation is vigorously entering the global market, with all its economic and cultural implications.

Talking briefly about generic profiles and epochs, many generations of Northern writing in English can be discerned, i.e. if we foreground the indigenous language literature dominated by Hausa, expectedly, as the lingua franca of the region then. Feeding on the Hausa classics of between the 1930s and 1950s, Hausa fiction in the eighties proliferated. We may mention the literary output of Shamsudeen Amali and his promotion of the Idoma language in his plays, some of which are bi-lingual—English and Idoma. His play *Onugbo Mi'oko*, is a bilingual, pioneering Idoma text meant to give fillip to the 'renaissance of the Idoma language and literature'.

Amali thus forms, by extension, a part of the first generation of creative writers of the 70s and 80s of the North of English expression, in a list that includes Muhammadu Sule, Lao Yari, Ibrahim Tahir, Ta Ahura, Adah Ugah, Zaynab Alkali, Olu Obafemi, Harry Hagher,

Abubakar Gimba, the late Mamman Vatsa, Joseph Mangut, Aliyu Jibia, Stella Oyedepo, Muhammad Tukur Garba, Mu'azu Maiwada and Segun Oyekunle. This list, by no means exhaustive, is drawn to reveal that, contrary to the scant picture of Northern writers of this period usually painted and marginally talked about in critical circles, there is a viable body of writers in the region of that period and beyond.

Another generation (or a generation-complex or motley) evolved and its emergence can be traced, in part, to the growth of creative writers' groups and clubs in Northern Universities such as Ahmadu Bello University, Zaria and Bayero University, Kano. For instance, *Dandali*, a literary journal meant to feature, promote and provide a forum for Northern writers, helped 'unearth' some of the writers of this generation that include, among many others, Hauwa Kassam, Hadiza Amapa, Murja Iro, Rasheed Oniyangi, Audee T. Giwa, including older 'young' writers like Nereus Tadi, the late Aderemi Bamikunle and Yakubu Nasidi. Rasheed Na'Allah has laid a solid foundation for the expansion and growth of both the oral and written literature of Ilorin, based initially but now on a widened scope, on his profound study of Dadakuada. Other creative clubs, like the Association of Nigerian Authors, have exposed a number of other writers of this generation— Yusuf Adamu, Denja Abdullahi, Ibrahim Sheme, Helon Habila, Odoh Diego Okenyodo, Lizi Ashimole, Maria Ajima, Victoria Kankara, B. M. Dzukogi, Ahmed Maiwada, Crispin Oduobuk, Ismail Garba, Halima Sekula, Binta Salma Mohammed, Aisha Zakary, Sunday Ododo, Tunde Olusunle, Charles Bodunde, Tsenongo, Isiaka Aliagan and so on. This generation also threw up writers who, out of frustration of the dearth of publishing outfits, began to self- publish. Some of the writers mentioned above had to indulge in this practice. But very notable self-publishing writers include Nana Embaga, Ibrahim Malumfashi and Masud Abdulkadir. This generation is continuous and continuing and it is indeed a mistake to start name-calling, for I certainly have left out some of my numerous young friends who are writing well and publishing profusely. I draw this to make a point—that creative writing has developed and blossomed, rapidly, in Northern Nigeria.

The impression given above may be one of a need for complacency, since there is already a handsome body of Northern Nigerian writers to explode the myth of backwardness, or is it merely paucity, of creative writers in that zone of the country. True, but that is if the region is taken and considered in isolation, without reference to creative happenings elsewhere. That will be a really myopic exercise indeed! Hence, the germanises of this Summit focus on sustaining the creative writing enterprise of the region.

Sustaining and Nurturing

If you want to deploy literature as an instrument to recollect the positive aspects of the Northern concept and phenomenon, then a lot of effort has to be put in place to sustain that body of literature that has emerged, and is blossoming from the Northern States of Nigeria.

Writing, of the creative category, is lonesome, hazardous in health and political terms, and a challenging vocation indeed—given the inclement socio-economic and socio-political ambience in our country, and in which the business of creative writing is carried on. It is worsened by the tradition of grossly inadequate publishing outlets for the manuscripts produced with blood and sweat. It has been observed that nearly all the multinational publishers in Nigeria were/are based in Southern Nigeria. In addition, they hardly establish branches to promote literature in the North. Having made their names and gains on the bleeding creative backs of Achebe, Soyinka, Clark, Ekwensi and others, they turned their backs on literature and obeyed the economic law of demand and supply of publishing commercially viable curriculum text books for primary and secondary schools.

The writers in the North were therefore never really patronised by these multi-nationals. The writers had either to approach relatively unknown foreign publishers or to self-publish. The consequence of either practice is unsavoury for the writers and their environment. Some of the negatives include poor distribution and poor quality production. Most of the writers in the North are hardly on the curriculum in educational institutions in the South. Even in the North, self-publishing authors do not get read, except a few who are lecturers who can carry their works in "Ghana-Must-Go" and parade institutions where they go examining or conferencing. Such writers who can afford to get their initial works published overseas could hardly be read in Nigeria, when there are hardly opportunities for local production rights or domestic distribution of their texts. As Sani Abba graphically expressed, most of those writers who opt for self-publishing suffer a similar fate; their works are 'poorly publicised, inadequately reviewed, and rarely available in the book stores'.

Will these disadvantages hinder or eliminate self-publishing? It is hardly possible, given the prevailing sociology of writing and publishing in the country today. Young writers are in a hurry to bear the name of authors—a condition for even becoming member of the umbrella writers' organ—ANA. I have been a constant victim of this publishing hunger. I receive manuscripts with such injunctions as "Kindly help me, sir. The publisher wants to go to press next week" or "The launching of the work is in a month's time, my Chief Launcher will travel immediately after"! What's the use then, if the comments I may have will require a surgical re-work of the text! There was a particular occasion in which just as I was getting to read the text, its launching date was announced—in two days' time!!!

Some writers – young or old, or both – labour under the sad illusion that being an author is a passport to instant wealth. They need to do a little research as to why most authors today are not full-time writers. Some of us in the academia and the humanities must improve our CV—with evidence of published creative works, if they wish to be smiled upon by the Appointments and Promotion Committees. In any case, there are hungry publishers as there are hungry authors, in a mutual self-seeking game.

In spite of all these, and the inevitable proliferation of self-publishing, the nurturing of our literature is a factor, largely of its quality, of aesthetics of production, technical finish and content. Creative works must benefit from editing and objective assessment on publishability. Publishers, not printers, must do the job of book production, if our literature is to be sustained with enduring values.

For a blossoming literary culture to emerge and be sustained, some of these steps must be taken and maintained:

A. To stimulate and enhance literary creativity, literary competitions and contests, which used to be the practice in the colonial days, need to be resuscitated. The colonialists did it in the 1930s. It should involve all departments of creativity in indigenous and foreign languages—drama, prose, poetry, short stories, film and video, etc. Attractive material rewards should be attached to winning texts. The successful texts should be distributed. Government and corporate bodies must embark on a wide distribution of the winning texts in schools and public libraries. The winning texts must be toured and read in many public institutions. If the colonialists did it with the result of an appreciable growth in the writing and reading culture of the time, there is even a greater need for our governments here in the North and the country generally to do so.

B. Journals, magazines, newspapers should show greater interest in the publication and serialisation of literary texts. The growth of a literary and reading culture in the South benefitted tremendously from the spaces which literary journals and newspapers devoted to works of literature. *Black Orpheus, The Horn, Nigeria Magazine, Okike* and so on, consciously helped to nurture literature. The example of *Dandali,* which I mentioned earlier, is worth emulating. The defunct *New Nigerian* used to give focus to literature and to book reviews—especially under Abubakar Rasheed. The existing newspapers should be more vigorous in serving the course of literature. I must add here that *Daily Trust* has been more vigorous in its concern and engagement with literature—fictional and scholarly—in its staples and should be encouraged to do more.

C. Governments, voluntary agencies and organisations should endow writers' fellowships and offer literary prizes to motivate writers to train and write in a sustained and enduring manner. The fellowships should cater for writers' needs—feeding, accommodation and honoraria that will enable writers to complete creative works in progress with less difficulty than it is now.

D. Associations related to literature —writing and reading—should enhance their activities of promotion and nurturing. ANA has created many literary prizes and is collaborating with governments and corporate bodies on workshops, prizes, endowments and seminars. Others, like Readers' Association of Nigeria (RAN), the Literary Society of Nigeria (LSN) and the Academic and Non-Fiction Authors Association of Nigeria (ANFAAN) should work more conscientiously to promote literary awareness and help build a reading and writing culture,

E. Our libraries are virtually dead. There are only very few public libraries in this country. There are fewer reading rooms around. Government should adopt a policy of acquiring at least 1000 copies of one successful creative text of every Nigerian author registered with ANA and distribute them in libraries and reading rooms, which should now be rehabilitated or re-built as the case may be.

F. The electronic media have been of tremendous help to the growth of creativity in the North in the past. I have mentioned the role of the FRCN. The radio audience of the Hausa programmes for instance, is in millions. This could be replicated in the other languages of Tiv, Fulfulde, Kanuri, Idoma, Okun, Ebira, Nupe, Igala and so on. Radio Kaduna encouraged literary development by regularly broadcasting poems, short-stories, drama sketches and story-telling sessions. The broadcast of their creative works have availed the authors' access to wide audiences. My first dramatic text, *Pestle in the Mortar*, was broadcast on Radio Television Kaduna in 1974 and it was of tremendous inspiration to me. The Hausa Television Drama evolved out of the broadcast of radio plays by FRCN.

G. Literature is the soul of the society and no subsidy to develop, sustain and nurture it would be excessive. I thus urge the governments who are directly or indirectly involved in this all-important Summit to invest in the literature of this region and grant generous subsidies to literary institutions and literary people in their domains.

I did warn that this is a brief intervention—open to debate.

References

Lindfors, B. (1982). *Early Nigerian literature.* New York: Africana Pub.

Obafemi, O. (1999). *Pestle on the mortar: A play.* Ilorin: Haytee Pub.

Chapter 2

Dramatic Theatre: A Nexus for Resurgence in the Twenty-First Century Northern Nigeria

Abdullahi Salih Abubakar

Introduction

Northern Nigeria is arguably more cosmopolitan in nature compared to other regions. Its vast political terrain, diverse ethnic/cultural groups and multi-religiosity present a complexity, which effective management in the past had availed it the status of a strong influence on the socio-political direction of Nigeria as a nation. This diversity was an impetus at the formation stage, characterised by a resounding commitment to the development of the region and a healthy competition with its counterparts in the West and the East. The main thrust, then, was patriotism to the region, as 'goodness' or 'badness' of a policy was determined by the number of its beneficiaries. This translated into education for all eligible youths, irrespective of cultural, class or religious background. These, in turn, created a unified people with a common front. Although there was a dissenting view based on ideology, it was constructive and was not allowed to sway the northern agenda. The positive effects were conspicuous in the role played by the region in determining the suitable period for Nigeria's independence and its contribution to the general resource that saw Nigeria through the early stages of nationhood.

> The relative education backwardness and under-development of Northern Nigeria in the 1930s to 50s, compared to the

other regions, and its impact on the future progress and development of the country, was so serious and far-reaching that concerted and deliberate efforts were made to address the problem by the leaders of the time. With careful planning and good motivation, the Northern Regional Government provided so many opportunities and sufficient funds for the education and training of their manpower. This foresight ultimately yielded great result and benefits as has been carefully documented in this book. Many young people from all over the North benefited from these initiatives. This writing of this book is therefore not only an acknowledgment of the contributions of the great leaders at the time, but also of the beneficiaries (Gowon, 1996, p. xvi).

However, the situation currently contradicts the euphoria of the formation age.

Contestably, one can aver that the North is currently a congregation of clashing interests masquerading under ethno-religious disguises. This calls to mind some lines in W. B. Yeats' poem, 'The Second Coming' (1921):

> The falcon cannot hear the falconer;
> Things fall apart; the centre cannot hold;
> Mere anarchy is loosed upon the world,
> The blood-dimmed tide is loosed, and everywhere.

Several factors are responsible key among these is the disruption of set values such as integration, purposeful leadership, patriotism, unity of purpose etc. What are the factors responsible for the gradual disintegration of the ideals of the founding fathers? What is the extent of damage by disguised ethnic and religious upsurges to the development of the region? How can dramatic theatre serve as a nexus for resurging the region? To answer these questions, the paper adopts Utilitarianism as a theory to analyse and suggest possible ways dramatic theatre can mediate in the resurgence of the region.

The Utilitarian Theory

Effects of actions constitute the focus of Utilitarianism as propounded by Jeremy Bentham. The theory is based on the concept that the judgement on every action resides in its overall effect on a greater number of people as individuals. This is in terms of its pleasant or unpleasant consequences on the majority. The main focus of Bentham is 'act utilitarian', which emphasises the worth of individual action on his immediate community or humanity in general. John Stuart Mill disagrees with Bentham on how happiness can be determined based on individual feelings. Instead, he suggests a collective concept of what should constitute happiness to a people and the means by which every citizen should comply. He is of the opinion that democracy, by virtue of participation, is the ideal, hence, his concept of 'rule utilitarian'.

Eggleston (2012) identifies the characteristics of utilitarianism as Aggregation (summing of individual's value in a given state), Consequentialism (value of an act being dependent on consequential facts), Individualism (value placed on persons and animals), Maximisation (optimising value), Utilitarianism (rightness or wrongness, measured by overall well-being) and Welfarism (emphasis on welfare). Based on the five concepts of Utilitarianism above, this paper shall attempt to analyse the incongruity that currently characterises the state of affairs in Northern Nigeria, in spite of the fact that most of its current leaders were beneficiaries of the laudable and progressive efforts of the founding fathers.

Individualism/Aggregation and Resurgence in Northern Nigeria: A Dramatic Theatre Intervention

Going by aggregation, the value attached to the life of an average northerner is far from being humane. This assumption is based on the poor quality of living among the majority as a result of denial of basic amenities and the denial of access to quality education to more than seventy per cent of children of school age. Consequently, begging, drug abuse, hooliganism and petty criminality constitute the habit of the young ones. What used to be restrictive anti-social habits in the 80s have become so popular such that they are exhibited without constraints. Also, these anti-social habits have defied class and sex discriminations. Recruits into the fold require diverse "qualifications" to cover a wide range of activities. Members of deviant groups are domiciled in different and sensitive parts of the community such as schools, streets, markets, offices of political stalwarts etc. where they freely operate or resort to harassment to have their ways. When such groups are pressed by their addictions, they resort to all means to fulfil their desire. The gradual loss of reasoning and concern for others make the youths easy recruits for ethnic, religious or political bigotry. The multiple effects of these are intolerance, violence, chaos and all other forms of lawlessness, which lay the foundation for insurgence. According to Tella (2015, p. 31),

> due to poverty, many youths, particularly so in the Northeast, have been denied choices and opportunities to go to better schools, hospitals, houses, basic social life as well as participate actively in the society.... In view of these they (victims) may join any violence (sic.) groups as majority of them are ill informed politically, socially, religiously, economically etc. As a result, most of the arm(ed) robbers, terrorist groups, Boko-Haram members, particularly so the foot soldiers, came from poor masses (sic).

In response to the above, Olu Obafemi's *Suicide Syndrome* aggregates the quality of life and draws attention to the incongruous style of living in the society, especially the north. He portrays majority of the citizens in endemic poverty while a very few number swim in excess. As characteristic of all oppressors, the elites responsible for the situation detest any move to awaken the consciousness of the oppressed. Thus, if the tendency to oppress is human, not to resist is unnatural. The playwright shows that more often than not, the dominant group adopts all means to perpetuate the dominated group in its slumber through religious and other forms of bigotry. It is the victims of injustice that should resist this. Hence, when the stooge of the leaders responsible for the deteriorating conditions of the people proposes a stage-managed play production to sell the unpopular policies of the incumbent, the people-oriented troupe is made to resist this; and instead, it proposes that the masses be allowed to participate in the play production, in order to provide first-hand information about their experiences under the administration.

This then gives insights into the lifestyles of two extreme divides in the same community: the excessively rich and the incredibly impoverished. The text exhibits the tendency in the younger generation of the latter group to resist the lopsidedness instead of being easily swayed by any argument.

SON: I mean, Mama. You, papa, my sister and me. We are hungry and poor....

DAUGHTER: Yes, mama, tell us. Why do the children of people over there, the minister, and the Alhaji, come to school in their posh cars, each with a driver while we go to school without shoes on?....

MAMA: (*Now impatient*) Now shut up and listen. You're different... But what is the use of raking up painful memories? What is the need? Things will soon get better.

SON: Mama, I don't understand. Is anything more inhuman than for some people to eat well and have leftovers for their animals, while others like us live on a cup of *gari* a day? Is that human?...

SON: When, mama? When? We both can't go to school tomorrow, no school fees. No books. No money to pay levies (Obafemi, 2012, pp. 15-17).

The scenario painted above is a prelude to the brutal consequence of failing to aggregate the lives of the individual; impunity remains a justifiable means of self-aggrandisement without recourse to the value attached to each citizen's life as a member of the community.

Consequentialism/Utilitarianism in the Dramatic Expositions of Selected Northern Nigerian Playwrights

These two concepts are taken together because they are based on judgement and its quality, determinable by what is accruable to the majority. Hence, there is no doubt that the existing polarity among the citizens of the North, in terms of opportunities to realise individuals' potentialities, is a far cry from justice. Thus, the elites, a product of yesteryears' foresight, have not reciprocated same. This could be likened to a breach of contributory scheme of sustainability, having failed to pay back what accrued to them as beneficiaries of free education, careful planning and good motivation. The discriminatory tendency of looking down on the masses as mere objects of exploitation by contemporary Northern elites contradicts the seeming egalitarianism of the formation stage, which provided a plain ground for all citizens, regardless of their family backgrounds. The elites are not only guilty of lack of reciprocity, but they are also culpable of nepotistic tendency of over protecting their offspring. They usurp the chances meant for all citizens with impunity. This has led to a waste of human resources as intelligent youths are denied access to develop their potentials, just because of their poor background and in spite of the huge resources available to cater for all. The disposition of the generation of educated northerners since the 70s, either as civil servants, judicial officers, political leaders etc., are egoistic because they are far from the overall well-being of the majority. They perceive their positions as privileges to enrich themselves and build empires by disenfranchising the people on whose platform they rose. The consequential facts of these are captured by Mike (2017) thus:

> Unemployment in [Northern] Nigeria would have been eradicated... [but] companies that would have invested in Nigeria are afraid because they do not know if the corrupt practice will ruin their industries in time. Because of this, they refuse to invest in Nigeria....When the heads of public service are busy laundering the money that is supposed to be used to create employment for the masses and reduce poverty, what happens is that there will be a rise in the poverty level of the country. ...When Nigerians keep on shifting the country's currency to foreign countries, there will be less economic development in Nigeria....The insecurity in Nigeria brought about by Boko Haram is a consequence of corruption.

Going by the utilitarian theory, the activities of the educated elite in the north are overbearing and are basically responsible for the negative impacts on the majority of northerners.

The Northern elites' hypocritical posture forms the thrust of Abdullahi Abubakar's *Sirens and Whispers*. It focuses on the dual dispositions of an unemployed graduate, Akowe, whose dwelling among beggars and labourers convinces them that they have values, in spite of being homeless. His words and activities inspire them to re-evaluate themselves and understand that their condition is a by-product of nefarious activities of co-citizens who have turned them into carriers of societal burdens. This 'saviour' of the street dwellers is arrested for allegedly causing public disorder. However, as the street dwellers plan on how to rescue Akowe from the police custody, Agbojulogun, a politician, discovers the potential in the latter for his political career. The head of thugs, who wants to settle scores with the politician for using and abandoning his group, leaks the secret about the cordiality between Agbojulogun and Akowe to the street dwellers. Meanwhile, intelligence report reveals the plan of the street dwellers to stage a demonstration. Based on this, the politician accuses Akowe of double standards. Akowe offers to convince the politician of his loyalty by meeting with the dwellers but he meets a brick wall. The beggars, thugs and other inhabitants of the street attack Akowe and his team with sachets of pure water, stones, bowls, etc. (p. 40).

The focus in this paper is on the unreliable nature of Akowe, which is a manifestation of the general attitude of the Northern elites towards their communities and people. They exploit the people and societal resources to achieve their set goals and later dump the people. This is manifest in Akowe's identifying with the street dwellers as an unemployed graduate, his using their platform to gain recognition, and his eventual betrayal of the people. Compare the following submissions by Akowe:

> A street with beggars on both sides. People are moving about their daily businesses: school children, workers, hawkers, etc.; many ignore the beggars....An old retiree struts on stage, dresses neatly but the material appears faded and worn-out. He moves to a beggar and gives her money to change into smaller denominations. The beggar obliges him; the retiree tosses five naira at her; as he makes to walk away, the beggar pulls his cloth.

BEGGAR I: Ah! Ah! Oga, master, only five naira? ...After all the efforts! What can five naira buy these days?...

AKOWE: (This) is harder for people like me, who believed that life was a bed of roses (to believe); now I know better... (Abubakar, 2013, p. 19).

and

AGBOJULOGUN: (*Solemnly*) you heard about the plans by the beggars to stage a protest over your arrest, so you have been meeting them to sabotage our efforts, in spite of what we have done to raise you from the dust. Elders have said that no matter how many times you rinse the *ebolo* vegetable, it will never stop smelling.

AKOWE: (*Sweating*) since the day of my arrest which marked the U-turn in my life, courtesy of your generosity, I have ever been loyal to you and shall remain so. I would appeal to you to give me a chance to handle the situation (Abubakar, 2013, p. 35)..

The consequential effect of Akowe's actions is distrust, which leads to suspicion, acrimony and chaos. The rights of the majority are trampled upon with impunity to the advantage of the few educated. Thus, under the concept of utilitarianism, the action is adjudged wrong and should attract punitive measures in line with the principle that '... the rightness and wrongness of acts depend entirely on facts about the consequences of acts' (Eggleston, 2012, p. 453). In the same vein, the maximum value expected from an informed mind is lacking in Akowe and, by implication, the educated Northern Nigerians. This constitutes another critical aspect. It points to the dearth of value in the outcome of the huge resources expended on the educated. Rather than build the region, they mastermind its destruction through greed and lack of vision; the resultant effect is complete absence of maximisation of resources to ensure the overall well-being of the people.

Dramatic Response to the Need for Maximisation/ Welfarism in Resurging Northern Nigeria

A glossary assessment of the living standard of people in the Northern region, whose prosperity as an agrarian society in the 50s and 60s was enormous, shows a drastic drop in the welfare of the individual six decades later. Thus, the aggregation of well-being through what accrues to each citizen of the north today indicates a drastic degeneration in the value attached to life and its survival. Instead of maximising the human and material resources for the development of the people in the region (as initiated by the founding fathers), the succeeding leaders and the bureaucrats corner the resources, to the detriment of the vast growing population. The state of facilities in the region presents a precarious situation of gross neglect of basic social amenities like water, health, education etc. necessary for the welfare of the citizenry. There are no corresponding indices in population growth and public utilities, to provide for and protect the interests of the common people. Rather, a clear disparity characterises the quality of life; this ranges from people living in mansions as against the street dwellers; those in excessive pleasure as against those in abject poverty; few citizens with numerous options as against many with no option to develop personal potentials etc. With the increase in the number of the disadvantaged, tension definitely rises between the extreme opposites. Ibrahim (2008) observes that:

> A typical spectacle in the streets of most of the cities and towns of Northern Nigeria looks like this: multiple streams of school age children roaming about with begging bowls if they are boys and with tray loads balanced on their heads selling trifles if they are girls. If they are youths, aged 20 and above or thereabout the males are likely to be selling petrol measured in jerry cans in the black market or loafing idly and the females will have small or big basins doling out food to buyers on the streets. Those middle-aged or older reclining tiredly on mats spread on street corners are likely to be beggars with no discrimination to gender. There is more to the above. On the same streets, the latest brand of Hummers, luxury

Honda or Mercedes cars sure to draw a long glance will be purring softly as it traverses pot-hole-filled roads with its expensively dressed occupants. In virtually every street, even in the poorest neighborhoods, there will be the usual big mansion looming over dilapidated houses that have seen better days. There are school children too, either coming from or going to school. This is a caricature of the two worlds which combine to make up the North today - one of abject poverty, disease and illiteracy and the other of stupendous wealth and sophistication.

This yawning gap, no doubt, attracts desperate reactions from the underprivileged whose rights are trampled upon, hence, the increasing tension and violence in different guises such as herdsmen/farmers clash and Boko Haram insurgency. They are products of an unjust system and after a long year of retreat, they decide to fight back; but unfortunately, these groups have been hijacked by the jackals in an intraclass tussle for power, which has worsened the situation of the common citizens in the region. Daily activities are truncated by fear, as death tolls in market places, mines, farms etc. escalate.

The possibility of capitalising on the differences arising from group interests is explored in Abubakar's *Citizens or Strangers*. It centres on the farmers/herdsmen skirmishes, which have recently assumed a scary dimension of mass killings in different parts of the region. Durow, an unemployed graduate of Fulani origin, drives a commercial vehicle, and is chartered to carry Ehohi, the daughter of a Member of the Lower Chamber, representing the constituency where Durow hails from. The journey is truncated by flood which forces the two and other road users to abandon their vehicles in order to escape from wild sea animals flushed by water. The duo go up on top of a hill where they cite a settlement and decide to take refuge there. The reception by the inhabitants is hostile because they suspect both to be spies and therefore lock them up. The unfolding events reveal series of political killings disguised in the farmers/herdsmen clashes. Ediga, the Honourable and father to Ehohi, confesses on capitalising on the existing disagreement.

> EDIGA: It wasn't all my fault. As the then Commissioner for Agriculture in the state,... I got a huge amount made from a fertilizer scam; so I decided to engage in irrigation farming...for which a loan of ten billion naira could be secured..., using my good office. I usurped the land beside the river...claiming government interest in it and... warned against trespass. But the herdsmen would not heed, claiming scarcity of water for their animals.... One day, a herdsman allowed his animals to encroach into my farm...near the river. The damage was too much and... coming just a day before the World Bank...assessment committee for loan, I got mad. I set my boys loose on the family; ...and members of the Reebo family were wiped out. This started the whole crisis (Abubakar, 2015, p. 52).

The above submission, if viewed intelligently, raises a suspicion on the sudden ferocity of farmers/herdsmen clashes that have often been resolved amicably in the past. Several other clashes with ethnic and religious tilts have become recurring in the northern region shortly after the commencement of the 4th Republic. The organised nature of the attacks and the sophisticated weapons used corroborate the assumption that the groups surely have sponsors and trainers.

The menace would have been easily put under control if the judicial system had not been infiltrated. The system which should serve the purpose of ensuring and securing everyone's hope has long been compromised. The recent investigations by anti-graft agencies of the federation have revealed the extent to which the judiciary has been overwhelmed by corrupt practices, thereby denying the poor the last hope for justice. This has also halted the maximisation of state benefits, as the judiciary colludes with politicians and business gurus to manipulate affairs against the masses. Thus, the concept of equality before the law only exists in print. In practice, the rich manipulates the judicial system to their favour, leaving the poor with no option than to resort to violence. Also, there exist situations where accused persons are arraigned and names of stalwarts are mentioned as their sponsors or leaders. The judicial officers are either influenced to discountenance the evidence or throw the case out for huge sums; the victims whose rights are trampled upon face another intimidation for reporting or filing a case at all, from the freed assailers. Having lost hope in the judiciary for justice, people, especially the youths, resort to personal vendetta by forming violent groups. This can take the form of cultism in tertiary institutions, kidnap gangs, armed robbery, religious extremism etc. to have their own back against the system which denies them a right to protection in all its ramifications as bona fide citizens. Daniel (2016) reports:

> In a nationwide crackdown, the Federal Government… began rounding up judges suspected to have aided and abetted corruption over the years. But, the arrest of the judges, which was carried out by operatives from the Department of Security Services, was in relation to those who allegedly took huge cash to pervert the cause of Justice.

Obafemi's *Dark Times Are Over?* (2015) was first published in 2005. It projects how the judiciary aided and abetted criminality based on class discrimination. Yepa I and Yepa II are members of a secret cult on the campus of a tertiary institution. The anti-social activities of the gang, with the full support of stalwarts who assist them with fund and protect them from the full wrath of the law, have devastating effects on the inhabitants of the campus and the city generally. In trying to curtail their menace, different groups on campus stand up to the challenge. Christian and Muslim groups provide succour to the victims through prayer and counselling. But, to Obafemi this is a docile approach to a volatile situation which needs a more aggressive step to control. Hence, the various paramilitary groups on campus are challenged to have more proactive measure of preventing rather than managing the tension caused by the terror group. Through this effort, members of the cult are arrested and arraigned before a court of law. The judge happens to have a link with the parents of Yepa II. Using his own influence with the Police, the judge facilitates the escape of Yepa II from Police custody and is later flown abroad. On the day the case comes up, only Yepa I appears before the judge. On his insistence that his co-accused person must be presented because they both committed the said offence, the judge adjourns the case in anger.

The playwright institutes a people's court where the audience chooses an ideal judge, Agbe, to continue the case after the exit of the judicial officers. The outcome is indicative of the people's expectation from the judicial system if the society is to be prosperous. Agbe submits:

> AGBE: ....Our court of law in Odaju Land is an appendage to the larger rotten system, out there. It is a place where justice has been sold for a mesh of porridge by a rotten, corrupt and nepotistic leadership.... No doubt, Yepa 1 is guilty... It is laudable to rid our society of rogues like Yepa 1; but is there justice, if two separate laws are erected in the society...? Those laws keep the poor down and weaken his resolve to be upright and decent. He is open to temptation through frustration and despair. He is consigned by our unjust society to poverty, crime and cultism (Obafemi, 2015, pp. 42-43).

The submissions by the selected playwrights allude to the fact that the crises that bedevil Northern Nigeria today are by-products of the lopsidedness in wealth distribution and its maximization for the use of all institutions established for its aggregation. Thus, the elites, saddled with the responsibility of advancing the system, unmake it by creating antithesis to its progress through injustice.

Conclusion

The paper has attempted to discuss the efforts of playwrights from the North to resurge the region, using selected plays from two of them to accentuate the integral role dramatic theatre can play in stabilising the polity. It dwells on how the literary genre can impact on the move to resurge the northern region from the current insecurity and economic challenges that have dwindled its fortune. But, this impact has not been properly felt due to the lackadaisical attitude of academics to make the genre complimentary to oral performance in regulating the society, since the latter has gradually been rendered inactive by modern challenges. It is not a gainsay that exemplifications from the play texts above would appear to many Northerners as a mere academic exercise. This is due to the fact that in most parts of the region, play texts are taken for reading materials like other genres of literature. The unpopularity of the genre is evident from the inactive nature of the dramatic society at the secondary and tertiary levels of education, a platform that used to draw students from different disciplines because of its enhancement of aptitude, competence and communication skills. However, the conception of any play is for production, either in live theatre situation or recorded form. Thus, for dramatic theatre to perform its assigned role of stabilising the society like the oral performance, there is the need to revive the dramatic society, which used to serve as the medium for training both instructors and students in schools. With that, available plays, that address various aspects that pose challenges to the resurgence of the North, should be interpreted to suit specific situations by directors for the purpose of production, communally and for academic purpose, to serve as behavioural codes. One may be tempted to claim that the home video producers have filled this vacuum. But that is a wrong assumption, considering the fact that the primary target of home video makers is profit; there is the temptation to prioritise the desires of the audience over a criticism of such. Thus, comparatively, there is a higher level of objectivity and quality in producing play scripts by the academics. Therefore, there is the urgent need to revive the dramatic society to impart positively on the school age population and the society in geeral.

References

Abubakar, A. (2006). *A critical study of revolutionary dialectics and context in Osofisan's Drama* (Ph.D. Thesis). Department of English, University of Ilorin, Ilorin, Nigeria.

Abubakar, A. (2013). *Sirens and whispers* (Performing Arts Creative Writing Series 16). Ilorin: University of Ilorin Press.

Abubakar, A. (2015). *Citizens or strangers?* (Performing Arts Creative Writing Series 25). Ilorin: University of Ilorin Press.

Daniel, S. (2016). Two Supreme court judges, 5 others arrested over alleged corruption. Retrieved from https://www.vanguardngr.com/2016/10/two-supreme-court-judges-5-others-arrested-alleged-corruption

Eggleston, B. (2012). Utilitarianism. In *Encyclopaedia of applied ethics* (Second Edition),*4*.

Gowon, Y. (1996). Introduction. In I. M. Mora, *New foundation: Preparing the future leaders.* Zaria: Northern Nigerian Publishing Company.

Ibrahim, H. J. (2008). North's vicious circle of poverty. Retrieved from http://nigeriavillagesquare.com/forum/threads/poverty-in-northern-nigeria-full-disclosure.21688 (originally published in *Daily Trust.*)

Mike, U. (2017). Corruption in Nigeria: Review, causes, effects and solutions. Retrieved from https://soapboxie.com/world-politics/Corruption-in-Nigeria

Obafemi, O. (2012). *Suicide syndrome.* Ibadan: Haytee Press.

Obafemi, O. (2015). *Dark times are over?* Ilorin: University of Ilorin Press.

Tella, M. C. (2015). Insecurity in Northern Nigeria: Causes, consequences and resolutions. *International Journal of Peace and Conflict Studies, 2*(4), 23-36.

Yeats, W. B. (1921).The collected poems. B. Retrieved from http://wordsbloom.com/uploads/files/Download%20(1).pdf

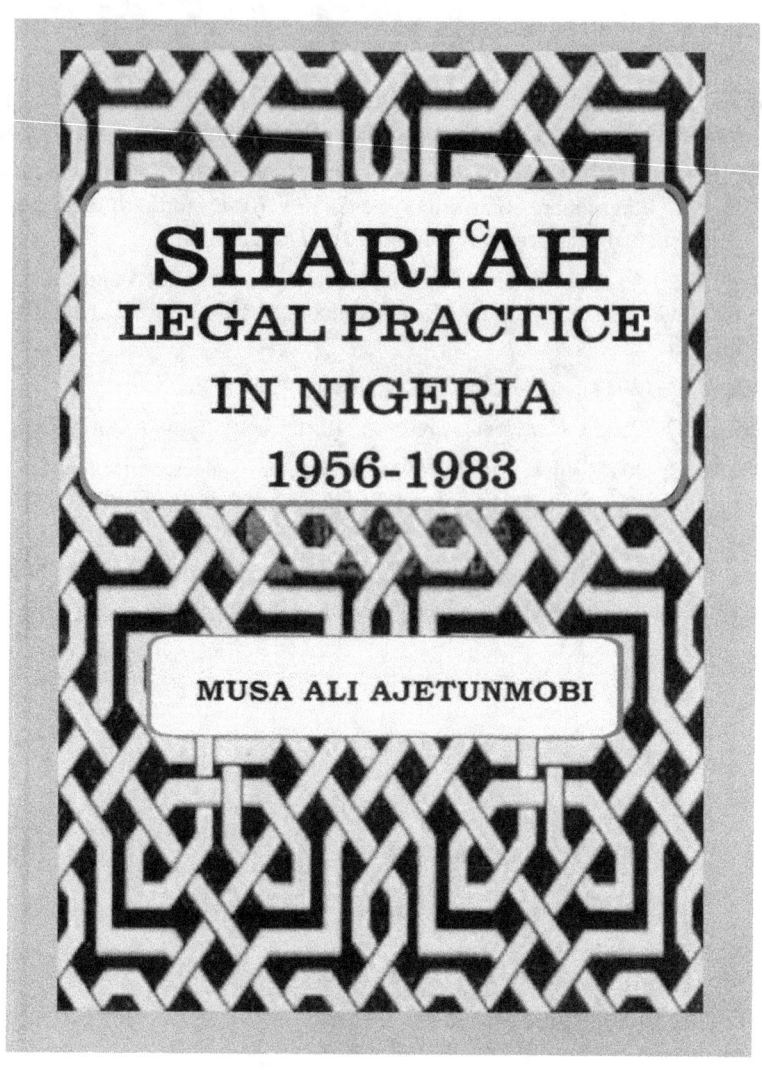

ISBN 978-978-927-592-2

To obtain your copy, please contact:

Kwara State University Press
Kwara State University, Malete
PMB 1530, Ilorin, Kwara State, Nigeria
Email: kwasupress@kwasu.edu.ng; kwasupress@gmail.com

Chapter 3

Northernism in Northern Nigerian Literature: A Study of al-Yāqūtī's *'Abarātul-Amal*

Abdulrazaq M. Katibi and *Aliyu O. Ahmad*

Introduction

Northern Nigeria as a geopolitical entity was, prior to the amalgamation, an autonomous division within what is known today as Nigeria, It was distinctly different from other parts of the country. The region had independent customs, foreign relations, educational system and security structures before it became a British protectorate between 1900 and 1913. Although the advent of Islam influenced most of the prevalent customs in this part of the country, the diverse ethnic groups coming from different socio-cultural, linguistic and religious backgrounds have what can be referred to as an identity or ideology. This identity or ideology is expressed politically, socially, economically, culturally and linguistically through various means.

However, to preserve this identity, the role of literature takes centre stage. The reason is not far-fetched, as against certain opinions that literature, like other arts, is a mere play of imagination, it preserves the ideals of people, connects individuals with the larger society and relieves writers and readers from the pressure of emotion. This paper, therefore, is an attempt to survey the expressions related to Northern sentiments, norms and values as contained in Abdul-Azeez Muhammad Salman al-Yaqūtī *'Abarātul-'Amal* (Tears of Hope): The paper also attempts to prove that literature in the North reflects the socio-cultural and political ideology of Northern Nigeria regardless of the linguistic and religious diversities.

Northernism in Selected Literary Works

In conceptualising the term 'Northernism' one may need to ask what approach is needed to view it: political, economic, linguistic, cultural etc. A dictionary meaning of the term, as found in *Encarta Dictionaries* (2009) comes with the linguistic dimension. It is "a pronunciation, word or other linguistic construction characteristic of the northern region of a country." Consequently, Northernism, in this context, can be defined as beliefs, norms and values characteristic of the northern part of a country or region, Nigeria in this context. By implication, Northernism is a concept that depicts the identities, beliefs, norms and values prevalent in the Northern part of Nigeria commonly referred to as '*Arewa*'.

This concept has for long been expressed in different forms, such as symbols designed into facades, bright and colourful palaces since the existence of the nomenclature '*Arewa*' as a geopolitical entity and value. It has culminated into the formation and founding of political, economic and socio-cultural fora to harness both human and natural resources for greater synergy among those who identify themselves with the region. The formation of Northern People's Congress (NPC) in June 1949, the successor organisation, Arewa Consultative Forum (ACF), in 2000, the forum of Northern States, the Northern Nigeria Development Company (NNDC), the Arewa Hotels, the Arewa Textile Industry etc. are attempts to actualise the Northern dream. However, the choice of 'Northernism' to represent the concept instead of '*Arewa*' as used in this paper, is born out of the fact that the latter refers to North or Northern, and this might not completely portray the philosophy in the former.

Although, literary scholars and critics have shown little concern in expressing these norms and values in their writings, a few of them have consciously or unconsciously done just that. For this study, three literary works on poetry are examined. These are: *Poems of Black Africa* edited and introduced by Wole Soyinka (1981), *Khalajātun wa Nabadhāt* (Emotions and Heartbeats) by Ibrahim Saeed Ahmad al-Gambari (2012), and *Danladi's Doggerels* by Saliu Danladi Yusuf (2010).

1. *Poems of Black Africa*

This literary work is an African Writer's Series (171) book and a collection of two hundred and forty-one poems written by Africans under various titles of African perspectives. In this collection, a poem titled 'The Fulani Creation Story' is the only poem that appears to express a concept that is attributed to Northern Nigeria. It is a traditional Fulani oral poem rendered into English. It sums up the myth surrounding the creation of the world, according to the Fulani belief. Though this might not be common to all Northerners in Nigeria, it constitutes part of the Northern ideology. Below are a few lines of the poem:

> At the beginning, there was a huge drop of milk.
> Then Doondari came and he created the stone.
> The stone created iron;
> And iron created fire;
> And fire created water (pp. 57-58).

It goes on in that manner to the creation of air, man, blindness, sleep, worry and death, then concludes thus:

> Doondari descended for the third time,
> And he came as Gueno, the eternal one,
> And *Gueno* defeated death.

This poem suggests that the first thing that ever existed on earth is milk, which is associated with the Fulani cattle. With this belief, the Fulanis lay claim to *Gueno*'s recognition of their profession of cattle rearing and milking the cow, which preceded the existence of man himself. The poem also explains the Fulani belief in the 'Eternal One' called *Gueno*, the first and the last.

2. *Khalajātun wa Nabadhāt (Emotions and Heartbeats)*

Written in Arabic the work is a collection of poems written in Arabic by Ibrahim Saeed Ahmad al-Gambari (Ibrahim, 2012) on several diverse but topical issues. One of these poems expresses a blameworthy habit common to the northern part of Nigeria: the act of street begging or the *Almajiri* phenomenon. The poem is titled '*Ilā*

Maqarrish-Sheikh' (To the Abode of the Sheikh), and portrays the writer's emotional reaction towards this act as these few lines make clear (pp. 40-41):

ت مبينة بل وهي أبهـــــاها	خلال رحلتنا إني أشاهد آيــا
نّ صورتهم فالفقر شـــــواها	على الطريق يا لعيشهمــــو وإ
كانت صغيرتهم تنشق رجلاها	أما الصغير فحاف ثم أكبرهم
عونا فألهم رب النفس تقـــواها	يمد أيديهم نحوي ويســـــألني
نتنا أيا أسفا فالجوع دســـاها	وكان ثوبهمو طمرا وجلــدهمو

During our journey, certainly I witnessed;
Clear proofs, yet the most magnificent.
On the roads, how pitiful is their lives;
And their appearance engulfed in poverty.
As for the young (male), and the most elderly as well;
The legs of the young (female) are tattered.
Extending their hands towards me begging;
For assistance, and the Lord of the soul inspired its fear.
And their cloths rags, and their skin;
Smelling bad, regrettably hunger instills corruption.

This writer expresses the menace of *almajiri* phenomenon which is a typical scene on streets, major and minor roads, as well as market places of Northern Nigeria. The poem was written after the writer's journey to Sokoto (the seat of Caliphate), where he experienced activities of the *almajiris*, a scene that is inimical to the whole of Northern Nigeria.

3. *Danladi's Doggerels*

This is yet another collection of poems composed by Saliu Danladi Yusuf (Yusuf, 2010). It contains about sixty poems under various titles. Many Northern norms and values are expressed in some of these poems, such as the use of '*Haba*'! '*Haba*'!! a Hausa word which usage is common among Northerners, sometimes to disprove or reject an action. Danladi while reflecting on Vancouver, states:

Vancouver?
Haba! Haba!!
The banality of the venality (pp. 30-31).

The word '*Magajis*' is also used in another poem under the title 'My Village Well' '*Magaji*' is a compound head and in some towns in the Northern Nigeria, represents a traditional title.

In addition to the above, while tracing the origin of Ilorin he expressed the fact that the turban is the crest of the regalia of the Emir in Ilorin, and characteristic of Northern Emirs, as opposed to the crown which is prevalent in the Southern and Eastern parts of Nigeria:

Turban is the crest of his regalia.
From the time of his forebears.
Whose head was a flag-bearer.
In the Southernmost frontier (pp. 37-38).

He also expresses a norm common among children in the Northern part of the country; that is the creation of temporary mosques with the use of stones within compounds during the months of Ramadan. This appears in his poem under the title 'Ramadan' when he says:

In thy anticipation,
Children, now deft masons.
In a frenzy.
Plant the foundation stones
Of a temporary but ethereal
House of God (pp. 46-47)

These attempts are no doubt embodiments of some aspects of the norms and values of Northern Nigeria, and a reflection on the activities of the people that distinguish them as an entity. The work '*Abarātul-'Amal* by Abdul-Azeez al-Yāqūtīis another work of literature in which Northernism is expressed in different ways.

Abdul-Azeez al-Yāqūtī's Biography

The author, Abdul-Azeez Muhammad Salman al-Yāqūtī is a native of the ancient city of Ilorin, the Kwara State Capital. Born in Ilorin to a family of repute in the 1970s, he grew up under the tutelage of his father, who later sent him to learn Qur'ānic recitation under the late Sheikh Muhammad Thānī Akanbi Olosan of Adangba area in the city. Interestingly, the combined efforts of his father and the late Sheikh developed in the young Abdul-Azeez good moral values such as sincerity, trust, good social relations and interest in learning.

His Educational Background

Abdul-Azeez started his journey towards attaining greatness in the field of Arabic and Islamic Studies at *Dārus-Sa'ādah* for Arabic and Islamic Education, Onikijikpa, in Omoda area of Ilorin, where he obtained his Elementary School Certificate. Afterwards, he enrolled at *Dārul-Ulūm,* Ilorin, from where he bagged his *I'dādiyyah* (preparatory) and *Thānawiyyah* (secondary) certificates in 1997 and 2000, respectively with excellent performance. He was at the Faculty of Education and Humanities, Adewole, Ilorin (now al-Hikmah University) from where he obtained a Diploma Certificate in Arabic and Islamic Studies in 2001. In that same year, he gained a scholarship to study Arabic Language and Literature in Abomey-Kalavi University, Republic of Benin, from where he obtained his Bachelor of Arts degree in 2005. This scholarship did not come on a platter of gold, rather, it was a result of hard work, prayers and a great favour from the Almighty Allah, being the only successful candidate from Kwara State after the admission screening process in that year.

During his National Youth Service Corps programme in Zamfara State between 2006 and 2007, he continued his educational pursuit by getting himself enrolled at the Federal College of Education, Kano, for a Postgraduate Diploma in Education, which he completed in 2007. Abdul-Azeez al-Yāqūtī went further in his quest for higher education and was admitted into Nasarawa State University, Keffi, in 2010 for a Master of Arts degree in Arabic Language and Literature. This, he completed in 2013.

His Literary Works

Abdul-Azeez al-Yāqūtī is a talented and inspired literary artist who has made great and ingenious contributions to literature in both prose and poetry. He has written occasional poems on various topics that were either presented orally or published, such as: '*Ma'assahābahal-Kirām*', in *Majallah at-Tarīq*, '*Ayyām al-Ijāzah*', in *Hasād al-Ma'dubah* and other poems in al-bīnīniyyāt (Collection of Poems by Nigerian Students in Benin Republic). His literary productions are epitome of wisdom, imagination, clarity and mastery of the Arabic language.

The work under study ('*Abarātul-'Amal*) is a remarkable achievement. In addition to this, the writer has some unpublished works that include '*Ad-da'nul-Aswad*' or 'The Black Sheep' (a story book), '*As-sadā*' or 'The Echo' (a collection of poems) and '*Wahyul-Khayāl*' or 'Inspiration of Imagination' (a collection of poems). He also has to his credit a number of scholarly articles published in reputable journals.

Synopsis of '*Abarātul-'Amal* (Tears of Hope)

The story is an artistic autobiography written in Arabic. It is a story of one hundred and forty-five pages and narrated in twenty-one parts. Major characters in the story include '*Na'īm*' (the main actor), his parents, Ayinla (an uncle to *Na'īm* and a weaver), his teachers in Arabic Language and Literature as well as Islamic Studies (Shaykh Adam al-Ilori and others), his two close friends (not named), an old devout woman, colleagues on a trip to Republic of Benin (not named) and Baba Oyẹ.

The story commences with a beautiful description of the universe and the beautiful things it contains. This is followed immediately by glorifications and adorations to Almighty God who has subjugated other creatures for the benefit of mankind, and a brief description of the main character (*Na'īm*).

The writer attempts to give a picture of years of struggle and tribulations in the life of '*Na'īm*' who grows up under the shackles of poverty. He starts as an apprentice in the weaving industry, an occupation of some of his relatives, and later as a hawker, selling chewing sticks concurrently with his primary school and Qur'ānic Studies.

The story also portrays the life of '*Na'īm*' as a student of Arabic at *Dārus-Sa'ādah* and *Dārul-Ulūm,* Ilorin, respectively and records the encouragement received from his mentor, Shaykh Adam al-Ilori, and other teachers, and the challenges he faces (health and economic) throughout his struggle towards becoming great in life. One major challenge he faces is how to secure admission into the university which, to him, is for the rich and influential. However, hope is rekindled as he comes to know that a Libyan University situated in Abomey Kalavi, Republic of Benin, grants scholarships to students wishing to study Arabic and Islamic Studies from within and outside the country. This, of course, requires travelling to the campus to take part in both oral and written examinations which determines, whether the grant would be his. Preparing for the trip constitutes another crisis on its own, trying to raise fund, and troubles along the way. All the same, he succeeds in crossing the hurdle and returns home safely; and finally emerges to be the only candidate from Kwara State to succeed in winning the scholarship. With this, *Na'īm's* dream is actualised, even though there are obstacles he has to contend with during the process. He graduates from the University in flying colours.

Meanwhile, the tears in the title of the story are a usual thing in the life of '*Na'īm*' as a distressed young man. His father is also prone to shedding tears on simple matters; and as such crying is considered to be hereditary so much that their house is called '*Ojuekun*' (weeping face). Although *Naīm*'s were not those of pain or grief, rather they are those of happiness and hope, born out of praise and glorification to God Almighty who see him through his *thānawiyyah* (secondary) education in Arabic studies.

Northernism as Expressed in *'Abarātul-Amal*

As stated earlier, Northernism as a concept is the standard pattern of behaviour that is considered normal in the Northern part of the country. It is also a set of common socio-cultural beliefs about what is right and wrong and what is important in life. These are the norms and values that are typical to Northern Nigeria. The concept is expressed by the writer, either consciously or otherwise, at different levels, going by the context of the story as discussed below:

a. *Physical Features*

The cover page of the literary work has three distinct features that are typical to the Northern part of Nigeria. These features are:

I: The Northern symbol or logo, otherwise known as the Northern Knot, which appears at the top right hand corner of the page. The logo is found in almost every part of Northern Nigeria, placed conspicuously in public and some private buildings, on signposts and even included in the logos of some Northern States to express affinity with this part of the country.

Fig. 1: Northern Knot   *Fig. 2:* horsemanwith

II: The horseman with full regalia riding on a well-dressed horse appears at the mid bottom of the cover page. This is a common characteristic of most parts of the Northern part of Nigeria, particularly during ceremonies like the 'Durbar' and other traditional celebrations. It is considered a royal right of traditional rulers, and one of the Northern identities.

b. *Norms and Values*

The Northern norms and values expressed in the story are as follows:

1 - *Recognition and respect for the leaders*

In this part of the world, it is an accepted practice that people duly recognise and pay respect to their leaders no matter the situation. This has been expressed in the story while recognising Alhaji Sir Ahmadu Bello, the Sardauna of Sokoto and first Premier of Northern Nigeria, as a political leader, linking him to notable figures such Ibn Khaldūn as a model of History, al-Ghazāli as an icon of philosophy. al-Yāqūtī (2015, p. 18) stated:

وجهباذ البراعة، المتخذ ابن خلدون أمثولة في التاريخ، والإمام السيوطي أنموذجا في التأليف، والغزالي قبلة في الفلسفة، وحسن البنّا قدوة في الجهاد،وأحمد بلّو [سردونا] إماما في السياسة.

> and (hoping to be) skillful, and taking Ibn Khaldūn a model in historiography, Imām As-sayūtī an example in authorship, al-Ghazālī a target in philosophy, Hasan Albannā a model in jihād (struggle)and Ahmadu Bello [Sardauna] a leader in politics ...

Alhaji Sir Ahmadu Bello's leadership qualities made him an icon in the whole of Northern Nigeria, his legacies indelible and records unbeaten. He is therefore being immortalised by way of recognising his roles in building this part of the country and respecting his personality regardless of religious and ethnic affinity.

2 - *Prayer Sessions at Palaces*

It is the norm by scholars to organise and arrange prayer sessions at the palaces of Emirs and District Heads at certain periods. During these sessions, the whole of the Qur'ān is recited and supplications made for the success of the leader and for peace and tranquillity in his domain. This sometimes takes days to be completed. al-Yāqūtī (2015, p. 34) expresses this common norm in these words:

استدعى الإمام طائفة متميّزين من الزملاء لجلسة دعاء في قصر أمير المؤمنين الحادي عشر للإمارة الإسلامية بالمدينة.

and the Imam invited a selected group of colleagues for a prayer session at the palace of the 11th leader of the faithfuls of the Islamic Emirate in the city.

3. *Respect for Privacy of Women*

Women are accorded respect and are guarded against assault. Foreigners are therefore not allowed to intrude on their privacy, a norm that makes many Northerners to keep their women in seclusion. This means that any person, particularly visitors need to wait for permission to be granted before entering upon a woman. This norm is expressed in the story by al-Yāqūtī (2015, p. 40) as:

وبعد لأي من الوقت، أُذن لهم بالدخول إلى الباب الأول قبل النزول إلى محراب الشيخة.

and after sometime, they were granted permission to enter through the first door, before being allowed into the (prayer) niche of the old woman.

4 - *Traditional Security Outfit for the Emirs*

It has been the norms and values of the North that traditional rulers possess their traditional security outfit that is easily recognised through their multi-coloured dress. This group of men guard the Emir while at home and abroad. This security outfit serves as personal guards providing security afore and behind them. This is expressed by al-Yāqūtī (2015, p. 35) in the following words:

فدخل الأمير وأمامه ووراءه عدد من عساكره في أزيائهم الرسمية المتلونة.

And the Emir entered and afore and behind him are his military dressed in their official multi-coloured dresses.

5 – Strong Belief in Predestination

It is not strange to anybody in Nigeria that people of Northern Nigeria (*Arewa*) are known for their strong belief in predestination. The Hausas are predominantly used to the words '*Allah ne yakawo*', meaning 'it's from Allah'. Therefore, the issue of attributing any misfortune or calamity to any creature would not arise. At a time '*Naʿīm*' faces a health challenge and whenever he rubbed over his head during ablution for the dawn prayer, he would observe reddishness on both hands. Could it be blood gushing out of his body as an attack by demons or magicians? He develops a strong faith that whatever it is, God Almighty has the full knowledge and He would see him through the problem. This doctrine is expressed in the story by al-Yāqūtī (2015, p. 65) in this manner:

أنه متى مسح رأسه عند الوضوء لصلاة الصبح يرى أن يديه تتلونان بلون أحمر!

and whenever he (*Naʿīm*) rubs his head during ablution for the dawn prayer he sees that his hands are coloured in red!

رأى أن سداد التخطيط أمام هذه المشكلة ملازمة الأذكار، مزاوجا بالصيام.

he decided that the only plan against this problem is to be in constant supplication supported with fasting.

6 - The Language

The Hausa language, considered as language of *Arewa,* is common in usage among the people of Northern Nigeria. Some languages are already endangered at the expense of Hausa, which has influenced and continues to influence many other languages in the region. Cases of Hausa interference has been documented in most of these languages. Regardless of religious and ethnic differences, the language has become an identity. It has been noticed that some traditional titles of Hausa background are not limited to Hausa/Muslim communities but rather, extend to non-Hausas outside the core Hausa States and even within some Christian dominated areas in the Northern Nigeria. For instance, in Nasarawa state, the Wakilin Agwatashi (Solomon Adokwe) and the MutawallinLafia (Daudakigbu) are non-Hausas and non-Muslims. Similarly, Jeremiah Oseni doubles as the Sardauna of Plateau and Wakilin Lantang, while Professor Jerry Gana is KakakinNupe. And in Adamawa State, the titles of Magatakardan Adamawa, Masanin Adamawa and Talban Adamawa are currently held by James Barka, Andrew P. Sawa and Emmanuel Mbuala respectively. This is an indication that a great importance is attached to the language in this part of the country. Such importance is manifested in the story, as scores of Hausa words are used in it. These include:

- [تٌوْ] '*to*' (A word of acceptance and approval, meaning 'ok')

This word in Hausa is mostly used in Northern Nigeria to express one's acceptance of an issue, particularly during conversations, to mean 'ok'. In *Oxford Advanced Learner's Dictionary* (2005), 'ok' could mean 'alright; acceptable; permission etc. It is also used to check that somebody agrees with you or understands you, or to stop people arguing or criticising you, or used to attract somebody's attention or as an exclamation. Basically, all these connotations of this word apply to the Hausa '*to*'. The word is used in the story by an old devout woman to whom *Na'īm* and his school friends present a symbolic gift for her concern over their future and prayers for their success in life. She says: "'*to*', may God reward you in abundance" (p. 62), showing her acceptance of the present. Sometimes, it is lengthened as '*toooo*' just as 'ok'.

- [سَرِكِنْ مَالَمِي] '*sarikin malami*' (Head of Islamic scholars)

The use of this expression in Hausa language is common in cities, towns and villages of Northern Nigeria, particularly among the Muslim communities, where it is a title given to the head of the learned in Islam as a mark of honour.

- [تُوْ] 'A meal made of maize/corn flour'

This is a kind of meal that is prepared from corn flour or from rice. It is a staple food in most parts of Northern Nigeria. Even though the meal is now known in other parts of the country, it is most common among Northern communities. The writer uses this word at the premises of *Na'īm*'s school (*Dārul-Ulūm*, Isale Koto, Ilorin) on a day the students voluntarily contributed for a new block of classrooms, including those that had already registered at the *'tuwo'* restaurant (p. 62).

- [بَا لَيْفِي] *'baa laifi'* (No problem)

This expression is typical with people of the northern part of Nigeria. It is used to express satisfaction about an issue or to express unhappiness over an issue, though this largely depends on the context. The expression is used in the story by the sheikh who teaches *Na'īm* the Qur'ān when he informs the former of his plan to travel to the Republic of Benin for admission screening (p. 78).

Conclusion

Northernism as a concept and ideology has been the focus of this paper, with particular reference to the way it is expressed by literary writers, and using *'Abarātul-'Amal* (Tears of Hope) by Abdul-Azeez Muhammad Salman al-Yāqūtī as a case study. The paper attempted to survey how Northern ideology in terms of norms and values are expressed in this literary work. In this process, the concepts of ideology and Northernism are briefly discussed. Also discussed are expressions of Northernism in some literary works. Our findings in this direction have revealed that the writer – consciously or unconsciously – expressed the concept of Northernism in two ways: the physical features that are characteristic of Northern Nigeria on the cover page, and the norms and values prevalent in this part of the country. We thereby recommend to the teaming Northern Nigerian writers to use their God given abilities to further capture the norms and values of Northern Nigeria through different literary genres to preserve them.

References

Al-Yāqūtī, Abdul-Azeez M. S. (2015). *'Abarāt al-amal* (Tears of Hope). Ilorin: Al-Mudeef Press.

Ibrahim, Saeed A. Al-Gambari. (2012). *Khalajātun wa nabadhāt* (Emotions and Heartbeats). Ilorin. Kewu Damilola Press.

Northernism. (2009). In *Encarta dictionaries*. Microsoft Encarta. Redmond, WA. Microsoft Corporation.

OK. (2005). *Oxford advanced learner's dictionary of current English* (7th ed.). Oxford. Oxford University Press.

Soyinka, Wole. (Ed.). (1981). *Poems of black Africa*. London: Heinemann.

Yusuf, S. D. (2010). *Danladi's doggerels*. Ilorin: News International.

ISSN 2315-5523

To obtain your copy, please contact:

Kwara State University Press
Kwara State University, Malete
PMB 1530, Ilorin, Kwara State, Nigeria
Email: kwasupress@kwasu.edu.ng; kwasupress@gmail.com

Chapter 4

Traditional Songs as Catalysts for Integration: A Study of Selected Ilọrin Traditional Songs

Hakeem Ọláwálé

Introduction

Traditional singers in African societies are like historians in many cases. Themes and allusions in their renditions reveal a lot of facts which in turn proffer solutions to many issues. This is in line with Bọ́láńlé Awẹ́'s opinion cited in Adéẹ̀kọ́ that:

> historians of non-literate societies should view oral traditions as valuable sources for chronicling the evolution of African social and cultural consciousness, because, in societies without permanent archives, creative oratures do capture the mentalities of their milieu of production and consumption (2001, p. 181).

Okafor (2005) locates the authenticity of music as a mirror through which a society is viewed when he says:

> music is a human activity as part of human existence. This existence comprises and implicates various activities in an environment. The totality is what is loosely defined as culture ...It is well known that man in his different environment produces different cultures. Consequently, music will have different purposes, characteristics and implications in different cultures and environments. In African culture, music is an entity, rather than a mere

mental creation or conception. It reflects and interprets the man in a specific environment and is often the key, which opens the gate to spiritual, mental, emotional, psychological, social and mystic realms (pp. 87-88).

The above opinion of Okafor refers to the prominent roles African music play in virtually all aspects of the society. Music and society are interwoven because music is usually all about what has happened and is also presently happening in the society. This is because the interactions of people in the society bring about what artistes compose into songs.

Akpabot in *Foundation of Nigeria Traditional Music* also opines that:

> Music does not exist in vacuum, rather it influences and it is influenced by a variety of factors within its socio-political and geographical context. As an element of culture, music connects to the culture of a people among which it evolves. The association of music with social and ritual ceremonies has been observed as one of the chief characteristics of African Music (1986, p. 1).

The opinion of Akpabot stresses that music, most especially in African society, is the productof what happens in the people's every day life. The connection of music with all that happens in the society is seriously interwoven because music does not just exist in a vacuum. This is also confirmed by Ajíbádé (2005) in his 'Is There no Man with Penis in this World' he says that songs are an important component of the folklore of many African groups. This implies that songs are an integral part of the African life.

The Emirate of Ìlọrin and the Combination of Its People

The Ìlọrin Emirate is recognised as one of the Muslim cities in Nigeria. Its emergence as an Islamic city dates back to the 17th Century when Islam spread to the city (Ṣọlagbẹru, 2013, p. 1). The geographical location of Ìlọrin is paramount for its uniqueness as the capital of Kwara State. It is considered to be one of the Hausa Banza Bakwai, or copycats of the Hausa Kingdom. At the start of the 19th century, Ìlọrin was a border town of the North-East Òyọ́ Empire, with a mainly Yorùbá population, but with many Hausas-Fulani immigrants or slaves. It was the headquarter of an Òyọ́ General, Àfọ̀njá, who rebelled against the Òyọ́ Empire and helped bring about its collapse with the assistance of the Fulani. The rebellion was powered by Hausa, Nupe and Bornu Muslim slaves. Àfọ̀njá was assisted by Saliu Janta, also called Sheu Alimi, a leader of the local Fulani. In 1824, Àfọ̀njá was assassinated and Alimi's son, Abdulsalami, became the Emir, Ìlọrin thus became an Emirate of Sokoto Caliphate (wikipedia, free encyclopedia: 12/10/2014).

Ìlọrin, as a distinct community comprising of people of diverse cultures and origins, speaks Yorùbá as the common and popular language. The choice of Yorùbá can be attributed to the fact that when it was formerly recognised in 1832 as an administrative entity, the Ìlọrin Emirate consisted of four Yorùbá speaking groups: the Ìlọrins, the Ìgbómìnàs, the Èkìtìs and the Ìbọ̀lọ́s (Nigeria Gazette, 1952, p. 980). Presently, Ìlọrin Emirate has been reduced to five Local Government Areas, namely: Ìlọrin West, Ìlọrin East, Ìlọrin South, Asà and Mórò Local Governments. All the towns and villages under these various Local Goverments are under the rulership of the Emir of Ìlọrin, being the Chairman of the traditional rulers in Kwara State and the paramount ruler over Ìlọrin Emirate. He appoints the Chiefs, the Balóguns, Aláǹgúás, Magàjís and many other subordinate chiefs under the Emirate of Ìlọrin. As reflected in Ọládọṣù (2013, p. 55), the Emirate is reputed for its Islamic orientation and this reflects in the culture and worldview.

Jimọh, in his book, *Ìlọrin: The Journey So Far*, attributes the cosmopolitan nature of contemporary Ìlọrin Emirate to a number of factors:

> It was a massive influx of people of assorted cultural backgrounds, after the Islamic governance has been firmly established that conditioned the demographic size, composition and texture of Ìlọrin. With the resultant ethnic and cultural heterogeneity, Islam became the common denominator and unifying factor. It facilitated intermingling, socialisation and integration among the various people. Consequently, a unique Islamic culture into which

the diverse cultures melted, emerged. However,... Yorùbá language became the lingua franca (1994, pp. 9-10).

Being a multi-ethnic community, Ìlọrin witnessed the influx of many groups, majority of whom were Muslims. This favoured the establishment of an Islamic system of government which flourishes till today. In the songs of the traditional artists of Ìlọrin community, a lot of issues are mentioned which reveal facts and through which some family members became integrated and re-united. According to a Yorùbá proverb, " Okùn kò ní gùn títí kó má ní ibi tí a ti fà á wá" (A rope must surely have its source no matter how long it is). For example,the core families in Àgbajì, namely Ilé Sáúrà, Ilé Àbùro, Ilé Bàbá Sàárẹ̀ , Ilé Àgòrò and Ilé Imam Àgbajì were originally Sudanese Arabs from a town called Ar-Baji on the Blue Nile... Members of Ibrahim Bàtúrè at Òkè Apòmù are Arabs by origin. They migrated to Ìlọrin from Àgades in Niger Republic. The Òjíbárá family in the same area are of Fúlàní descent... The Ṣọlágbẹrú family at Àgbajì, the Ọ̀nágun family of Ìta-Ẹ̀gbá , the members of Ilé-Olóyin (formerly called Ilé-Igbọ́n) at Ìta-Ẹlẹ́pà, the Gíwá family of Pópó Gíwá and the Mèkábárà family of Ìta-Ògúnbọ̀ are Kànúrì migrants. Ṣọlágbẹrú migrated from Bámá in Bornu and was the founder of ancient Òkèsúnà...The family of Magaji Kúǹtú are Boko-Barubas paternally but Fulani maternally, while members of Ilé Ẹlẹ́ran, Àdáǹgbá are Barubas...Membrs of the following families are Hausa by ancestry: Ilé Alálìkíńlá at Ìta Ògúnbọ̀, Ilé Shírù at Òde Alfa Nda, Ilé Saba'ani at Òde Aláúsá and Ilé Saba'ani at Ìdí-Òrombó, Ilé Jáwòǹdó at Ìta Ògúnbọ̀ and Ilé Alfa Ajóǹgọ́lọ̀ which was formerly called Ilé Alápatà... (Jimọh, 1994, pp. 10-11).

The Traditional Songs of Ìlọrin and Some Notable Artistes

Ìlọrin is a big metropolitan city which encompasses some smaller towns and vilages as part of the emirate. The interactions and social activities, coupled with cultural and religious activities of the people of different origins, brought about many traditional songs which can be categorised under several typology according to peculiar characteristics. Such categories are youth-based songs, male-based songs, female-based songs, aged-based songs, vituperative songs, religious-based song, palace songs, social-based song, nuptial or epithalamium songs among others (Ọláwálé, 2015, pp. 104-112).

Traditional songs among Ìlọrin people are many and they are used for different occasions and purposes. Such music are dàdàkúàdà, bàlúù, Ọlọ́mó-ọba song, kàkàkí/bẹ̀ǹbẹ́, kèǹgbè, wákà, agbè, pamúpamù, pàkenke, Yemọja song, sẹnwẹlẹ, ìyá-mi –lóìlóò and wéré. The artistes of dàdàkúàdà are mainly male while bàlúù is its female counterpart, both of which originated from pàkenke song according to Adéọlá (1995, p. 7) and Abiodun (1999:58). Notable among the dàdàkúàdà singers are Jáígbadé Àlàó, the late Odòlayé Àrẹ̀mú, Ọmọékeé Àmọ̀ó, Àrẹ̀mú Òsé , Kọ́lá Olóoru, among others. Among the bàlúù singers in Ìlọrin are Àlàájà Ìyábọ̀ Bàlúù, ÀlàájàSùwébátù Àmọ̀pé, Ọmọ-Ìyá-Tamíwò, among many others. The wákà song, which is a religious cum cultural type of song is popular especially during traditional weddings.Àlàájì Àlàbí Làbáékà, Bàbá Olóbì, Àlàájà Rúkàyátù Báatimolúwasí, Àlàájà Áfúsát Onísèsé and Àlàájà Kẹ́hìndé Ọláńrewáju are some of the prominent waka musicians.

Women-based songs performed in the palace are called orin-ọlọ́mọ-ọba Ìlọrin. This is mainly for the Emir and the entire royal family of Ìlọrin. It is mainly performed by old and middle-aged women who are either wives or daughters of Ìlọrin royal family. Performance of this type of song comes up during wedding programmes for the royal sons and daughters. They also perform for the Emir on special occasions. At the time of this research, an aged woman, Àlàájà Sàdía Èjìdé of Pópó Ọlọ́mọ-ọba Street, Bàábòkò, in Ìlọrin, is the leader of the sole group of that Ìlọrin traditional song.

The kàkàkí/bẹ̀ńbẹ́ song is another music genre in Ìlọrin, which is categorised as youth-based, Ọláwálé (2015, p. 114). It is very useful in virtually all occasions among Ìlọrin people because of its popularity. There is the special "Támbàrí", otherwise known as "Gbádidi", which is specially performed for the Emir on Fridays. This starts from early in the morning till after the Jumat service on every Friday. It is to entertain the Emir and his household on Fridays, being a special day in Ìlọrin and for Muslims at large. It is also used to escort the Emir to and fro the mosque with horse riders entertaing people as well. The blowing of kàkàkí (trumpet) is peculiar and reserved for the Emir alone, while the àlùgétà and bèǹbẹ́ drums can be performed in some other occasions in Ìlọrin. Àlàájì Ismaila Ibrahim Àrẹ̀mú, of Balógun Fúlàní area of Ìlọrin is the leader of the bèǹbẹ́ artistes in Ìlọrin and its environs. Some other notable kàkàkí/ bèǹbẹ́ or Àlùgétà artists in Ìlọrin are Sámbò Ìyandá Bèǹbẹ́, Ràmọ́nù Àwẹ̀dá Bèǹbẹ́, Àlàájì Ísúmáílà Àtàndá Alálugétà, among others.

Agbè song is another musical genre in Ìlọrin in which the artistes beat the big rattles (agbè/ṣẹ̀kẹ̀rẹ̀), sing and perform poetic renditions and perform, do acrobatic acts to entertain their audience. Notable among them are Ọlọ́hun-lọ́-gbọ́n Àjàdí Kúrè, Káríkáná Bùhárí Àjàdí Kúrè, Núúrù Àjàdí Kúrè and some others. Further more, there is also kèǹgbè song which is mostly performed for a new bride by her peer-group during her wedding eve and some days later as a farewell and solidarity support song for her forthcoming household challenges. They also sing many verses of songs to advise for bride to be a good wife in her new home. However, there are lots of vituperative verses in the songs as well. Hajia Ramat Lawal waxed some kèǹgbè records, which is quite useful as data source for research purposes. There is pamúpamù song among the songs in Ìlọrin, which is useful in virtually all the social ceremonies in Ìlọrin. Notable among the artists of this musical genre is Àlàájì Pélé Wúrà, who has modified the genre to include avertisements and sensitisation on many societal issues.

Àlàájà Àwáwù Àlàkẹ́, popularly known as Ìyáládùkẹ́ and Múkáílà Ẹṣínrógunjó, are some of the popular sẹnwẹlẹ singers. This type of music is full of humorous verses and mostly depict women's life and weaknesses in the society. Ìyá-mi-lóìlóò and wéré are trado-religious songs in Ìlọrin. This is because, they are purely religious songs and both originated from the activities related to the religion of Islam, which is the main and popular religion of Ìlọrin indigenes. Wéré originated in Ìlọrin to wake Muslim faithfuls up for early morning food (Sahur) during the month of Ramadan, while Ìyá-mi-lóìlóò is performed by the youth at night after the Tarawih prayer during the month of Ramadan, most especially to sensitise people about the nearness of Eid-el-Fitri festival to mark the end of Ramadan fast. All these different songs of Ìlọrin community serve different purposes. The songs are embedded with different facts which allow people to know more about the cultural heritage, historical antecedents and activities of Ìlọrin people.

Concerning the Emirship throne of Ìlọrin, an excerpt from dàdàkúàdà song of Àrẹ̀mú Òsé goes thus:

Wòlíì Dáń Báwà	Friend of God, Of Báwà family
Ààfáà Ṣééhù	Senior Cleric
Ìṣọlá Òpó ọmọ Sùbéérù ní Sókótó	Ìsọlá Òpó, son of Sùbéérù of Sókótó
Àá tí ń jọba nílùú 'Lọrin	We have been having kings in Ìlọrin
Ọjọ́ tọ́ pẹ́ ni	Long time ago
Irú Bùràímọ̀ Ìṣọ̀lá	The type of Bùràímọ̀ Ìṣọ̀lá
Irú rẹ̀ è tíì jẹ	Has never been enthroned
Ìṣọlá ọmọ Bùrẹ̀ẹ́mọ̀ aráa Ṣókótó	Ìṣọ̀lá the son of Bùrẹ̀ẹ́mọ̀ of Sókótó origin
Ìṣọ̀lá Òpó	Ìṣọlá of Òpómúléró lineage
Ọmọ Àkáádì aráa Ṣókótó	Son of Àkáádì from Sókótó
Ọmọ-ọmọ Ayélabówó	Grandson of Ayélabówó
Ọmọ ọmọ Sàídù Àlàó	Grandson of Sàídù Àlàó
Ọmọ Gògó Àlùkò...	Son of Gògó Àlùkò

The singer is trying to praise the eleventh Emir whose name is Bùrẹ̀ẹ́mọ̀ (Ibraheem) Ìṣọ̀lá Òpó. The song reveals that he is one of the distinct Emirs of Ìlọrin and of Sókótó descent. He was referred to as Ìṣọlá Òpó, son of Quadri from Sókótó, grandson of Ayélabówó, Sàídù Àlàó and son of Gògó Àlùkò. Though, the Emirs family of Ìlọrin are of Fúlàní origin from Sókótó, bearing Yorùbá names, cognomens or agnomens by virtually all the Emirs of Ìlọrin indicates and signifies the total assimilation and integration of other ethnic groups to form a formidable Ìlọrin.

Below is an excerpt from the kàkàkí/bẹ̀nbẹ́ song of Ismaila Àtàndá (Àpọ́nlé Ọba wa) which affirms the name of an Ilọrin king as Ayélabówó and Gàmbàrí, a collective name for the people of non-Yorùbá ethnic group in Northern Nigeria (Jimoh, 1994, p. 353).

Lílé: *Ayélabówó dé o o o o o*	Àyélabówó has come
Ègbè: *Gàmbàrí dé o o o o*	Gàmbàrí has come
Lílé: *Ayélabówó dé o o o o*	Àyélabówó has come

Ègbè: *Gàmbàrí dé o o o*   Gàmbàrí has come
Lílé: *Ayélabówó dé bíí tíí dé*   Ayélabówó has come as usual
Ègbè: *Gàmbàrí dé bíí tíí dé*   Gàmbàrí has come as usual.

The above excerpt shows the integration of different cultures whereby a Gàmbàrí man from Northern Nigeria is also called Ayélabówó, a Yorùbá name of South-Western Nigeria. This is a sign of total assimilation and integration of cultures.

In the same àlùgétà/bẹ̀nbẹ́ song of Ismaila Àtàndá, "Àpọ́nlé Ọba wa", there is a depiction of occupations and some peculiar characteristics:

Lílé: *Ẹ dákẹ́ ẹ má pariwo*   Be calm and don't make a noise
      Ẹ dákẹ́, ẹ má pariwo   Be calm and don't make a noise
      Agbo Fúlàní la wà yìí   We are in the Fúlàní party
      Wàrà tútù la ó fi ṣomi   We will drink raw milk

Lílé: *Wọ́n ní Fílàní le jẹun*   They accused Fúlàní of too much food
      Wọ̀n nì Fílàní le jẹun   They accused Fúlàní of too much food
      Yàtọ̀ sí tàwọn òpònú o o   If not for the fools
      Ẹ̀kọ kan ti yó gbogbo wa   We are all satisfied with only one pap

The above verses of the song indicate that Fulani tribe are known for cattle rearing, therefore they are proud of having enough fresh milk and cheese whenever they have any feast, function or festivities. It also reveals Fúlàní people as not fond of too much food.

More over, Ìdí-Àpẹ́ Quarters is one of the prominent and historical areas in Ìlọrin due to the fact that the inhabitants of the area are the descendants of the war Generalismo, Àfọ̀njá Ààrẹ-Ọ̀nà-Kakaǹfò, whose contribution in the establishment and the entire history of Ìlọrin can never be over-emphasised. In the excerpt of àlùgétà/bẹ̀nbẹ́ song below, the traditional religion of their forefathers is depicted:

Lílé: *Iyemọja nídìí Apẹ́, Iyemọja*   River goddess at Ìdí-Àpẹ́, river goddess
      Ògùnmọ̀ yéé yeè yé, Iyemọja   Ògùnmọ̀ yéé yeè yé, river goddess
Ègbè: *Iyemọja nídìí Àpẹ́, Iyemọja*   River goddess of Ìdí-Àpẹ́
      Ògùnmọ̀ yéé yeè yé, Iyemọja   Ògùnmọ̀ yéé yeè yé river goddess
Lílé: *Ọmọ Láderin*   Son of Láderin
Ègbè: *Ọmọ Láderin*   Son of Láderin
Lílé: *Ẹ wá wọmọ Láderin*   Come and see Láderin's descendants
Ègbè: *Ẹ wá wọmọ Láderin*   Come and see Láderin's descendants

The above genre of Ìlọrin traditional music reveals that Iyemọja, river goddess, was the major traditional religion of Àfọ̀njá and his people in the olden days. Though, the religion of Islam has overtaken a lot of things, yet, whenever they are singing or chanting their lineage descriptive poetry, they usually pour water on one another at a point as a sign and to remember their forefathers as Iyemoja worshippers. The mention was also made of Láderin, who was the father of Pàsín, the father of Alùgbìn who was the father of Àfọ̀njá.

About the relevance of the musicians in the African societies as educators who have a lot of roles to play to sensitise people on different issues about their society, some facts that may be hidden to so many people can be got from the traditional songs especially from the musicians who are well-versed in the norms, culture, ethics and the historical antecedents of their society. Okafor (2005, pp. 6-7) therefore goes thus:

> The musician has a role as a keeper of public conscience and as a man who has his hands in the social control lever. He guides the society, drawing, of course, from the collective wisdom and pool of knowledge and proverbs of his people... The musicians, therefore, have an acceptable role in many of our traditional societies... The musicians is an educator. Many of our social comments, moral codes and guides are couched in music and songs.

In the excerpt of Àrẹ̀mú Òsé dàdàkúàdà song from his record tagged "Àrẹ̀mú Gbàwọ́ọ́dù, music was used historically to explain the detailed relationships of the present Emir of Ìlọrin with the past Emirs, both paternally and maternally. It goes thus:

Àtọlẹ̀dọ́lẹ̀ n tàdán,	Foetus inside foetus is that of bat
Kò ní í hun ọ́, ìran baba rẹ̀ ní í jọba	It shall never turn against you, your fore-fathers are Kings
Ilé ìyá rẹ̀, Ilé Ọba Ìlọrin ni	Your maternal family are Kings in Ìlọrin
Ilé baba rẹ̀, ilé ọba Ìlọrin ni	Your paternal family are kings in Ìlọrin
Àlíù Baba Àgbà,	Àlíù Baba Àgbà
Ẹ̀gbọ́n mọmọ rẹ ni,	Is your mother's uncle
Ọ́ jọba Ìlọrin.	He was enthroned in Ìlọrin
Àbùdùkáádírì,	Àbùdùkáádírì

Baba mọ̀mọ́ rẹ̀ ni,	Is your maternal grand-father
Ọ́ jọba Ìlọrin.	He was enthroned in Ìlọrin
Báwà tó bí Káádì,	Báwà the father of Káádì
Baba-baba mọ̀mọ́ rẹ̀ ni,	Is your maternal great grand-father
Ọ́ jọba Ìlọrin	He was an Emir of Ìlọrin
Súlú baba rẹ,	Súlú ,your father
Ọ́ jọba Ìlọrin	He was an Emir of Ìlọrin
Báwà tó bí Láòfẹ̀,	Báwà, the father of Láòfẹ̀
Baba-baba rẹ ni,	Is your paternal grand-father
Ọ́ jọba Ìlọrin,	He was an Emir of Ìlọrin
Ọ́ wáá terí i Lọ́ọ́yà,	You graduated from being a Lawyer
Ọ bọ́ sérí Adájọ́	To being a Chief Judge
Ọ torí Adájọ́,	From Chief Judge
Ọ bọ́ sérí ọba	You became an Emir
Aséèjoyè ọmọ Súlú ọmọ Bọ́láńtà	Àséèjoyè, son of Súlú,son of Bọ́láńtà

The above excerpt from the song of Àrẹ̀mú Òsé explains a lot about the detailed relationship of the Emir of Ìlọrin and his progenitors. It points it out that he is a bonafide royal family member and would be successful on the throne. It is known that both his paternal and maternal families are entitled to the throne of Ìlọrin Emirship. Furthermore, his mother's uncle, his grand-father, his great-grand-father and his own biological father who were past Emirs of Ìlọrin, are mentioned. With all these facts that are embedded in traditional music, it can be clearly seen that in any society, oral literature can never be over-emphasised because it is like the mirror to see the society and establish many facts.

One excerpt from Orin Ọlọmọ-Ọba Ìlọrin is an allusion which is full of meaning on the history of the enthronement of the fifth Emir of Ìlọrin, called "Mọ́mọ́", shortened from "Mọ́mọ́lọ́ṣọ́ọ́" (the immaculate),derived from his complexion and handsomeness. His real name is Abdul-Salam, the eldest son of Ọba Zubair Ayélabówó, who was the third Emir of Ìlọrin. He was installed right from the battle field during the siege on Ọ̀fà around 1891. The song goes thus:

Ọ̀fà ló ti móyèe o o o	He was enthroned from Ọ̀fà
Ọ̀fà ló ti móyè	He was enthroned from Ọ̀fà
Ọba wa Mọ́mọ́ òokú o o	Our king Mọ́mọ́ kudos to you
Ọ̀fà ló ti móyè o o	He was enthroned from Ọ̀fà

This song simply reveals that the fifth Emir of Ìlọrin was chosen and installed by the Balóguns of Ìlọrin from the battle field as the next Emir when the stool became vacant after the demise of Ọba Aliyu, the fourth Emir of Ìlọrin, who reigned between 1868-1891. Jimoh (1994, p. 143) affirms this when he says:

While at the war front, Prince Mọ́mọ́ was the darling of all his associates. His handsome look, his courage in battle and his amiable disposition endeared him to all those who knew or had contact with him. He was therefore, a popular choice for the emirship when the stool became vacant. He was chosen accordingly by the Balóguns to succeed the late Ọba Àlíyù.

In one of the dàdàkúàdà songs of the popular Ìlọrin artiste, Jáígbadé Àlàó, in his "Ká fayé ṣe rere" record, he points out an historical fact on how the line of the Bawa Ruling House of Ìlọrin have successively ruling the Emirate. The excerpt of the song goes thus:

Wọ́n ní ìtì ọ̀gẹ̀dẹ̀ èé so lẹ́ẹ̀mejì	They said plantain tree doesn't
Mo ní láyé Súlú kọ́	Produce friuts twice
Ìtì ọ̀gẹ̀dẹ̀ Ìṣọ̀lá Òpó ti so lẹ́ẹ̀mẹrin léraa wọn	I said , not in Súlú regime
Torí Báwà lọba ìjẹrin	Plantain tree of
Báwà lọba ìjẹta	Ìṣọ̀lá Òpó has produce friuts four times in succession
Báwà lọba tàná tọ́ lọ	Four days ago king was Báwà
Ìṣọ̀lá Òpó, Báwà lọba tòní tó tún dé	Three days ago king was Báwà

Conclusion

This paper, which is an exploration of the themes of some traditional songs of Ìlọrin, sheds light on some historical ambiguities and helps to reconstruct history where possible. The study shows that language is powerful to integrate people of diverse cultures together. Yorùbá is the language of the traditional songs of Ìlọrin, despite the fact that majority of the artistes are not originally Yorùbás. The use of Yorùbá language as a medium of composing the traditional songs in Ìlọrin, is a sign of harmonious integration of many tribes who formed the formidable Ìlọrin, with some distinct dialectal variations. The study therefore points it out that language is one of the powerful tools that can reintegrate people of diverse cultures to become one. Different types of traditional musical instruments of diverse cultures came together and were utilised interchangeably in different cultural outings which, is another sign of successful cultural integration. The study also shows that though the past and the present Emirs of Ìlọrin are originally Fúlànís from Sókótó, but they have Yorùbá names, cognomens and agnomens and many other tribes in Ìlọrin are bearing Yorùbá names and some other cultural traits are today interwoven, which is an evidence of integration. The study shows that a lot of hidden facts are embedded in the traditional music of any society, which can be used as a repertoire of knowledge and to be relied upon in many instances to get many historical facts for possible historical reconstructions.

References

Adéẹ̀kọ́, Adélékè̩. (2001). Oral poetry and hegemony: Yorùbá oríkì. *Dialectical Anthropology, 26*(3-4), 181-192.

Adéọlá, Taiye. (1995). *Dàdàkúàdà: A socio-musical study*. Saarbrücken, Germany: LAP LAMBERT Academic Publishing GMBH & Co.

Ajíbádé, Olúṣọlá. (2005). Is there no man with penis in this land? Eroticism and performance in Yoruba nuptial song. *African Study Monographs, 26*(2), 99-113.

Akpabot, S. (1986). *Foundation of Nigeria traditional music*. Ìbàdàn: Spectrum Books Limited.

Jimoh, L.A.K. (1994). *Ìlọrin: The journey so far*. Ìlọrin: Atoto Press Ltd.

Nigerian Gazette (1952). *Decision of his excellency, the Governor on the claim for a revision of inter-regional boundry between the Northern and Western regions* (Govt. Notice No.1161). Lagos.

Okafor, R.C. (2005). *Music in Nigerian society*. Enugu: New Generation Books.

Ọládosù, A.G.A.S. (Ed.). (2013). *Ìlọrin: History, culture and lessons of peaceful co-existence*. Ìlọrin: Centre for Ìlọrin Studies, University of Ìlọrin.

Ọláwálé, Hakeem. (2015). *'Àgbéyẹ̀wò orin ìbílẹ̀ Yorùbá ní Ìlọrin* (Ph.D. Thesis). Department of Linguistics and African Languages, Ọbafẹmi Awolọwọ University, Ile-Ifẹ.

Sọlágbẹrú, Abdul-Razzaq M. Balogun. (2013). Sufi versus anti Sufi in Ìlọrin, Nigeria: A struggle for Supremacy. In A.G.A.S. Ọládosù et al. (Eds.), *Ìlọrin: History, culture, and lessons of peaceful co-existence*(pp. 1-24). Ìlọrin: Centre for Ìlọrin Studies, University of Ìlọrin.

Wikipedia, free Encyclopedia 12/10/2014.

Audio CDs and Recorded Songs

Àrẹ̀mú Gba Àwọ́ọ̀dù (no date)

Alhaji Ismaila Àtàndá & His Kàkàkí/Bẹ̀ǹbẹ́ Group (Title: Àpọ́nlé Ọba wa). Y. Success Digital Production. G. 37, Gàmbàrí Ìta-Àjíà Road, Ìlọrin.

Jáígbadé Àlàó (Ẹ jẹ́ ká fayé ṣe rere) 2014.

Orin Ọlọ́mọ-Ọba níbi ìgbéyàwó Saadat Àdùkẹ́ Alégẹ, Ìkókóró Compound, Ìlọrin. Life Recording as a participant. 2nd December, 2014.

ISBN 978-978-53920-4-3

To obtain your copy, please contact:

Kwara State University Press
Kwara State University, Malete
PMB 1530, Ilorin, Kwara State, Nigeria
Email: kwasupress@kwasu.edu.ng; kwasupress@gmail.com

Chapter 5

Language and Ideology in Tuface Idibia's Music

Oluwatomi Adeoti and *Moshood Zakariyah*

Introduction

Music has been known, from the ancient times, to be a means of expression of human thoughts and perceptions especially of issues or particular states of affairs. This expression could be a reaction to some social, political, religious or other issues relating directly or indirectly to man's existence and which affect his wellbeing. Music is also held to be a part of a people's culture; an indication of their beliefs, values and customs. Music can therefore be said to be a reflection of the environment (i.e. social, political, etc.) from which it emanates. Nigeria has witnessed the birth and reign of many music styles, ranging from local beats such as Afrobeat, juju and highlife, to the more Western and contemporary beats like funk, rock, hip hop, rap and R&B. The hip-hop and R&B genre has, for many years, remained popular among young and upcoming musicians, just as it has remained popular in the West.

Nigeria is known for her cultural and linguistic heterogeneity. This has its attendant issues and benefits. This heterogeneity has however become a source of division, rather than a unifying feature and has prevented the harnessing of the peculiarities of the diversity to the benefit of the country. The three major tribes, Hausa, Igbo and Yoruba, are constantly suspecting one another marginalisation while the remaining over 350 culture groups are constantly fighting the appellation of being the minority groups. This situation has informed some of the ideologies that we share, whether consciously or subconsciously, as a nation and this has also, consequently, informed the lyrics of many Nigerian musicians who, at some point or the other, have tried to use music, a universal language, to unite the dissenting views and opinions of Nigerians, preaching the gospel of love, trust, hope and oneness in spite of our diversity as a people.

Having stated the above that music is a part of a people's culture, it can be suggested that their ideologies are expressed and reflected in the ideas expressed in their music and also the choice of language items in expressing those ideas. Consequently, the cultural, political, religious, etc. ideologies of a people are mirrored in the songs, which reflect the ways the people think and perceive issues, their environment, their leaders, other people around them and their perception of the world at large. This is based on the description of ideologies as fundamental beliefs that underlie the shared social representations of particular social groups, social representations, contexts, the choice of lexical items in varying discourses, among others. One of such vanguards, promoting the message of peace, oneness, and accountability in leadership and justice in Nigeria through music is Tuface Idibia. Through his music, Tuface challenges the perceived phlegmatic disposition of Nigerian leaders and the apparent misconception of superiority that informs some Nigerians' perception of other Nigerians (and in a more general sense, fellow humans). He demands that leaders to be true to their duties and promises and that everyman should learn to live at peace with his fellow man, relating with one another in one love and in the spirit of mutual understanding which, ultimately, fosters respect and peaceful coexistence. These positions inform his worldview, his ideology which, in turn, informs the conscious and specific lexical choices in passing his messages through his music.

Language use and Ideology

The concept 'ideology' is adapted from the social sciences and philosophy into the study of language in use. Koerner (1999, p. 1) posits that the term 'ideologie' is credited to the French philosopher,

Destutt de Tracy, who, in 1976, used it to refer to "the theories of ideas conceived within a sensorialist view of mind in the tradition of condillac with practical and socially beneficial intentions." This suggests that the original notion of ideology represented a system of ideas, rather than being a core language issue. The 'ideas' or issues projected by the ideology is encoded and expressed by language.

By way of definition, Fairclough presents ideologies as "representations of aspects of the world which can be shown to contribute to establishing, maintaining and changing social relations of power, domination and exploitation"; they are thus implicit assumptions held in interaction (2003, p. 9; 2001). Van Dijk posits that ideologies are "a special form of social cognition shared by social groups. Ideologies thus form the basis of social representation and practices of group members, including their discourse, which at the same time serves as the means of ideological production, reproduction and challenge" (2001, p. 12). This definition presents ideology to be a product of social cognition and the property of a group. The result of this social cognition is the creation of a mental set in the individuals in the society which fits into the expectation of the dominant or power holding group (van Dijk, 1993). This invariably serves as a basis for social practice which consequently affects the disposition of an individual or a group to the idea being presented to them.

Oorhan, (2007, pp. 10-11) identifies four main functions of ideology in the society:

1. Ideologies provide a perspective through which the world is understood and explained. People hardly see the world as it is, only as they expect it to be. This means that people see the world through a veil of ingrained beliefs, opinions and assumptions;
2. Ideologies help to shape the nature of political systems. The political systems are established upon a given set of principles;
3. Ideologies play a crucial role in either upholding the prevailing power structure by portraying it as fair, natural, rightful or whatever; or in weakening it, by highlighting its inequities or injustices and drawing attention to the attractions of alternative power structures.

4. Ideologies can act as forms of social cement, providing social groups and indeed societies with a set of unifying beliefs and values.

The point in 4 above is reiterated in the submission of Bloor & Bloor (2007) in their definition of ideology as being "a set of beliefs or attitudes shared by members of a particular social group" (p. 10) or communities. Discourse by members of such communities is therefore ideologically rooted and/ or structured towards communicating particular ideologies. Oorhan's submission that " ideologies provide a perspective through which the world is understood and explained..." is relevant to this study as the ideological leanings/ projections of Tuface suggests his perception of or representations of his perception of the expectations of the society in which he lives. His music thus suggests how he sees the world, "through a veil of ingrained beliefs, opinions and assumptions." Johnstone (2008) explains that CDA seeks to unearth the ways in which discourses and ideology are intricately linked. Our talks are a reflection of our thoughts and these thoughts can be influenced by choices about grammar, style, wording and every aspect of discourse. When writers write, they have choices, and their choices have several effects. Writers use their choices to create points of views via the choice of what to say and how to say it. They use words to create worlds and, according to Johnstone, "particular choices can come to stand for a whole new way of seeing things, whole new ways of being, and those new ways of seeing things can come to seem natural, unchallengeable and right." Choice in language use is therefore strategic, for that choice was made for a purpose. This position is aptly relevant to the conception of ideology in music, as Tuface is seen to make specific and strategic choices in his lyrics for his communicative purpose.

About Tuface Idibia

Tuface - Innocent Ujah Idibia was born on September 18, 1975 in Jos, Plateau State, Nigeria. He is from the Idoma tribe of the Benue State and he celebrates his roots, as he usually sings in his native language/ dialect. Most people do not, however, know or remember his given name, as his stage name, Tuface (or TuBaba), has come to be a brand name in the Nigerian music industry and beyond. Tuface is a singer, songwriter, record producer and entrepreneur whose style is quite peculiar. With a distinctive voice that sets him apart from the pack, Tuface's creativity and focus distinguishes his music from others, endearing him to many. He is mostly associated with the R& B, Hip hop, Reggae and Afrobeat music genres, and has been in the music industry since 1994. He was a member of the defunct music group Plantashun Boyz, and has since gone solo since the disbanding of the group in 2004. Tuface has had a prolific music career and he is acclaimed to be one of the most decorated and successful Afro pop artists in Africa, going by his many awards (one MTV Europe Music Award, one World Music Award, five Headies Awards [Hip-hop award], four Channel O Music Video Awards, and one BET Award, four MTV Africa Music Awards, one MOBO Award, one KORA Award, and numerous additional nominations) and recognitions. He also has to his credit six Albums and numerous singles. The NGO 2Face Idibia Reach-out Foundation is his way of giving back to the society, as he does a great "Service to Humanity" through his acts of philanthropy in the NGO (Wikipedia.org).

Theoretical Background

This study employs the Critical Discourse Analysis (CDA) to the approach of ideology, given that there are several conceptions of ideology. In a CDA stance to ideology, van Dijk (2000) presents a practical heuristic which connects underlying social beliefs to their expression in discourse. The strategy is what he calls the 'ideological square', which may be applied to the analysis of all levels of discourse. The ideological square contains four principles/ possibilities viz: emphasise positive things about Us, emphasise negative things about Them, de-emphasise negative things about Us, de-emphasise positive things about them. These possibilities within the ideological square can be used to analyse discourse on many levels of discourse, which include meaning, propositional structures, formal structures, sentence syntax, discourse forms, argumentation, rhetoric and action and interaction. The discursive work of the singer (Tuface) can therefore be interpreted on these levels of discourse, all of which are, in some way or the other, identifiable parts of Tuface's music. At the core of ideologies are a specific world-view, a mental system of beliefs and values, which underlie their linguistic norms, guides their perception of issues and ultimately the people's definition of the world. This 'global' perception of ideology is in line with Wodak et al. (1990) discourse-historical approach to CDA. This method submits that language manifests social processes and interactions and constitutes those processes as well. The theoretical anchor of the discourse-historical method is the theory of text planning, "by means of which the intentions of the speaker and extra-linguistic factors in the text production are identified" (Titscher et al., 2000, p. 154). This theory grew out of a perceived inadequacy in the theory of linguistic activity. Highlighting the place of historical and social aspects of discourse, Wodak explains that the speech situation, status of the participants, time and place, sociolinguistic variables such as group membership and age, and psychological determinants, play an essential role in speech production, and in our example, the production of the music and lyrics that make up the songs. The socio-psychological, cognitive and linguistic dimensions of text production which informs and underlies the concept of frames (global patterns which encapsulate our general knowledge of some situation) and schemata (exact patterns for the concrete realisation of a situation or text), are therefore of great significance in the analysis of ideological texts (Wodak et. al., 1990).

The discourse-historical approach is thus based on a theory of context which takes into account the immediate language or the local interactive processes of negotiation, the intertextual and interdiscursive relationship between utterances, texts and discourses, the language and other social variables and institutional frames of the particular context of situation and the broader socio-political and historical context in which the discursive practices are related to and embedded in (Titscher et al., 2000). Matouschek, Wodak and Januschek (1995, p. 60) provide a three-dimensional analytical model for the adaptation of the discourse historical method.

The first level (content level) explains the construction of "discourse of difference i.e. the constitution of 'we' and how 'self is positively portrayed', through lexical choices such as grammatically cohesive elements. This level precipitates the second level which exemplifies techniques of 'defamation and devaluation of the 'Other's viewpoint'. The third level presents examples of the linguistic forms through which the first two levels are actualised. These include the creation of unreal scenarios, use of generalisations, quotations, and vagueness among others. The three parts of the model operate, not as a series of steps in an operational activity. Rather, they systematically and recursively work in sync in relation to the entirety of contextual

In the context of this current study, the discourse-historical method presents a context-based approach to the consideration of discourse texts. It consequently provides insights into the understanding of how the music of Tuface, which is informed and invested societal expectations, which are also a part of certain ideologies, further project these ideologies and more in his music.

Data Presentation and Analysis

The data consist of examples drawn from four tracks of Tuface titled: See me So, One Love, For Instance and Vote, not Fight. The identified behavioural patterns are discussed below:

A. *Leadership Ideology (Deception as a Leadership Ideological Trait)*

Leadership style as it relates to Nigerian politicians, is observed in the music of Tuface as being one of deception. Here, Tuface challenges the status quo by reminding the government of their standing promises that are yet to be fulfilled. In stanza two of *E be like Say*, he expresses his position:

> See, all I want to say is that
> They don't really care about us
> Because all they want to do is to get in touch with big bucks
> Because they think the money gives them the power
> But the power is nothing
> If your people cannot get quality education
> The power is nothing
> If your people keep on dying of disease and starvation

> The power is nothing
> If your people have no peace (no peace)
> The power is nothing
> If your people cannot live in unity (eh)
> See, why do you keep deceiving the people, my brother, my sister
> See, why you make all this people to dey fight one another
> Only God can judge you now [x4]
> And now you want my vote once more.

The we-you discourse level involves the use of social polarisation (van Dijk, 2000) between Us and Them, a form of in-group and out-group classification, with social consequences. This strategy is used to establish solidarity; through the constitution of 'we' and also to discredit the other while positive self-portrayal is pursued. In the opening line of stanza two above, Tuface says... "I want to say is that they don't really care about us." 'Us' here is immediately seen as being used to establish an in-group identity, viz: we, us. Vs you, they and them. 'Us' can therefore be said to be Tuface and any other person that he or his ideas represent. His use of 'they' is seen as an attempt at dissociating himself from them. Tuface further expresses this ideology in the line where he says, *"why do you keep deceiving the people, my brother, my sister."* These suggest to us the ideological investments in this song.

The lyrics in *e be like say* further presents the ideology of Nigerian leadership as one of deception. In the first stanza, he expresses a recurring trend of lies and the referent (the government or people vying for political offices) reneging on their promises. He says:

> E be like say you want to tell me another story again
> e be like say you want to act another movie again
> e be like say you want to code another coding again...

And in the last line of the song, he says "And now you want my vote once more." The referent(s) 'you' in this song is therefore presented as being deceptive and possibly unaccountable. This is also taken to be the belief of the group that Tuface represents, thereby making it an ideologically invested position.

B. *Eroding of Oneness and Peaceful Co-existence*

The theme of oneness and peaceful co-existence is seen to be an ideological leaning in the music of Tuface. His lyrics promote the need for the people of Nigeria, and the world at large, to live in peaceful coexistence which can happen only if there is love, one love. In *One Love*, he expresses an overwhelming concern at the brutal killings he saw on CNN. He asks, is this love, is this hate…"…

This is almost difficult, as the government does not foster oneness but through their actions and inactions, promote division. The obvious ideological standpoint of the artist, which also represents the position of the masses, is that political leaders in Nigeria device a divide-and-rule principle for their personal political gains. The underlying reality of the ethnic composition of the Nigeria-State makes this strategy effective, as Nigerians are easily divided along ethnic, culture, region, and religion affiliations. It is highly ironical that the leaders who are supposed to champion the need for peaceful co-existence in the society are the ones fuelling ethno-tribal and religious tension through divide-and-rule for their inordinate political gains. In the words of Tuface:

> Why do you keep deceiving the people
> Why you make all these people go de
> Fight one another
> Only God can judge you now
> Another year has come
> And now you want my vote once more

The first two lines above question the resolve of bad leadership towards deceiving people and making them take up arms against each other. Line three seeks supernatural power in solving the problem as this suggest that resolving the problem of bad leadership is beyond the masses, hence the reliance on God for intervention. The idea of "another year has come" and "my vote once more" indicates that soliciting the masses' votes has been happening from time-to-time without anything positive to show for it. The above submission is also echoed in several other instances of Tuface's song.

C. Impunity and Corruption

Tuface, like the Nigerian masses, believes that the major factor militating against social and economic development in the country is corruption. There are widely reported and documented cases of corruption in Nigeria. It is a common trend for the Nigerian politicians not only to embezzle the tax payer's money but also to keep it illegally in foreign countries. Tuface asserts thus:

> I dedicate this one to all the shady politicians
> Wey go promise and fail and make the people live in harsh condition
> I dedicate this one to all the shady politicians
> Why don't you change your ways?
> Change your ways now
> Make the people live the way they are supposed to live

The choice of lexical items such as "shady politicians," "promise and fail," and "harsh condition" in the above data are carefully chosen to project the negative image of the typical Nigerian politicians. It is also no coincidence that the track, according to the artist, is dedicated to "all the shady politicians" who have every apparatus needed to put things right, to provide good roads, hospitals, shelter, and more. On the one hand, the Nigerian politicians are depicted as the "alpha and omega," determining the destiny of the common man. On the other hand, the Nigerian politicians are projected as greedy, corrupt, insensitive and non-responsive to the sufferings of the masses. Having described the typical Nigerian politician, Tuface identifies money laundering as one of the major causes of underdevelopment in Nigeria. He posits thus

> For instance
> I go create a scenery where better go plenty
> Make we de give chance
> Instead to de pack money go France
> To make suffer to full in abundance

The artist wishes to have the opportunity to put the wrong right, to stop the sufferings of the masses, to put an end to starvation, and generally to improve the masses' standard of living. As the dream of the founding fathers or the heroes past of Nigeria, the artist wishes to create a country of people's. To make this become a reality, the artist (line 3) suggests that the age-long bad leadership style should pave way for a purposeful and responsive leadership style that is visionary and operates with the fear of God. This is more beneficial than keeping the stolen money in foreign land (line 4). Stashing the country's resources in foreign countries in this manner can only multiply poverty and suffering of the masses in Nigeria. The condition of the common man is graphically understood through the following lines:

> This kind of life
> That we living
> All my people
> Them be suffering and smiling
> Smiling smiling
> This ghetto life
> That we living
> Living living
> Them be suffering and smiling
> Smiling smiling

The above lines present a stark irony, as the Nigerian people who are seriously suffering are also seriously smiling. Attention needs to be paid to the use of personal pronoun "we" (line 1) which Tuface deliberately employs to emphasise his ideological standpoint on hardship being caused by bad leadership style in Nigeria. Also, the expression "all my people" (line 2) is an indication that there is no part of the country where there is no suffering, where the poor do not outnumbered the rich, where people are not dying of hunger and starvation, and where people are not being sent to their early graves because of poorly equipped hospitals. This implies that the bad leadership situation is hopeless, as there is absolutely nothing within the control of the masses to salvage the ugly situation. The hopelessness of the situation partly accounts for why the artist calls for God's intervention in putting an end to bad leadership style in Nigeria. He asserts thus:

> How come our country
> Be like this
> We want to run

> But we never crawl
> Its like putting the cart
> Before the horse
> Only God can save us now
> Save us now

However, in spite of the artist's reliance on God for a pragmatic solution, there seems to be no end in sight. This is because, according to the artist, there is no certainty as to when the problem of bad leadership would come to an end.

> Every day and night
> Na chaos for our area
> How long shall we
> Keep on living like this

It is revealed in the above lines that chaos, civic unrest, poverty, illness, and killing of innocent people for political gains are the order of the day. Also, the problems rocking Nigeria are not time specific, as they occur at all times, day and night. The above lines are a clear indication that there is no end in sight as far as the sufferings of the masses are concerned. This pessimistic idea of Tuface is ideologically coined to reflect the view of the masses generally, and that of the artist in particular.

Conclusion

So far, this study has demonstrated that music is a potent weapon not only for entertainment but also for criticising social vices. This is particularly true of the concept of the idea of bad leadership as evident in the music Tuface Idibia, who, according to many, is a social critic and the mouth-piece of the commoners. In addition, music is greatly influenced by the ideological position of the singer, depending on where he/she stands on a particular issue of common interest. Through music, Tuface, projects the leadership style in Nigeria negatively, with emphasis on the uncaring and irresponsible nature of the people in various positions of responsibility in the country. In addition, the study has demonstrated that linguistic theories can be used for the analysis of oral literature, including music.

References

Bloor, M. & Bloor, T. (2007). *The practice of critical discourse analysis: An introduction.* London: Hodder Education.

Fairclough, N. (2001). *Language and power.* London: Pearson Education Ltd.

Fairclough, N. (2003). *Analysing discourse: Textual analysis for social research.* London: Routledge.

Koerner, E. F. K. (1999). Linguistics and ideology in the study of language. From http://www.tulane.edu/~howard/LangIdeo/Koerner/Koerner.html

Titscher, S., Meyer, M., Wodak, R. & Vetter, E. (2000). *Methods of text and discourse analysis.* London: SAGE publications.

van Dijk, T. (1993). Principles of critical discourse analysis. *Discourse & society,* 4 (2), 249–283. Retrieved 5th May, 2014 from http://www.discourse.org/OldArticles/Principle%20%0f%20critical%20discourse%20analysis.pdf

van Dijk, T. (2000). *Ideology and discourse: A multidisciplinary introduction* (Unpublished English version of an internet course for the Universitat Oberta de Catalunya).

van Dijk, T. (2001). Critical discourse analysis. In D. Tannem, D. Schriffin, & H. Hamilton, (Eds.), *Handbook of discourse analysis* (pp. 352–371). Oxford: Blackwell. Retrieved from www.discourses.org/oldarticles/criticaldiscourseanalysispdf

Wodak, R., Nowak, P., Pelikan, J., Gruber, H., de Zilia, R., & Mitten, R. (1990). Wir sind alle unschuldige tater: Diskur-historische studien zum nachkriegsantisemitismus. Frankfurt: Suhrkamp. www.allwritefictionadvice.blogspot.in2011/05/repetition-how-to-use-it-effectively.html?m=1

Èṣù Elẹ́gbára

*Change, Chance, Uncertainty
In Yorùbá Mythology*

AYỌDELE OGUNDIPẸ

With Introduction by Jacob Olupona

ISBN 978-978-972-590-8

To obtain your copy, please contact:

Kwara State University Press
Kwara State University, Malete
PMB 1530, Ilorin, Kwara State, Nigeria
Email: kwasupress@kwasu.edu.ng; kwasupress@gmail.com

Chapter 6

Sunnie Ododo's *Broken Pitchers* and the (Im)possibilities of National Resurgence

Kayode Niyi Afolayan

Introduction

Scholarly interests in Nigerian poetry have always used the parameters of history and aesthetics to indicate the different movements in its evolution. For instance, Oyeniyi Okunoye (2008) examines the poetry of decolonisation in his essay, "Modern African Poetry as Counter-Discursive Practice" and draws a relationship between history and aesthetics in the "four phases" within a period (pp. 73-93). In his "An Appraisal of the Critical Legacies of the 1980 Revolution in Nigerian Poetry," Wole Ogundele (2008) argues from the perspective of history and connects the first generation of poets, like Christopher Okigbo, Wole Soyinka and John Pepper Clark to the pre-civil war period and others to the post war era (pp. 136-154). Ogundele (2008) also makes a distinction between the aesthetics of two generations of poets. Citing Chinweizu, Onwuchekwa, Jemie and Ihechukwu Madubuike (1980), he distinguishes between what he calls the first and second generations of poets in Nigeria. While Chinweizu, Jemie and Madubuike (1980) characterise poets of the first generation as lacking in commitment, being "obsess[ed] with private grief and emotions ... elitism ... over intellectualism ... willful obscurantism, Eurocentrism and aestheticism" (p. 139), they describe the second generation poets (e.g. Odia Ofeimun, Tanure Ojaide and Niyi Osundare) as being more socially responsive with their "poetry of orality ... [that is] socially anchored... [and] functional" (p. 140).

The era of military leaders, like Generals Mohammadu Buhari, Ibrahim Babangida, Sanni Abacha and Abdulsalami Abubakar, has been adjudged quite important in the study of modern poetry in Nigeria. Okunoye, in "Writing resistance: Dissidence and Visions of Healing in Nigerian Poetry of the Military Era," captures the importance of the period in relation to the evolution of poetry in Nigeria:

> Anyone familiar with the growth of Nigerian literature after the civil war will have no difficulty appreciating why the genre of poetry dominated Nigerian writing, especially from the mid-1980s to the late 1990s. In a sense, the prevailing political climate in the country created the atmosphere for it to thrive. Proof that Nigerian poetry has been very dynamic is that it has drawn on a variety of experiences. But of the three major events that have significantly impacted on it – the Nigerian crisis of the 1960s, the Nigerian civil war (1967–1970) and military rule (1966–1979; 1983–99) (Okunoye, 2011, pp. 64- 85).

It seems obvious that the political situation in the country made it pertinent for writers to make thematic such issues as abuse of human rights, corruption and even the intimidation of artists. Although all the military regimes had a common dictatorial tendency, each military regime had a peculiar orientation that called for a different variety of poetry. During the Buhari regime, there was the obnoxious Decree 4 which curtailed press freedom and rights of expression. Notwithstanding, creative writers were not silenced. Newspaper poetry became very popular and a poet like Niyi Osundare had a poetry column in the *National Tribune,* through which he satirised the social conditions of the era. Even though the Babangida regime pretended to be social friendly, state war against writers continued. The horrifying murder of Dele Giwa, a seasoned journalist, which was allegedly linked to the state, exemplifies this. There was also the killing of Mamman Vatsa over an alleged coup plot. This was followed by the annulment of the 1993 presidential election believed to have been won by Moshood Abiola.

The time of Abacha as Head of State witnessed the writing of more poems that highlighted the worsening of rights violations. Writers were incarcerated without fair trial. Some like Soyinka had to leave the country on exile. The Niger Delta imbroglio culminated in the judicial murder of Ken Saro Wiwa, another notable creative writer and activist. As a result of this state-empowered persecution, prison notes/diaries, exile-experience-induced poems and Niger Delta poetry emerged and became very popular.

Okunoye (2011) compresses these forms into three main phases:

> The first coincides with the work of Odia Ofeimun and constitutes the foundation for the tradition in the sense of inaugurating the basic discursive foundation for it. The second was a development in the eighties which saw many poets building on the foundation that had been laid, while the third, in part an extension of the second, largely chronicles the losses and social dislocations – personal and collective – occasioned by the last phase of military dictatorship (pp. 66-67).

Okunoye's division has some merit but falls short in presenting the dynamics of folklore and the innovation its uses brought to bear on the poetry of the period. This has special influence on the emerging, younger poets, majority of who were born a few years before or after the nation's independence. Apart from the trauma of the Biafra-Nigeria war, they had the benefit of the oil boom and its impact on the economy. They have also witnessed the philandering and squandering of the riches of the oil boom. Sunnie Ododo, while giving the background to *Broken Pitchers*, alludes to this dilemma in an interview with this author:

> The poems in *Broken Pitchers* were not written deliberately to form a volume. I was just writing the way ideas occurred to me. I have tried to put them in three thematic concerns- "Tension", "Titillation" and "Tutti-Fruiti"- they are purely informed by my environment, structures, institutions and governance. For me, we have a nation at independence that all of us were happy about and were trying to make the best we could out of it. Along

the line, for whatever went wrong, we began to hit at that treasure of nationhood, siphoning and dissipating it until it looks like there is nothing left. Many of the poems give concern to disillusionment as captured by the title (Afolayan, 2010, p. 297).

Through these three sections - "Tension", "Titillation" and "Tutti-frutti" - Ododo mirrors the terrible condition of things in the nation. The poet's rigorous engagement and sense of disillusionment are predicated on the hopelessness evident in the title. However, this cannot be said of the last two sections where the poet grapples more with personal experience.

Ododo and the Satire of Collective Dilemma

T. S. Eliot's clarifies how shifts between 'old' and 'new' practices offer distinctions in this manner:

> No poet, no artist of any art, has his complete meaning alone. His significance, his appreciation is the appreciation of his reaction to the dead poet and artists. You cannot value him alone; you must set him for contrast and comparison.... When a new work of art is created it is something that happens simultaneously to all the works of art which preceded it. The existing monuments form an ideal among themselves which is modified by the introduction of the new.... The existing order is complete before the new work arrives, for order to persist after the supervention of novelty, the whole existing order must be... altered; and so the relations, proportions, values of each work of art toward the whole are readjusted; and this is conformity between the old and the new (p. 37).

Abiola Irele explains further that "tradition *is* not so much an abiding, permanent, immutable stock of beliefs and symbols but is the constant refinement and extension of these in a way which relates them to an experience that is felt as being at once continuous and significantly new" (p. 4). But, at the level of the poet, the allocation and association of fixed time frames can be problematic especially when a writer's life spans through different historical periods and experiences. Therefore, it appears safer to look at a particular period and examine how poets or writers have responded to the situations that prevailed. As expected, military leaders, owing to their misrule, dictatorial inclinations and abuse, came under serious criticism. Although, the tone of writing fluctuates between pessimism and hope,

[the] Nigerian poetry of the military era is not just about the military; it is as much about the nation and the people, the helpless witnesses of the oddities that characterized the era. It represents the people in their resilience and resolve to invent a new nation out of the rot and immortalizes those who dared to confront the dictators, those represented as the martyrs of the struggle. It thus constitutes the literary expression of resistance to the chaotic state of affairs that the Nigerian experience of military rule precipitated (Okunoye, 2011, p. 83).

Indeed, the sense of nationalism is triggered by the failure in leadership and a pallid sense of hopelessness that feeds on an irascible resignation and stoicism of the led. The social condition in the country was very paramount in the mind of Ododo when he wrote most of the poems in *Broken Pitchers*. Perhaps, more relevant are the fifteen (p. 15) poems in "Tension" in which he exposes the condition of his nation at the time. In "Quarter of a Cent" (the first poem in the collection) the silver jubilee anniversary of his country provides the expediency for an assessment that is quite auspicious:

> Clothed and simmered in reddish pool,
> Umbilical cord holding tight to mentor,
> With gradual tribulation, that frees itself.
>
> A teething child groping to find its bearing
> Tottering feet here and there; falls and wails
> Manages to survive adolescent incubation;
>
> A promising youth foretelling foetal future;
> You joined conclave of elders at twenty one
> Plying and moulding your designed destiny;
>
> At 25, crises cry loud in your kingdom,
> Quartet score scoring quarter of a cent
> Jubilant music heralds silky silver cent
> That colourizes the hair with wisdom –
> A guiding trait to a Golden Medal (pp. 11-12).

In this poem, the poet presents his own testament of the history of a crises riddled nation that is rendered susceptible to disintegration. The last line of the poem ("It is still a slim silver juggling jubilee!") laments the diminution of the euphoria that ought to mark the celebration of twenty-five years of independence. The issue is that instead of the nation to utilise its human and material resources for sustainable growth, it is bedevilled with debilitating socio-economic and political crises.

The poet continues, in "Purgatory of Race", to lament the sad condition of a nation that began with very bright prospects. His dirge is captured in some flora and fauna imagery:

> That was its primehood,
> A flourishing phase.
> A viable wisdom germinated
> Barrels of juice exchanged
> For foreign currencies.
> Now a repressive wisdom has taken over,
> The juicy fruits becoming stones;
> Birds becoming imprudent;
> Yellowish vegetation descended,
> Hardship illuminated
> By threatening, hard brown shuttles
> Hanging precariously;
> The territory once loved and cherished
> Is now shattered, tattered and wretched (pp. 13-14).

The allusion to Nigeria's oil wealth, which has since ceased to be a blessing indicates the misappropriation of natural values and its attendant adverse effect on the citizens who are supposed to be beneficiaries.

The metaphor of the famished tree at the end of the poem is an apparent expression of melancholy. This explains the poet's repetitive use of "there" (which means "at this point or stage") to amplify the present state of neglect and the cloud of misery that enveloped his nation:

> There
> There now stands
> A haggard shadowless structure
> With stunted criss-crossed arms

> Like a map's routes
> Scorched hearth tapping its roots,
> Squeezing nutrients of life to death.
>
> Is it too far from redemption?
> Where is its hope?... Where? (p. 15)

For the poet, the people live in a nation whose "Sedimentary Riches" have ceased to be a blessing. His allusion to the broken [and by implication, useless] pitcher is indicative of a shattered collective dream, propelled by wanton plunder of the nation's wealth. The poet's anger against the ruling class is hinged on their lack of vision. For instance, he is disgusted with the maximum rulers who pretend to be interested in ameliorating the suffering of the people while compounding it. Their response to the problem of shelter is puzzling; laudable, poverty-alleviating policies and projects are often abandoned while the completed ones become available only to the rich. For instance, the poor have become "Souls without bodies", as the low cost housing units (LCHU) originally meant for them are allocated to weeds, animals and hoodlums who are usually active at night:

> LCHU – a solace of paradox
> Lucrative Cosy Heavenly Units –
> Cost too huge for ordinary man's reach,
> But fertile homes for weeds and wildlife;
> Safe heavens for nocturnal hoodlums...
> Hardly a befitting tale of a race
> Of mammoth means and measure
> Festering nests of prodigal culture,
> But wearing pallid lace of disgrace (p. 19).

The economic policy of government also comes under the poet's close scrutiny. The Structural Adjustment Program (SAP) of the Babangida administration, put in place to revamp the ailing economy is against the people and falls short of the ability to solve the problem that necessitates its making and implementation. In "Twigs of furies" the poet generates alternative meanings to the acronym, SAP, to show the negative implications of the policy:

> Structural AIDS Policy
> State Advancement in Pain
> Satanic Addendum for the People
> Systematic Acquisition of Poverty
> Siphoning of Abundant *Petronaira* (p. 20).

The refusal of government to abolish this scheme is the preoccupation of the poet in "Babangidaquin". Using a combination of *Babangida* and the *Queen*, in the title index, the poet condemns neo-colonialism. In broad terms, Babangida represents the black African leaders who are visionless while "Queen" represents the West whose long term interest is to sustain the impoverishment of the African people. The poverty is so palpable that it weakens the people physically and spiritually:

> Stomachs are grumbling
> Limbs are limping
> Sights are failing
> Systems are crumbling
> While
> SAP saps the *sappables* (p. 22).

The diplomacy that puts the scheme in place is one that auctions our birth right for a plate of porridge:

> Talks: diplomatic jaw-jaw transpired
> Scribbles of ink spelt economic relief
> A nation of pounds promised dollars.
> Is the meeting of Babangida and the Queen
> The *Babangidaquin* for our *economaria*? (p. 22)

Another interesting dimension to the poet's thematic preoccupation is seen in "WAI's armoury" (p. 23) where the poet lampoons the programme set up by government to encourage environmental sanitation. But for the poet, the visible achievement of WAI (War Against Indiscipline) is that the common man is victimised as his fundamental right to free movement is curtailed while the larger filth in government quarters continue to putrefy the environment. WAI therefore becomes a repressive policy put in place to solve a problem by creating another. This condition of hopelessness, occasioned by misrule, is soon become the lot of a people under the siege of the military.

In "What a journey" (pp. 24-25), transition programmes are adjudged mere political exercises as they are programmed to fail and dash the hope of the people to transit to civil rule. As a result, the people come to realise that they are being deceived and this explains why the poet calls for a total abrogation of military rule:

> Now, I dream of freedom
> From this martial marching
> Full of gloom and doom.
> I am tired of whistling wicked sounds
> I am tired of extorting explosions
> I am tired of gushing gaudy sights
> My heart is tired of stricken stitches (pp. 26-27).

The poet anticipates that his appeal will amount to nothing:

> Please leave me alone,
> Foul or false, leave me alone
> To heal up my wounds
> And ply my pluvial destiny...
> Now that you have finally consented
> To retreat on my 32nd birthday,
> The only present I ask of you
> Is my total freedom, freedom forever,
> And never again poke into my palaver;
> No matter what! (p. 27).

There is usually a cloud of uncertainty concerning who takes over from the military. In "Who picks the baton?" (pp. 29-30) the preparation for transition to civil rule is rife. But the politicians appear not to have learnt anything from their failures in the past. Perhaps, to facilitate their quick return to power, the military deliberately establish ill-prepared electoral commissions to superintend over shabby electoral processes and cause bad leaders to be 'elected.' This ensures the return to dictatorial military rule. This situation is so worrisome to the poet that in "Leave Me Alone", he vents his anger on successive military regimes. For him, supernatural intervention is the only panacea:

> In 1998 just before the demise of Abacha, I wrote an opera, *To Return from the Void*, where after looking at

the situation in the country, I prophesised that it was only divine intervention that could save this country from total collapse. That, for me was the height of the prophetic duty of a writer because not quite long after that opera, Abacha died in a manner not understood till today. His death brought fresh breath to the nation.... So far, what has led us where we are today is the divine grace of God, we are yet to see that man with clear vision to lead us out of the woods; we are just gambling with the nation (Interview: p. 297).

Oral forms, nationalism and the Nigerian poet

Tradition and practice in modern African poetry cannot be discussed without mentioning the people's folklore as its precursor. Charles Bodunde (2001) demonstrates how individual African poets have used the medium of poetry to universalise or elevate the social and metaphysical credentials of indigenous idioms. However, Kayode Afolayan (2010) delineates the dimensions, import and usage of indigenous forms when he asserts that:

> [the] uses of folklore—for the African artist—have been through two stages which have produced four epochs. The first bothered on the apprehension and usage of folklore for its sake... The second category consist in those artists who sought the proactive use of folklore in their genius. In the third and last category we have poets ... whose delight is not only in the use of diverse forms of folklore but also in the integration of performance into poems of social mediation (pp. 132-145)

Sunnie Ododo uses the indigenous forms in *Broken Pitchers* to make statements about his people's folklore and he has continued to develop the form. Perhaps, an example that comes to mind here is Wole Soyinka whose use of Ogun, which began in *Idanre and other Poems* (1967) and has since reflected in *A Shuttle in the Crypt* (1972), *Ogun Abibiman* (1976), *Mandela's Earth and Other Poems* (1989), and *Samarkand and Other Markets I Have Known* (2002). Ododo initialises with statements that exhibit the stabilising and mediatory function of the "Ekwu" masquerade cult in the Ebira cultural milieu. Before this, he had considered the mytho-legendary features of the cult and, against the masquerade label, renamed it "facequerade." At least two poems give credence to this in *Broken Pitchers*. In "Okene" (30) the poet extols the traditional virtues of the Ebira people but laments the erosion of those sacred values by civilisation. The poet glowingly shows the candour of the flora and fauna of Ebiraland as well as the hospitable nature of the people:

> Hover in, and a mud face
> Dotted with modern architectural inks
> Greets you into the town,
> Trek in, and pebbles of riches
> Kiss your feet on ancient carpet.
> Pop up to reply and *Ireba*
> Arrests your sights to a standstill
> *Taruuu*! One utters in a great awe (p. 30).

His choice of "Ireba" and "Taruuu", in this excerpt, amplifies the synergy culture and a people in the sense that while *Ireba* symbolises primordial cultural landmarks, *Taruuu* between unveils the openness and tolerance of the community to visitors and strangers.

Unfortunately, the poet's lament in the end of the poem shows a negative trend that is eroding these classic values as:

> Cultural flavour fritters away into
> The oblivion like escaping smokes…
> Confusion creeps in on stilts
> Crashing down at the behest of the unknown (p. 30).

Beyond the physical strictures of nature, however, the poet also engages the metaphysics. This is mostly encapsulated in "Ajagu lives on" which is a poem that concludes the collection where one finds the following lines very relevant:

> Ajagu!
> Your critical hinges shall always creak
> Your pungest philosophies are undying
>
> As Ebira ancestors play the symphony of a holy day.
> The sun and the rain unite in your name to the peak;
> With your legs beyond ….
> With your legacy here with us, live on (p. 63).

These lines are Ododo's posthumous tribute to Ajagu Obeito who was "the custodian of Achewuru Anavehi, one of the foremost Ebira 'facekuerade' performers, who died in 1989" (p. 62). The poet projects his attachment to the masquerade cult, not only for its aesthetic values but also for the mediatory role it plays in the society. In Ebiraland, the cult's stabilising roles extends from ordinary members of the society to the monarch. Ododo elucidates:

> every monarch wants to be friend of the "Ekwu" cult. It is not that the cult brings whip to flog anybody but the invectives in the words of their poetry annually. They are privy to the societal happenings, so they lampoon you, talk to you directly, so nobody is beyond their sharp tongues of criticism… In those days it was a stigma to be signposted by "Ekwu", such a person admonished will go on self- exile…. When the king is hit, he is either forced to abdicate the throne or change his ways. Sometimes it can incite mass action against the monarch (Interview: 304).

The inference that can be drawn from this not only compliments the artistic candour that the performance generates but the poet himself is the modern day "Ekwu" who hankers after probity and uses his art to assert truth and justice in a corrupt and hopeless society.

Sunnie Ododo's in *Broken Pitchers* sustains the legacy of African poets whose primary concern is to interrogate the failures of structures and institutions in their societies. The title index of the collection exhibits melancholy that is precipitated by failure of leadership in a way that queries the docility of the followership. The poet gives a faint impression of remedy but tragically nothing is being done or about to be done to fix the "pitchers" which, in metaphorical context, stands for the poet's nation. The poet's yearning for a democratic dispensation is predicated on anticipation for a just society. This reflects in his answer as to whether he prefers the military to civilian rule:

> How many years of military rule have we had? About three decades. Our nascent unbroken democracy from 1999 to date is only 13 years. Comparatively, one cannot give a straight answer but I must tell you that the worst democracy is better that the best military regime. We are learning, take it or leave it. In spite of our inadequacies, fights in the national

and state assemblies here and there, at least there is a forum for people to disagree and fight. The military ruled by fiat and the opinion of the people never really counted. We shall get to that point when fights shall no longer be physical but by elocution of language only (Interview: 302).

The antidote that Ododo prescribes is inspired by a social vision that seeks to mend those social structures rendered inept by the leaders and the led in his country. His lines challenge the masses who, sadly have become used to suffering, to join with the progressives in the task of rebuilding the nation. He gives an insight into how to achieve this when he calls for the galvanisation of progressive forces:

> There is disharmony in the voices of the masses, until all these voices are harmonised and unified to speak against the common enemy, there cannot be a meaningful change. We need an organized thrust to infiltrate the structure of government. Soyinka, for instance wore the garb of politics when he feels his drama or poetry is not enough for his social crusade. This is not a job for one person. The carrier syndrome cannot solve the problem (Interview: 299).

One credits the poet's bluntness in his evocation which challenges his compatriots to harness the potential of the nation but this will not happen until the pitcher has been fixed and placed in the hands of those who will use it creditably. But the poet is still faced with a daunting task as robust exploration of the tendencies and relevance of the 'Ekwu' masquerade to the dilemmas of the post military era must be exhibited in his subsequent are expected.

Conclusion

This paper has critically examined the values of Sunnie Ododo's *Broken Pitchers* by pointing out its social relevance. The writer has harnessed the discussions on the subjects of politics and folklore which form the basic essences of the collection. Whereas, the writer has observed the realities presented by the poet in his discussions of social themes, the paper is of the opinion that the poet needs to expose more 'mysteries' of the 'Ekwu' masquerade and bring it in line with contemporary conditions of national and universal appeals.

References

Afolayan, Kayode Niyi. (2010). Mythic strands, orature and social mediation in Olu Obafemi's Illumination: Songs, dances, from the belly of time. *US-China Foreign Languages, 8*(11), 132 –145.

Bodunde, Charles. (2001). *Oral traditions and aesthetic transfer: Creativity and social vision in contemporary African poetry.* Bayreuth: Bayreuth African Studies.

Chinweizu, Onwuchekwa Jemie, & Ihechukwu Madubuike (Eds.) (1980). *Toward the decolonization of African literature.* Enugu: Fourth Dimension Publishers.

Eliot, T. S. (1982). Tradition and the individual talent. *Perspecta, 19,* 36-42.

Irele, Abiola (2000). Tradition and the Yoruba writer: D. O. Fagunwa, Amos Tutuola and Wole Soyinka. In Biodun Jeyifo (Ed.), *Perspectives on Wole Soyinka: Freedom and complexity* (pp. 3-26). United States: University of Mississippi Press.

Ododo, Sunnie. (2012). *Broken pitchers.* Ibadan: Kraft Books.

Ogundele, Wole. (2008). An appraisal of the critical legacies of the 1980s revolution in Nigerian poetry in English. In Aderemi Raji-Oyelade & Oyeniyi Okunoye (Eds.), *The postcolonial lamp: Essays in Honour of Dan Izevbaye* (pp. 136-154). Ibadan: Bookcraft.

Okunoye, Oyeniyi. (2008). Modern African poetry as counter discursive practice. In Aderemi Raji-Oyelade & Oyeniyi Okunoye (Eds.), *The postcolonial lamp: Essays in honour of Dan Izevbaye* (pp. 79-93). Ibadan: Bookcraft.

Okunoye, Oyeniyi. (2011). Writing resistance: Dissidence and visions of healing in Nigerian poetry of the military era. *Tydskrif Vir Letterkunde, 48*(1), 64-85.

Soyinka, Wole. (1967). *Idanre and other poems.* London: Eyre Methuen.

Soyinka, Wole. (1972). *A shuttle in the crypt.* London: Rex Collins/ Eyre Methuen.

Soyinka, Wole. (1976). *Ogun Abibiman.* London: Rex Collins.

Soyinka, Wole. (1989). *Mandela's earth and other poems.* Ibadan: Fountain Publications.

Soyinka, Wole. (2002). *Samarkand and other markets I have known.* Lagos: Crucible Publishers Limited.

Chapter 7

Originality in Absentia: A Study of Selected Kannywood Films

Muhammad Muhsin Ibrahim

Introduction

For over a century since the beginning of cinema, much has changed in the technology, style, theme and subject of film. One thing, arguably, remains constant, and this is called adaptation and/or appropriation, though the two are slightly different. Sanders (2006, pp. 23-26), defines adaptation as "a cinematic version of canonical plays and novels," while appropriation refers to a process that "frequently affects a more decisive journey away from the informing source into a wholly new cultural product and domain." Many, if not most, stories told in films are, according to Welsh and Lev (2007, p. xiii), "appropriated from literary or dramatic sources, as much as 85% by some calculations and accounts." The percentage is very high, thus many scholars, such as Stam (2000), Bane (2006) and Venuti (2007), criticise the practice. This paper seeks to discover whether or not the practice threatens originality.

The Problem with Originality

Originality is a concept that is bound in time and place. Originality is about being new and different in a good way (Leitch, 2003). Major film industries of the world are said to be running out of creativity and originality. More than 70% Academy and Emmy Award-winning films and television dramas are adaptations of novels, poems, short stories, plays, and nonfiction books. Bane (2006, p. 4) notes that "of the 240 Best Picture Nominees since 1957, 153 have been adaptations. Of the 48 actual Best Picture Winners, 33 have been adaptations. In fact, in the entire 77-year history of the Academy Awards, 70% (54 films) of the winning films have been adapted from literary sources." But what is original is highly dialectical.

Since its inception in the late 19th century, Film has been more or less reliant on Literature. It, in fact, used to be under the domain of Literature for decades. It was much later that Film gained autonomy in some institutions. A prominent film scholar and critic, Robert Stam (2000), calls this an "axiomatic superiority of literary art to film", inferring an upper hand of Literature over Film. Leitch (2003) also notes that the basis for the assumption that literary texts have value in terms of originality is clarified by considering the apparently exceptional case of William Shakespeare. Many of his plays are allegedly adaptations; hence, many critics question his originality and integrity. Leitch (2003, p. 163) further notes:

> The originality of Shakespeare, his defenders asseverate, depends precisely on his seeing the artistic potential of inert source materials; he is an alchemist, not an adapter, as one can see by comparing any of his plays with its base original. But this defence demonstrates only that some adaptations are better than others, not that the best adaptations aren't really adaptations at all. Nor does it demonstrate that only writers can escape the label of adapter, since there are several noted film adapters sanctified by the name of auteur.

However, adaptation is as old as the cinema itself (Bane, 2006). Venuti (2007, pp. 25-43) calls it a "second-order creation", while several others reject the strategy per se on the basis of fidelity and infidelity issues. This is pervasive in the local film industries in India, Nigeria and other places where film thrives as a business. Stories are 'adapted' without any consent, or changed extensively, altering the intended thematic preoccupation of its original writer, and so on. These and other reasons have resulted to numerous lawsuits between the story owners and the film directors/producers.

The American Experience

The nascent American films drew much from the 18th century novels of Charles Dickens, Jane Austin and Charlotte Bronte. Filmmakers, like the famous D.W. Griffith, equally took from poems of Alfred Lord Tennyson's Victorian poems as well as others (Eisenstein, 1947, p. 144). Corrigan (2012, pp. 12-13) points out that in those early years, literature greatly served as the sort of attraction to filmmakers. There are three important dimensions to film practice: (1) film practice and its connection with literature follow the social and aesthetic directions and developments established in the nineteenth century, especially the demands for realism and a class-oriented fascination with spectacle; (2) early cinema tends to find its formal literary precedents in the staged perspective of the theatre and less in narrative traditions; and (3) even at this early stage, film turns to literary materials of all kinds for subject matter.

However, adaptation and appropriation have today gone far beyond those levels. Film critics like Stam (2000), express dissatisfaction over the current trend in adaptation and appropriation. To him, what obtains is not practical adaptation, but something else. He states that film adaptations "are caught up in the ongoing whirl of textual reference and transformation, of texts generating other texts in an endless process of *recycling, transformation, and transmutation*, with no clear point of origin" (Stam, 2000, p. 66) (Italics added).

It is a wonder to many that even the mighty Hollywood draws – plagiarises, if you like - much from mostly French filmmakers. In an interview with *The New York Times*, an entertainment lawyer, Pierce O'Donnell (1992) said "Idea theft is a cancer in Hollywood. In an industry where imagination and creativity is the key to success, idea theft is grand larceny. And it is prevalent."

The Indian Experience

It is difficult to trace the origin of all stories filmed in Bollywood. The origin of the stories is sometimes obvious, and at other times hidden. In several instances, however, the stories are what Stam (2000) described as recycled, transformed, and transmuted. They are largely, according to some critics, best qualified as plagiarised. According to

Desai and Dudrah (2008, p. 5), several charges of plagiarism were, and continue to be, lobbied against Bollywood's borrowings from other cinemas such as Hollywood, Hong Kong, Chinese, Japanese, Korean, or Soviet cinemas in its remakes of famous films such as *A Star is Born* as *Abhimaan* (Pride, 1973, dir. Hrishikesh Mukherjee) or the Korean film *Oldboy* as *Zinda* (Alive, 2006, dir. Sanjay Gupta). Khalid as cited in Orfall (2009, p. 3) argued:

> Originality never has been and perhaps never will be the strong point of Indian cinema. Not only are the stories liberally pinched, but in every department of film-making a definite Western stamp is more than visible. Hence, the technical excellence, we speak of with such pride, is nothing more than a facsimile of the Western films. The trend to emulate the West began right from our silent cinema, with carbon copies of Flash Gordon serials hitting the Indian screen.

Shah (2012, p. 458) also estimates that in 2008 alone, forty-six percent of Bollywood films copied Hollywood films. Of those copies, "only [two] were authorised adapted screenplays." Shah (2012) elsewhere states that "in recent years, nearly eight out of every ten Bollywood scripts have been 'inspired' by one or more Hollywood films."

The Nigerian (Kannywood) Experience

Adaptation/appropriation is more rampant in local film industries, for an author or director will remain ignorant of his work being copied. This raises more questions. A young, though burgeoning film industry called Kannywood based in Kano but which operates across the Hausa speaking north and beyond, is a quintessential example. A Professor of Media and Cultural Communication, Abdalla Uba Adamu, in an interview with the BBC Hausa, said that he alone has more than 150 such films (Adamu, 2014). In a separate instance, Adamu (2006, p. 43) mentions that due to the rampant nature of the practice, "the Hausa video [...] filmmakers fall over themselves to copy a Hindi film. For instance, *Nagin* (1976) a Hindi film (which itself was appropriated from a Pakistani film of the same name) was further adapted into *Macijiya* (snake) and *Kububuwa* (cobra) by Hausa filmmakers."

The division of Nigeria along religious lines brought about the remarkable difference in the films produced in the two major geographical divides. Film makers from the south make films in English and a few other languages. These films showcase mostly Western and Christian motifs and contents, and are seen as more or less the national film industry. Film makers from the north draw significantly from Indian and Arab cinemas and portray what they perceive as 'Islamic', or, at least, 'less un-Islamic'. Adamu (2007, p. 76) observes that "the religious divide and the 'Islamicate' environment in Northern Nigeria created a preference for eastern-flavoured visual entertainment due to perceived similarities between eastern cultures and Hausa Muslim cultures – at least in the public space of Islam."

Indian cinema has the biggest influence on Kannywood (Larkin, 2000; Adamu, 2006; 2007; Haynes, 2007, and Muhammed, 1992). The Hindi films have a long history, as they were initially imported by earliest resident Lebanese merchants and shown in their theatres throughout Northern Nigeria, and eventually shown by the state-controlled television stations as 'Weekend Television'. Indian films share a lot of similarities with the peoples' way of life in areas like love, marriage, dressing conflict between the bourgeois and masses, and using magic, among other things (Ibrahim, 2013).

Then the trend changed as Larkin (1997, p. 1) observes:

> For years, Indian movies have been an accepted, admired part of Hausa popular culture compared favourably with the negative effects of Western media. Indian movies offered an alternative style of fashion and romance that Hausa youth could follow without the ideological baggage of "becoming western". But as the style of Bollywood has begun to change over the last few years this acceptance is becoming more questioned. Contemporary films are more sexually explicit and violent. Nigerian viewers comment on this when they compare older Indian films of the 1950s and 1960s that "had" culture to newer ones which are more Westernized. One friend complained about this saying that "when I was young, the Indian films we used to see were

based on their tradition. But now Indian films are just like American films. They go to discos, make gangs, they'll do anything in a hotel and they play rough in romantic scenes where before you could never see things like that."

The shift served as an impetus to the local filmmakers to provide the audience with things such as commercial gain, a better substitute. Films like *Sangaya, Taskar Rayuwa, Salsala, Kansakali, Ibro Awilo, Mujadala,* etc., succeeded precisely because of their song and dance routines adapted from Indian films, rather than the strength of their storylines or their messages (Adamu, 2007). Although they largely draw much from the Indian cinema, Kannywood films are more 'sanitised' as there are minimal body contact between male and female actors. This is a practice considered indecent by the general northern public. This is the genesis of the massive appropriation of Bollywood films that has now become problematic, as some marketers go beyond appropriation to simply dubbing the Hindi films.

Larkin (1997); Maikaba (2004); Hynes (2007); Adamu (2007 and 2014) have traced how Kannywood takes Bollywood ethos such as song and dance routine, choreography, storyline, music and theme tone, etc. as their creative templates at the expense of their local circumstances and creativity. Maikaba (2004, p. 102) is even very categorical as he concludes thus: "it is abundantly clear that the Hausa home video industry was influenced more than any other section by Indian cinema Industry.

Hausa Video Film	Appropriated Hindi Film	Appropriated Element
Al'ajabi	Ram Balram (1980)	Song
Alaqa	Suhaag (1940), Mann (1999)	Songs
Aljannar Mace	Gunda Raj (1995)	Songs
Bakace	Tere Naam (2003)	Storyline
Burin Zuciya	Raazia Sultaan (1961)	Storyline
Ciwon Ido	Devdas (2002)	Storyline
Dafa'i	Ghayal (1990)	Storyline

Danshi	Bazigar (1993)	Storyline
Dijengala	Khoon Bhari Maang (1988)	Storyline
Hisabi	Gunda Raj (1995), Angarkshak (1995)	Songs
Ibro Dan Indiya	Mohabbat (1997), Rakshak (1996)	Songs
Inuwar Rayuwa	Main Pyar Kiya (1989)	Storyline
Jazaman	Lahu Ke Do Rang (1997)	Songs
Khusufi	Taal (1999)	Storyline/song/poster
Sharadi	Dilwale Dulhania Le Jayenge (1995)	Songs
Shaukin So	Pyar Ishq Aur Mohabbat (2001)	Scenes/Songs
So Bayan Ki	Kuch Kuch Hota Hai (1998)	Songs
Tanadi	Judaai (1997)	Storyline
Zabari	Mein Khiladi Tu Anari (1996), Mohra (1998)	Choreography
Zo Mu Zauna	Khabie Khushi Khabi Gain (2001)	Storyline

Fig. 1: Appropriated Hindi films in Hausa
Source: Adamu (2007)

Inuwa (2016) has found more of such appropriated films in his PhD thesis proposal, thus:

SN	Hindi Film (Source)	Director	Year	Hausa Film (Remake)	Director	Year
1	Jan Tak Hai Jaan	Yash Chopra	2012	Ni da ke mun dace	Ali Nuhu	2013
2	Swades	Ashutosh Gowarike	2004	Kudi a duhu	Ali Nuhu	2013
3	Bombay to Goa	Raj Pendurkar	2007	Hanyar Kano	Iliyasu Abdulmumin	2014
4	Rawdy Rathore	Prabhu Deva	2012	Ana haka	Iliyasu Abdulmumin	2015
5	Kick	Sajid Nadiadwala	2014	Gwaska	Adam A. Zango	2015
6	Rakih vs Ladies	Yash Raj 2011	2011	Basaja	Adam A. Zango	2012

7	Bhoot	Ram Gopal Varma	2003	Almuru	Ahmed Biffa	2014
8	Raaz 3	Vikram Bhatt	2012	BakinKishi	Hafiz Bello	2013
9	Ankur Arora murder case	Suhail Tatari	2013	Asibiti	Mansur Sadik	2015
10	Chori Chori Chupke Chupke	Mustan Burmawalla & Abbas Burmawalla	2001	Furuci	Sadiq N. Mafia	2016

Fig. 2: Appropriated Hindi films in Hausa
Source: *Inuwa* (2016)

Others are more carefree as to plagiarise their Nollywood counterparts, e.g. Kannywood's *Nai Miki Uzuri* (dir. Ali Gumzak 2016) ripped off *Kokomma* (dir. Tomrobson 2012). Hollywood films, too, are appropriated, though not as much as Bollywood's. For instance, *Masoyiyata Titanic* (dir. Farouk Ashu Brown 2003), *Romeo da Jamila* (dir. Yakubu Muhammad 2013) are obviously influenced by *Titanic* (dir. James Cameron 1997) and William Shakespeare's *Romeo and Juliet*, respectively. The cloned posters below (Plate 1) show such an instance. Therefore, the above tables are by no means exhaustive, for the practice still thrives.

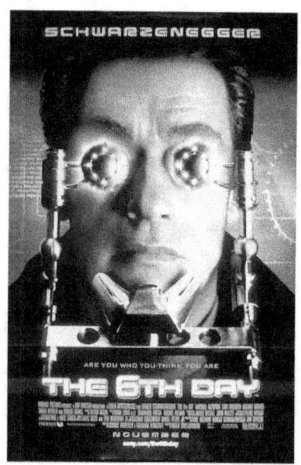
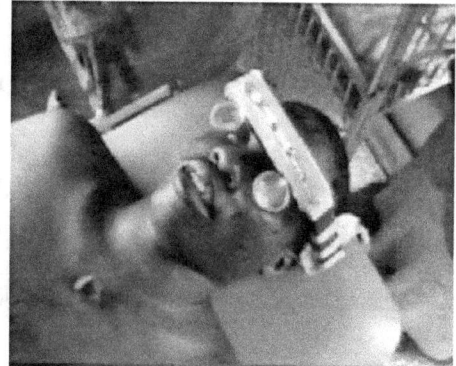

Fig 3: Plate 1 (Adamu 2007, p. 40)   *Fig 4: Qarni*

Relatively, Hausa writers too are accused of adapting, appropriating and transmuting many Indian films. Malumfashi (1999) claims that:

> Bala Anas Babinlata's (novel) *Sara Da Sassaka* is an adaptation of the Indian film *Iqlik De Khaliya* (sic) while his *Rashin Sani* is another transmutation of another Indian film, *Dostana*, etc.

These are the same books that are sometimes 'adapted' into films by the same writers. This fits the description of what Genette (1982) calls "hypertextuality". Bala Anas Babinlata, along others such as Dan Azumi Baba, Balaraba Ramat Muhammad, Ado Ahmad Gidan-Dabino have adapted some of their books into films, though the books may not all be adapted from Bollywood.

However, in his paper titled: "Bollywood/Hollywood", Madhavi Sunder, a professor of Law, University of California, Davis, opens with a note, thus:

> Free flow of culture is not always fair flow of culture. A recent spate of copyright suits by Hollywood against Bollywood accuses the latter of ruthlessly copying movie themes and scenes from America. But claims of cultural appropriation go far back, and travel in multiple directions. The revered American director, Steven Spielberg, has been accused of copying the idea for *E.T. the Extra-Terrestrial* from legendary Indian filmmaker Satyajit Ray's 1962 script, *The Alien*. Disney's *The LionKing* bears striking similarities to Osamu Tezuka's Japanese anime series, *Kimba the White Lion* (2011, p. 75).

This demonstrates exceptionality in the practice of plagiarism and any form of idea theft among the filmmakers across the world. The theft can be obviously deliberate or accidental. Kannywood, Hollywood, Bollywood and any other film industries may not be the only guilty players. With globalisation and media making the world more of a village, the flow of cultures and cross cultural exchange cannot always be noticed. Again, Kannywood operates on a low budget and is only relatively popular, perhaps the reason for copying other "woods" with impunity. It cannot be an exaggeration if I say that no Kannywood filmmaker has ever sought for authorisation to remake, adapt, appropriate, etc any Indian or even Nollywood films. Not even for dubbing that has lately been the major cause of concern in the film industry.

A brief analysis of two Kannywood films: *Kudiri* (dir. Sadiq N. Mafia 2014) that explicitly caricatures a famous Indian film, *Aashiqui 2* (dir. Mohit Suri 2013); and *Nai Miki Uzuri* (dir. Ali Gumzak 2016) that ripped off a Nollywood film, *Kokomma* (dir. Tomrobson 2012) will be given below.

Sample 1:
Kudiri tells a story of a successful singer and a chronic alcoholic, Salim, who does not take his occupation serious. He fights with a rival singer during a show after which he meets a female bar singer, Nabila, who is singing his songs. She gets scared when she sees him, while he contrarily finds her melodious voice fascinating and immediately offers to employ her. As a girl from a poor family, Nabila wants to continue with her education but she cannot. That is why she sings at a bar, an undignified work for a lady. She quickly accepts the offer and quits her job.

Salim's manager cum friend does not like the manner his boss behaves. For Nabila, Salim leaves Kaduna to Kano. Unfortunately his rivals assaults him, as a result of which he is hospitalised for weeks. Nabila tries to contact him while his manager refuses to answer her calls. The now jobless Nabila brings nothing to her poor parents. Salim finally meets her after his recovery and soon gets a contract for her with a music company.

Nabila's career grows, while Salim's stagnate. This causes his relapse to alcoholism and despair. She relocates to his house to look after him. Her parents object to her decision but they give up after learning that Salim truly needs her around. Finally, Salim attempts suicide and leaves a note for her. He is nonetheless shown to have survived the car crash, and even wins a contract to perform at Hollywood.

Aashiqui 2 opens at a show in Goa. A large crowd has gathered to watch the performance of a chronic alcoholic and a famous singer and musician, Rahul Jaykar. He grudgingly comes onstage. A rival singer who thinks Rahul degrades his popularity disrupts the show. After the fight, he goes to a local bar and finds a bar singer, Aarohi singing his songs. He is impressed by her voice and potentials, and believes that bar singing is not dignified for her. He assures her to leave her job and follow him to Mumbai. She obliges. However, as soon as he goes back to Mumbai, Rahul is attacked. His friend cum manager, Vivek, thinks that the media should not be aware of the attack, and thus lies that he has travelled abroad.

The now jobless Aarohi tries everything possible to contact Rahul in Mumbai but she cannot. Vivek ignores her calls. This worries her parents. Rahul finally recovers and finds Aarohi himself. He fires Vivek. A deal with a record producer for Aarohi is signed. She soon becomes a successful singer. Everyone is happy; gossip sprouts that Rahul is misusing her. This goads him to return to his old habit of drug addiction and alcoholism.

She moves in to his house to assist in rehabilitating him. Her parents do not like that but they give up. Aarohi keeps on giving Rahul all the supports she can; she even vows not to sing again until he quits alcoholism and recovers. He remains adamant, and finally commits suicide. Aarohi is devastated but she is later encouraged to continue singing as that would please Rahul.

Sample 2:
Nai Miki Uzuri begins from a scene where Bilal follows Amira, demanding an explanation for her pregnancy. She hedges, refusing to respond to him until when he insists. She thus directs him to go back and ask his father. The story is then shown through a flashback.

Amira works as a maid in Bilal's house while he is away, studying abroad. His mother, Hajiya goes to work thereby leaving his father, Alhaji at home alone with the maid. Alhaji gradually begins to admire her. One-day, Alhaji chases away a guy, Jabir, who is fond of follows her home every day. Alhaji eventually rapes Amira. A few days after his return, Bilal falls in love with Amira. His mother objects to it, but he remains defiant. Unknown to him, she carries his father's unborn child. Hajiya eventually finds out that Amira is pregnant, and demands to know who is responsible. The flashback ends.

Although Bilal intends to marry her, it is Jabir who finally marries her. Hajiya is blamed for neglecting her duties as Alhaji's wife for her work. Amira is asked to stay and give birth in the house, and afterwards get married.

Kokomma is titled after a girl, the central character who is, from a poor family and who works as a maid in a wealthy family house in Lagos city. The housewife, Mrs. Margaret leaves home daily for her workplace and her husband, Mr. Enet, stays at home with the housemaid. One day, the guardsman of the house assaults Koko (shortened for Kokomma) and is sacked. But as the days pass by, Mr. Enet begins to admire Koko as his friend Moses advises him to. He eventually rapes her. His son, Usen, returns after finishing his studies abroad. He hardly settles when he falls in love with Koko (Kokumma). His mother doggedly objects to his choice and proposes another girl to him. He rejects her outrightly.

It finally comes out that Koko is pregnant. Margaret demands to know who is responsible. After much drama and threats, it is found out that Mr. Enet is the father of the unborn child. Usen vows to marry her, but she leaves the house and goes back to her parents. Margaret and Usen also desert Mr. Enet.

Discussion

The similitude between the aforementioned films goes beyond the intertexuality of Bakhtin and Julia Kristeve to what Gerard Genette in *Palimpsestes* (1982) calls *transtextuality*. Genette posits five types of transtextual relations, one of which bears relevance to the kind of appropriation we have above, and this is called "metatextuality". Metatextuality consists of "the critical relation between one text and another, whether the commented text is explicitly cited or only silently evoked" (Stam, 2000 in Corrigan 2012:82).

It is however a commonplace observation in copyright scholarship that "all creativity is derivative" (Sunder, 2011) in one way or the other. The filmmakers are a product of the same universe. That is why ever Hollywood, seen as an epitome of originality and pinnacle of ingenuity, has, at various instances, been charged with subtle plagiarism and unauthorised remakes; or for mining the works of past creators, or less popular film industries in some remote part of the world.

The examples of the aforementioned Kannywood films are pure plagiarism. Seger (1992, pp. 64-71) suggests that a film remake needs to do the following to qualify as good. The filmmakers need to contemporise the original, update the context, consider the value system (of the sourced text and theirs) and, above all, be creative. Adamu (2013), cited in Krings and Okome, (2013, p. 291) also adds that "for the remake to achieve its artistic objectives, the audience must be aware of the original (source text) and its offspring, that is, the remake." Some Kannywood producers employ a strategy of compiling various scenes from multiple Bollywood movies in an attempt to evade being easily identified, or copyright infringement suit, which is highly unlikely to happen (see Figures 1 & 2 above).

Although both sourced films are already contemporary, the context needs update, especially that of *Kudiri*. The filmmakers add very little or no subplots. It is slightly different in the case of *Nai Miki Uzuri* where a few characters are substituted; for instance, the guardsman in *Kokumma* with Jabir. The producers also try to 'Islamise' the ending by inviting an Islamic cleric at the end who admonishes the wife, Hajiya and informs the audience that the son can marry Amira, though she carries his father's unborn child.

Our society is so much different from Indian, thus the value system should be considered and adjusted to fit the conservative, puritanical one. For instance, the culture of music is unfolded and no decent girl will "move in" with another man. Creativity is also largely absent as the original stories are not expanded and the narratives (are) not extended. This is, perhaps, due to the fact that the filmmakers have run out of creativity, or are too lazy to work diligently on their products.

Recommendations

The following are some of the recommendations proffered:

As enshrined in the Copyright Acts of both the US, India and Nigeria, reproducing any work of art in a whole, or a substantial part thereof by duplication, imitation or simulation amounts to copyright infringement. Therefore, the film industries of the mentioned countries should act according to the law to avoid any legal action against them.

Where applicable, the original source of any adapted, appropriated and remade film should be duly acknowledged by the adapter. This is to respect and value the hard work of that owner and to appreciate their peculiar intellect, idea and imagination.

Where possible, a consent and/or authorisation should be legally obtained from the owner of any literary work that another person wants to adapt, appropriate, remake, etc.

This study believes that there is a need for cooperation and collaboration between Kannywood and Bollywood, and Nollywood film industries. There is already some collaborative effort between Kannywood and Nollywood, but that has significantly dwindled in the recent years. There is thus the need to strengthen it.

Conclusion

Kannywood filmmakers also are awre that their films lack originality. But for profit, they continue. Theirs, nonetheless, is a much smaller industry that produces films on mostly shoestring budget. This low profile status allows them to substantially copy, imitate, transmute and plagiarise Bollywood films with impunity. These filmmakers have always maintained that they do so for the satisfaction of their audience, and indeed, profit as the success story of the biggest hit films like *Sangaya, Mujadala, Ibro Awilo,* etc in Kannywood is always attached to their popular songs-and-dance sequences. In contrast, the audience, at least some, the government and the hegemonic religious scholars reject and condemn that. Adaptation and remake are lawful acts inasmuch as they are carried out in accordance with the practice. Originality is something elusive.

References

Adamu, A. U. (2006). Transglobal media flows and African popular culture: Revolution and reaction in Muslim Hausa popular culture. Mary Kingsley Zochonis lecture for the African Studies Association, UK Biennial Conference; School of African and Oriental Studies, University of London, London; 12th September.

Adamu, A. U. (2007). Currying favour: Eastern media influences and the Hausa video film. *Film International, 5*(4), 77-89.

Adamu, A. U. (2013). Transgressing boundaries: Reinterpretation of Nollywood films in Muslim Northern Nigeria. In M. Krings, & O. Okome, (Eds.) *Global Nollywood: The transnational dimension of an African video film industry.* Indianapolis: Indiana University Press.

Adamu, A. U. (2014, November 15). *Gane Mana Hanya.* A BBC Hausa Program at Noon; an interview with Professor A. U. Adamu on Dubbing in Kannywood, Audio.

Chapter 8

Odolaye Aremu's Multifunctional Genre and Songs of Exorcism

Kehinde Akano, Abbibah Zaka and *Garuba Giwa*

Introduction

Music falls in the repertoire of popular culture as a social product and social process which invariably impacts socially on the producers and the consumers as well. On the other hand, popular culture is also a subgenre of literature or popular literature which is acceptable to and consumed by a large percentage of readers or audience. It may be cheap and accessible but not inferior in quality and message. *The Encyclopedia Britannica* defines popular literature as

> the form of literature available to those who do not have the money to buy the classics of the time. The rise of popular press and literacy made working reaches wider audience so much. Cheap books are the major products of popular literature. The cheap books afford the audience easy communication and exchange of ideas among themselves (2012).

Pop culture is usually available for the consumption, pleasure and inspiration of the majority of people, especially community folks. Mass communication, mass appeal and mass accessibility are central to popular culture. With specific reference to the music of Odolaye Aremu, it is a traditional music that is popular among the Yoruba speaking people of Nigeria. There is easy access to Odolaye Aremu's music and it is also easy to decode the message. In providing evidence to the properties of popular culture, Ashley Crossman, a sociology expert, defines popular culture as:

> the accommodation of cultural products such as music, art, literature, fashion, dance, film, cyber culture, television and radio that are consumed by the majority of society's population. Popular culture has mass accessibility and appeal. The term "popular culture" was coined in the 19th century or earlier. Traditionally, it was associated with lower classes and poor education as opposed to the "official culture" of the upper class (2016).

Odolaye Aremu is a Yoruba musician who hails from Ilorin, the gateway to the south-western Nigeria. His brand of music falls into the category of a multi-media which relates to the totality of experience of a people.

The word 'music' refers to production of rhythmic melodious sounds which are voiced or rendered through musical instruments. Music could be written or printed symbols showing guide on how music should be played or sung. Music could be performance and creative in nature. In a more professional way, music could refer to "the science or art of ordering tones or sounds in succession, in combination and in relationship to produce a composition having unity and continuity" (www.WebsterDictionary). The production of music could be mechanical, vocal, rhythmic and instrumental. The production of sounds usually accompanied by drum beats or musical instruments for the purpose of producing melody or rhythm (euphony) pleasing to both the brain and ears.

In the North Central Zone of Nigeria, Ilorin is a mini North with migrants from both Northern and Western parts of Nigeria. In Ilorin, you would find Yoruba, Hausa, Fulani, Kanuri, Kembari, Nupe, Baruba and a host of others. But Yoruba language remains the lingua franca as the dominant mother tongue. The music of Odolaye Aremu is rendered in Yoruba language, although not without some instances of Hausa and Arabic vocabularies or expressions which could be a whole sentence or phrase.

The study is interested in the social relevance of the songs in its multi-functional modes; the aspects or features which are of paramount importance to the literariness or literary aesthetics of the songs in both form and content. It should be noted here that Odolaye Aremu's songs are imbued with both local and universal appeal put across to the audience through voicing and musical instruments.

Odolaye Aremu's Dadakuada Subgenre and Its Sociological Imperatives

The sociological background of Odolaye Aremu's songs and genre underline the relevance, appeal, style or features of the songs. From the lyrics and tones to the messages either subtly or directly given, there is an inferred extra-musical significance laced with aesthetics. The ultimate of Odolaye Aremu's music is to communicate effectively with his audience, but on a variety of issues. The selected song Album of the musician is titled "Olowe Mowe" (translated as the guilty is aware of his condemnation). It captures a satiric musicality with which the musician takes a swipe at certain social vices as well as their perpetrators. Thus, one would, hear or understand in the selected album of Odolaye Aremu a multifunctional genre and song of exorcism. The literariness of the songs explains the multi-various layers of the songs as poetry or ballad. Olabode Omojola (1994) gives an insightful overview of traditional music which captures both the texture and functionalism of Odolaye Aremu's songs.

> Music, in traditional Nigerian societies, is generally conceived as part of a multi-media, total theatre experience within which different aspects of the performing and visual arts such as poetry dance, drama often combine for effective communication. In its relationship with other aspects of the performing Arts, traditional Nigerian music is often conceived not just as an aesthetic experience but also as a medium through which societal issues of extra-musical significance are articulated. Traditional musical performances are therefore usually products of aesthetic and extra-aesthetic considerations (p. 147).

Odolaye Aremu has a number of albums in which he sings for the restoration of sanity and growth of the nation. His brand of music falls into the subgenre called Dadakuada, a brand which is peculiar to Kwara people and a more acceptable and broad sub-genre called rara – a slow chant often deployed in praise of notable individuals, people and communities. What actually distinguishes the musician's brand is his rhythmic and cascading voices partly invocatory and partly expressive as the musician is notable for his use of high and rising pitch and tonal vocalization of words of songs.

Listening to his music, especially the selected album, "Olowe Mowe", one encounters an artiste per excellence whose style of rendition gives him out as a poet. Evident in this album are copious but effective adoption of witty sayings, aphoristic statements, proverbs, invectives among others, woven into rhythmic songs and tonal renditions. Odolaye opens his songs with invocatory salutations with which he pays homage to a number of people and sects believed to be powerful enough to affect the success of his performance. Then he goes on to identify himself by singing about the originality of his songs. Excerpts of his opening glee of his songs in the album:

Ausubillahi minasaitonirojimi
Bisimillahi Ramoni Rohimi
Atiwaye ojo, iba lowo re o   I salute the breaking of the day
Atiwo oorun, iba lowo re o   I salute the setting of the sun
Aafa to yan to yanju, tinu e mo   I salute diligent and upright clerics
   to ya Woli, iba lowo eyin
Eyin te laye, iba lowo eyin o   I salute those of you who own the world
Eyin omo kekeke te se leyin wa   I salute the junior ones coming after us
   Iba lowo eyin o

Acknowledging that as an artist and a musician, he needs to pay homage to certain people, he notes that nobody is so powerful that cannot be intimidated or over-whelmed by the challenges of the planetary earth. To those who may harbour the feeling of invisibility which, of course, is tantamount to playing God, Odolaye Aremu condemns and jests about such individuals as useless and ignorant:

Kini anfani eni to sope owo aiye ole te oun, Titun njanu

What is the relevance of a person who says he cannot be intimidated; that he is boasting and 'making mouth'?

As one would find in the dramatic display of Hubert Ogunde and Duro Ladipo, he indulges in supplicatory opening glee by way of pleasing some forces who are likely to hinder his performance. Such style hints at the dramatic element of his musicality. "Do you permit me to sing on and carry on with my performance? Hope there is no problem?"

I salute and salute Dagoro, Ebora Labueke, Obadimeji with a big net... He goes on to salute in specific terms now –

> I salute and salute my mother
> Ajibola child of Edan.
> My mother, Edan, words that live in the shrine and sound yunmuyunmu
> This particular night (meaning the performance takes place in the evening)
> I salute Ajibola, a native of the town of smartness
> Abeni, native of charcoal (edu)
> A lizard with tining tail
> With black face and black mouth and receeding chin
> daring Dove which feeds among Orofo (other birds)
> A daring bird that feeds in the open glare
> Angua of Yoruba, Angua Yoruba
> May the land strengthen your path
> Child of Alayaba
> The useful one in the shrine,
> Child of Senior fraternal members

Odolaye Aremu's opening invocation or salutation follows the style of other traditional musicians in Ilorin whose list includes Alhaji Jaigbade Alao, Late Alhaji Aremu Ose, Alhaja Hassana Abake, Alhaja Yewande Abake, Alhaji Fatai Olowonyo, Mr. Raji Ile nla (Shao), Mr. Aiyemojuba (Shao), Alhaji Omokekere Amao and a host of others. Omojola identifies a broader sociological frame from which traditional music emerges and impacts in return. This aptly illustrates the sociological imperative of Odolaye Aremu's "Olowe Mowe" in its multifunctional attributes.

> Yoruba musicians have been able to establish an enviable tradition of music of social relevance within a total theatre frame work.... In addition to specific religious and social events, close rapport also exists between musical performances and everyday life activities. Examples of such renditions abound and include such categories as work songs (Orin Ise)... Praise songs (Oriki) and songs of social control (Orin ikoni ni janu). Special socio-religious occasions as well as day to-day activities therefore providing opportunity for communal music-making during which members of the community share a satisfying musical experience... providing forum for interaction among members of a given community, also helps to create the avenue for artistic articulation of societal norms, thereby revalidating communally-binding social values (n.d., pp. 147 – 149).

The aesthetic cum theoretical preview which gives impetus to the social and artistic relevance of the music of Odolaye Aremu as adopted in the study resides in sociology and humanism. The deployment of the music underlines the artiste's commitment to cultural and communal rejuvenation. In carrying out this task, Odolaye singles out some individuals notable in the community for praise while he satirises social vices and the likely perpetrators. These, among others, enlist the musician's musical antidote for a decadent society.

Songs for Moral Resurgence

A morally bankrupt society will be economically, politically and socially bankrupt, while moral standard is the bedrock of growth, discipline and development and the hallmarks of nationhood. Morality equally defines humanity which is at the centre of national life of a country. Morality has to do with the doctrine or system of moral conduct; the belief about the right behaviour or what constitutes wrong behaviour. It could mean the degree to which something is right and good; the moral goodness or badness of something.

A work of art or musical production that is imaginative and teaching moral lessons is applicable in this regard. Odolaye Aremu's "Olowe Mowe" contains quite a number of tracks teaching moral lessons geared in a deeper sense, towards national resurgence. To drive home the message, Ayo Banjo observes:

> The laws of a country are hopefully, based on ethical foundations. No country that we know of rewards individuals for committing murder or robbing their fellow citizens, but the state does not consider it its business to inquire into the morality of the citizens of a nation provided the laws of the land have at least been technically observed. All too often in the developing world, the state is more concerned for its citizens to be happy than for them to be good. And it concentrates, not on the pleasures of the intellect, but on those of the flesh (pp. 3-4).

Nigeria, of which Northern Nigeria is an integral part, is undergoing both moral and political degeneration. It is decadence that permeates the moral fabric of the national life. The ominous signs are palpable for all, not just to see but to feel and feel badly. Currently, the Federal Government of Nigeria, led by President Muhammadu Buhari and his Vice, Prof. Yemi Osinbajo is prosecuting anti-graft war. Of course, corruption is the greatest scourge most African nations are battling with as the bane of development. Again Ayo Banjo identifies the evils or causes of corruption which he tagged 'indices of materialism' based on a personality test on the internet. These are wealth seeking, preferring extravagance, being selfish, seeking status and power, regarding looking good as being important than comfort among others (pp. 5-6).

Odolaye labels morally bankrupt citizens by calling them all sorts of names and warning them to keep off the national scene.

Excerpt:

> Come and see, betrayers, backbiters, traitors, eavesdroppers, rebels, slanderers, jealous ones, war mongers, marauders we do not call on you, keep away from us.

A corrupt nation will be full of this group of people castigated and forewarned by the musician. His target is a free society; a society devoid of indiscipline and marauders and to such miscreants, he directs advices, to keep away from governance - and seats of power – presidency, National Assembly, State House, Local Government Council, among others. His song also targets both leadership and followership, which often constitute stumbling blocks to the societal walk to freedom and economic boom.

The musician goes further, particularly about those in government and the wealthy or at best those reaping or milking presently from the common wealth, warning them to be modest in their consumption or acquisition mode and the way they display or flaunt their wealth. Odolaye cautions against wastage of the nation's resources, high taste and uncontrollable avarice. This he puts across through songs in a rather aphoristic or proverbial way.

> Now we are in Lagos in one of the capital cities of Nigeria.
> We are now at Mushin, we are at the place of Eskenke, we are at the place of the son of Ahmadu's the great Ayinde's place,... Iyanda child of Adizat... Akodudu
> Please, let not what we have at hand be lost let not what we are holding under our feet be wasted.
> Pleaseeee, let not what remains on ground be more than what is in the mouth.
> For I have not seen what is so much that cannot be depleted

The musician's witty sayings are directed at the leaders and citizens alike who would stop at nothing to amass wealth even corruptly, and even flaunt such wealth to the displeasure of the majority and the masses. Odolaye's diatribe is to the rescue of humanity which is defined by nationhood.

A. E. Afigbo defines nation as:

> a word... used to designate a human community that is united by language and culture. Some students of that idea consider the nation and nationalism national social phenomena while some others consider them artificial creations of man (p. 81).

In the songs of Odolaye, Nigeria as a nation reflects in every part – Yoruba, Hausa, Igbo among others in the Western, Northern and Eastern parts. The musician distinguishes himself as a northerner as he sings of Ilorin, the Kwara State capital, as a place where God Almighty resides.

> Ilorin ooo, I will deliver your message
> Ilorin's issue cannot be ignored
> It is true that there is nowhere God does not exist
> But God lives in Ilorin
> A town without farm but the natives eat what they like

His Northern nativity is also evident in the array of his clients who hail from Ilorin. These are the late Emir of Ilorin, Alhaji Sulu Gambari, the late Jimoh Aboki of Adifa area, late Alkali Salawu and the reigning Emir of Ilorin, Alhaji Ibrahim Gambari Isola among others.

Excerpts:

> Sulu Gambari, Baba Isola, a brave man who could live in a massive building
> Baba Ciroma, father of a judge prince who marries a princess
> Hold tight to your portion prince that marries a princess
> The head that will be crowned hardly lives at home
> You judge fairly at Iyakangu Ibadan
> Beribepo, Aloba laanu (Prince with merciful kingship)
> The gift of God has nothing to do with smartness
> The son of Bolanta of Isale-Oja, Relation of Salami from Agodoyo.

In the opening track, Odolaye reiterates his commitment to morality songs and his avowed preparedness to expose social vices and warn or admonish leaders and followers (the citizenry) in Nigeria.

Olowe mowe, Orin Aremu mo eniti onbawi.

Meaning:

> The culprit or the satirised knows himself, the target of Aremu's songs is unmistakable.
> Aremu's songs know the culprits
> Nigeria, the wise know themselves

> It is the ignorant who do not know themselves
> But if you draw the attention of the ignorant
> You are inviting trouble

In exorcising the land full of decadence and evil, the singer goes on:

> If termites become careless the land will devour it
> The world (Nigeria) has become chaotic
> Look at the powerful and the highly placed individuals that are being brought down
> Those that helpless citizens will run to for help are taking to their heels as well; we should all be watchful
> Now that mysteries are happening
> For instance, Guinea Corn stem now brings forth Okro
> And Elegede (pumpkin) brings forth tangiri (a different specie)

But Odolaye warns that those who pillage the rabit's hole God will surely pillage their anus too.

The above songs capture the state of things in Nigeria – the topsy-turvy nature of the affairs of the nation – political, economic, social and even welfare and religion.

For some years now, Nigeria has been waging war on terrorism – Boko Haram, Niger Delta Militants, Kidnapping, Armed Robbery, Cultism and a host of other social calamities. Yet the nation is grappling with political and economic problems – the recession is killing the citizenry. Many States and Local Governmenst could not pay workers' salaries, apart from the backlog of arrears. The moral fabric of the nation has been torn without solution in sight. It is these myriad of social problems and economic woes being heightened by religious bigotry, political brigandage and corruption that Odolaye exposes and castigates in his album – "Olowe Mowe".

To cap it all, the traditional musician labels himself a watchdog of Kwara State:

> I am the dog of Kwara who does not bark for the fun of it
> It is either attacking human beings or animals

His strongest tracks contains his warning to all and sundry observing that:

Some behave as if they will not die again
but that death will meet them one day
And to the corrupt and criminally minded leaders
It is your children who will suffer
For your corruption and social vices
If you are good we will say
If you are not good we will say
Even if you are wealthy that you
Spread your father's wealth in the sun
It does not have effect on our vision

Conclusion

The paper has x-rayed Odolaye Aremu's music, in particular his album entitled "Olowe Mowe," to show the potency of music and the relevance of traditional music of this brand. The musician's morality songs which touch on self-discipline, behavioural tendencies, leadership and communal traits, and sense of regard for other human beings, have been discussed to emphasise the genuine concerns of the artiste. Of utmost importance is the portrait of an artiste as the watchdog always alerting members of the public by attacking the unscrupulous elements in the society. The selected album, "Olowe Mowe," actually contains tracks of exorcism through scathing satire of social vices and perpetrators.

References

Afigbo, A. E. (2000). Myth, history and national orientation in Nigeria. In A. Banjo (Ed.), *Humanity in context*. Ibadan: The Nigerian Academy of Letters.

Ayo, Banjo (2008). *The wages of obsessive materialism* (Olatunji Oloruntimehin, Ed.) Ibadan: The Nigerian Academy of Letters.

Crossman, Ashley. (2016). Sociological Definition of popular culture the history and genesis of pop culture Sept. 22, 2016.www.wikipedia.org

Odolaye Aremu (n.d.). *Olowe mowe*. Lagos: Ivory Music Limited.

Omojola, Olabode (1994). Music as the epicenter of African drama: The Yoruba example. In Olu Obafemi et al. (Eds.), *New introduction to literature* (pp. 147-158). Ibadan: Y-Books.

Popular culture. In *Encyclopedia Britannica.* http.www.britannica.com online.

Chapter 9

Religious Interpretations and Their Implications on the Society in Abubakar Gimba's *Sacred Apples* and Elnathan John's *Born on a Tuesday*

Sarat Adenike Salihu

Introduction

In most parts of the world today, every individual is expected to exercise the fundamental human right and freedom to practice whatever religion s/he desires. It is believed that religion helps improve social interaction, especially among people with the same religious beliefs, enhances moral development and ensures peaceful co-existence among citizens. However, religious mores have led to different religious interpretations and subsequent biases and different expressions. Thus, rather than being a tool for peace, religion has become an instrument for social malaise, conflict, wars and terrorist activities. Religious differences have been one of the reasons for the wars in different parts of the world, including Nigeria.

Northern Nigeria in particular has witnessed series of religious crises over the years, many of which are generally believed to be aided by religious ideology. Some of these conflicts include the Maitatsine crisis of 1980, the crisis in Birnin Kebbi in 1990, Kaduna uprising in 2000, and the one in Jos in 2001. The most recent of these crises is that of the Jama'atul Alhul Sunnah Lidda'wati wal Jihad popularly referred to as Boko Haram in the Northeastern part of Nigeria, which has become an international issue due to its terrorist and anti-human activities.

According to Nwaomah, religious conflicts are special and unique as a result of different doctrinal interpretations, religious values and sect identification (p. 97). Many adherents' attitudes and actions are generally believed to be based on the teachings of their religions. Hence, religious conflicts have been known to be predicated on different religious ideologies. In other words, biases and extremist fundamental views enhance and help influence different religious conflicts. These biases are encouraged through different religious loyalties expected of the adherents. Takaya (1992) notes that "Religion, at some point, is politics and is the most potent and long lasting political association. Moreover, religious creeds excite and extract the deepest possible emotional and physical loyalties from their adherents when in political competition with people of other faiths" (p. 10).

In addition, religious and political loyalties cannot be divorced completely from each other in different societies. Thus political figures use religious differences as a means to garner support from the group that would be in their favour. Jalingo avers that "the common man [needs] to know that their leaders want to use them for their selfish interests in the cover of religion. A lot of these leaders are only using religion to make money and to enrich themselves...." (cited in Boer, 1980, p. 72). Therefore, increase in religious conflicts and especially the rise of the Boko Haram sect, can be associated with the issues of poverty, ignorance and religious loyalties.

Between Literature and Religion

Literature is diverse, as it encompasses all aspects of human society. It transcends the physical and social postulations, as it also embraces human spiritual and metaphysical realms. Thus literature discusses issues related to the religions of the world, from the oral religion (beliefs in gods and goddesses) to Islam and Christianity. Religion has therefore been a veritable literary tool used by different writers in their discussion of societal issues.

African oral literature presents religion as sacred and various gods and goddesses and their priests are revered by their adherents. This is transferred to early African texts that have inclinations to pre-colonial and colonial periods in Africa such as Chinua Achebe's

Things Fall Apart, Ola Rotimi's *The Gods are not to Blame,* Wole Soyinka's *Death and the King's Horseman* and Elechi Amadi's *The Concubine*. These texts present an unadulterated African traditional belief in gods and goddesses and the need to reemphasise the availability of cultural religious practices before the advent of colonialism.

In later works, writers like Wole Soyinka, Olu Obafemi, Femi Osofisan, Nguigi wa Thiongo satirise and expose the hypocritical acts of religious leaders and the use of religion as ideological tools by leaders to perpetrate injustice in the land, dissuade and destabilise revolutionary struggles. Emerging writers following in their wake not only expose and satirise the hypocrisy by religious leaders, but also portray the effects it has on the adherents. Abubakar's *All for God* particularly focused on religious leaders and how each leader has re-interpreted religious tenets in order to amass wealth and engage in different atrocities. This paper thus seeks to evaluate how Abubakar Gimba and Elnathan John have portrayed religious issues in the selected texts.

Theoretical Framework

A viable literary tool for the evaluation of religious elements in literary works is the sociological literary theory. The sociology of literature accommodates every literary work that reflects the human society. It studies the social structures and social relations of a given society as reflected in literature. According to Ganga (2016):

> sociological study of literature proves very useful to understand the socioeconomic situations, political issues, the world view and creativity of the writers, the system of the social and political organisations, the relations between certain thoughts and cultural configurations in which they occur and determinants of a literary work (p. 15).

The sociology of literature helps to elucidate the contributions of individual writers to the sociological issues of the era in which they live and write (Ganga, 2016, p. 75). It justifies the belief that literature is a mirror for societal values and issues and not only isolated fictional imagination of the writer. Hence literary works are products of the human society.

As a scientific study of man, social institutions and social processes (Laurenson, & Swingewood, 1972, p. 11) sociology therefore helps to define, evaluate and critically access the various human phenomena in literary works. It seeks to explain human interactions and assist the reader to understand various human political, social, economic, religious, cultural and environmental processes reflected in literature. Thus, this paper adopts the sociological model to analyse the religious interpretations and societal implications which are products of the human society as reflected in Abubakar Gimba's *Sacred Apples* and Elnathan John's *Born on a Tuesday*.

These writers are both Nigerian authors who seek to use their literary works to critique societal ideological beliefs with a view to promoting change and enhance societal development, as African writers will want to do. This paper, therefore, explores how both have achieved this commitment in their works.

Synopsis of *Sacred Apples*

Abubakar Gimba's *Sacred Apples* tells the story of the travails and struggles of a woman, Zahra, and how she overcomes all of them through steadfastness, personal strength and self-actualisation. With series of flashbacks at the beginning of the story, Zahra is presented as a woman whose life has become shattered as a result of her recent divorce from her husband and first love, Yazid, and thus is on her way to her grandmother with her three children. Unfortunately, she encounters angry rioters who, due to some misunderstandings, kill the driver, and almost kill Zahra. Her car is burnt, supposedly with her children. However, the children escape as they are saved by Rashad and Miriam, a couple with military intelligence, who witness Zahrah's ordeals in the hands of the rioters. From here, Zahra, with the help of her brother, Ya Shareef, begins a journey of self-realisation. She becomes friendly with Miriam and start a career which she couldn't do while married to her first husband, Yazid. Zahra also remarries and experiences a polygamous lifestyle. This ends in sorrow as a result of her husband's death, and the eventual realisation of her self-worth and the need to be committed to her ideals and goals as a woman. *Sacred Apples* thus gives a gruelling tale of the life of a typical African woman whose life is filled with different struggles and the need to overcome it all despite male domination.

Religious Interpretations and Societal Implications in Gimba's *Sacred Apples*

Gimba's *Sacred Apples* transcends feminist ordeals. It encompasses sociological issues which abound in different societies. Written in the 90s, and set in an Islamic socio-cultural society, Gimba's work explores religious injunctions and their interpretation in the Nigerian society particularly the Northern region notable for its adherence to Islamic teachings. This is not to say that there are no adherents of Christianity in the novel, however, Islam is the dominant religion. Hence, Gimba (1994) presents different Islamic societal interpretations and basic representations.

Zahra is a divorced woman, a condition that is not encouraged in Islam. Despite its abhorrence by his religion, Yazid divorces his wife by proclaiming "I divorce you" (p. 29) to his wife not considering its rightness or wrongness. He divorces her according to his religious dictates but fails to adhere to instructions guiding the pronouncement and its religious implications. Zahra notes that "when it comes to dealing with women or their wives, many men are guided more by their whims and passions than by principles or religion" (Gimba, 1994, p. 29) Thus, Yazid negates his religious beliefs to satisfy his own selfish whims.

In an attempt to convince Zahra of the importance of marriage and the need to reconcile with her husband, Zubayda emphasises that "in the old days, we used to be told that, a woman's Paradise after death, starts from, and is assured by, her husband's home here on earth…" (p. 43). Ya Shareef, in Zahra's defence, responds that Zubayda's perspective "is more of a cultural construct, a social preservative for the chemistry of the marriage institution by men, than a religious witticism" (p. 43). He further emphasises that:

> our cultural orientation has been given a religious toga to make it seem that the woman should carry the greater burden... that's my quarrel with what Mamah said. When it comes to the affairs of the hereafter, I'm afraid... we are all on our own. Equal before God. That's my understanding of what our book teaches (p. 43).

The above thus suggests that many cultural beliefs have been given religious interpretations to further concretise cultural perceptions based on the fact that religious perceptions and tenets are sacred and people are wont to believe in them. Hence, creating a forceful interface between culture and religion which negates actual religious ideologies.

Another indication of a forceful interface between culture and religion is expressed by Zahra when she explicates the importance of unity and abhorrence of conflicts based on "seniority' in a polygamous home to her co-wives. She says:

> It's a cultural outgrowth, and a malignant one, on the institution of polygamy in our religion. The Holy Scripture exhorts men to treat women equally. Yet, here we are fighting each other for preferential treatment, wanting superiority over each other. Fighting for unequal treatment.... We are all equal before our man and God.... And the best of us is the one that is best in conduct in our dealings (p. 175).

From the above, it is implied that Islam preaches equality and justice and only man's quest for superiority and special treatment dissuades him from the actual religious truth. In addition, for many Muslims, a visit to Makkah implies the change in title to 'Alhaji or Alhaja or Hajia', as indicated when a confused police chief asks Ya Shareef, "but... you must at least be an Alhaj... or haven't you been to Makkah?"(p. 38). At the latter's request that he should be addressed plainly as Sharee, Ya Shareef responds that:

> I have... I've performed the pilgrimage three times now.... I was strictly speaking, an Alhaj, a pilgrim then while in the Holy Land. Back at home I'm no more a pilgrim. It's a religious obligation that is time-discreet...

not a continuum. Only the religion itself is.... These are descriptive identities. They shouldn't be hoisted as titles... (p. 39).

At the chief of police's insistence that many people would disagree with Ya Shareef's views, he (Ya Shareef) explains that "... I don't begrudge them their views on it... but I believe they are doing violence to modesty and logic" (p. 39). Hence religious logical reasoning and modesty are also abandoned for self-recognition and identification by many adherents of Islam.

Gimba also raises the reader's consciousness to the importance of education in Islamic jurisprudence. In a flashback, Zahra recalls how Ya Shareef had supported her decision to continue with her education at the university after her marriage to Yazid despite her grandmother's and father-in-law's objection to it. On their insistence that marriage was more important than education, Ya Shareef argues that:

> the first word revealed in our Book of Guidance is 'Read' and not 'Marry'. Marriage is therefore secondary to education....The exhortation to 'Read' is for mankind to seek for knowledge. Not just religious knowledge...but all types of knowledge. Boundless knowledge... the Book exhorts us to do much more... and the *hadith* that enjoins us to travel as far as China in search of knowledge if need be, entails that you must know how to get to China in the first place (p. 55).

Thus from the above, Gimba propagates the Islamic jurisprudence on education which should be encouraged and supported by all and sundry. He notes that the four walls of a school cannot effectively complete the necessary education a child needs, thus the responsibility falls on the parents to complete the missing aspects (p. 56).

He avers that man's search for self identification, recognition and importance is the sole basis of his different religious (mis) interpretations which has led to the various injustices in the society today. This is noted when Zubayda tells Zahra in a dream sequence after the former's death, that:

lust and greed, are the cause: Man is by nature possessive. Whatever does not serve that instinct is ignored, ridiculed, even reviled... some people even seek to rewrite God's laws... And they quote God's words to buttress their position... (p. 267).

Ya Shareef emphasises this purview when he notes that "the problem has not been with the blueprint [Islamic religion blueprint]. The problem has been the practice, adherence to the commandments. The misapplication and outright violation... such is the nature of mankind" (p. 304).

Mankind is thus the architect of religious misrepresentations in order to fulfil his own ignominious ambitions. Thus an understanding of religious injunctions gives an individual the desired and necessary peace of mind, as Zahra finds in her journey through self-realisation. Therefore, when adequate and correct interpretations, devoid of all selfish whims and caprices, are given to religious injunctions, there is bound to be equality, peace and development in any given society. In *Sacred Apples,* Gimba thus proclaims that many interpretations and religious perspectives are misconceptions arrived at as a result of the selfish ambitions of the interpreters and ignorance of the actual interpretations. It is not surprising therefore that there are religious conflicts in the society; conflicts between a husband and a wife, conflict between co-wives and conflicts between religious adherents.

Synopsis of *Born on a Tuesday*

Elnathan John's *Born on a Tuesday* sets in a Hausa community, is an eponymous story that gives a first person account of the life of an almajiri boy, Dantala, also known as Ahmad. Dantala gives a step-by-step account of his journey through life. As an almajiri boy at Bayan Layi where he is sent to learn how to read the Qur'an because his parents could not afford to feed him and his brothers (John, 2015, p. 43), Dantala joins a group of thugs after his Qur'anic education because he cannot afford the transport fare back home. As a thug, he has no home, sleeps under a Kuka tree, smokes weed and with the others in his group, is used by politicians to create societal disturbance, destroy people's properties and kill innocent individuals. Dantala and his groups' last raid meets with police resistance which leads to the death of the leader of Dantala's group. This makes him flee from Bayan Layi to Sokoto, enroute Dogon Icce, his home town. In Sokoto, Dantala meets Malam Abdul Nur (a Christian turned Muslim) who introduces him to Sheikh Jamal who eventually becomes his teacher and mentor. Later in the story, Malam Abdul Nur (subsequently referred to as Abdul Nur) turns against Sheikh Jamal (subsequently referred to as Sheikh) due to their different ideological beliefs and religious interpretations and Dantala is made the Sheikh's deputy. Abdul Nur creates his own different sect called 'Firqatul Mujahideen Li Ihyau Islam' or "Mujahideen,' which totally negates and rejects every form of Western education, an ideology synonymous with the ideology of the Boko Haram of Nigeria. This is opposition to Sheikh's group called 'Jama'atul Ihyau Islamil Haqiqiy,' or 'Haqiqiy' which means 'the Society for the Restoration of True Islam', which encourages all sorts of beneficial education. Abdul Nur's group has different clashes with the police. Hence, Sheikh is murdered, signalling a climax to societal chaos. Subsequently, there is military intervention and retaliation which leads to the incarceration of Dantala. After about nine months into his incarceration, Dantala is released and begins his life all over.

Religious Interpretations and Societal Implications in Elnathan John's *Born on a Tuesday*

Focusing on Dantala's life, John captures the lack of basic understanding that heralds the interpretation of religious tenets in Islam. As a teenage Muslim boy in Bayan Layi, Dantala believes that everything that happens to a human is by the will of Allah. For this reason, he justifies every act of atrocities committed by his gang as being according to the will of Allah. The merciless beating of a boy named Idowu and his eventual death (p. 4) is seen as an act of Allah. "See how Allah does his things-we didn't even beat him too much" (4), he says. The killing of the security man and the 'Big Party man" are also seen as deserving deaths (pp. 14-5). Dantala has no understanding of the difference between right and wrong, hence his interpretation of such acts as the will of Allah. Therefore it is implied that many a wrong deed is borne out of lack of proper understanding or misconception.

John also avers that one of the major causes of different atrocities committed by the youth is parental negligence and not assumed religious teachings, as the child acquires all sorts of knowledge (positive and negative) through the wrong processes. This is indicated through the major character, Dantala, and his brothers, Maccido, Hussein and Hassan. As a very young boy, Dantala was sent to Bayan Layi while his brothers were sent to Tashar Kanuri by their parents in order for them to have an Islamic education, which makes them 'almajiri'. At Bayan Layi, Dantala, after his education, became a thug because no one asked of him after he was sent away. "I wonder why Umma didn't send anyone to look for me" (p. 43), he says and his Malam never cared about him. Rather he made Dantala and others like him work on his farm and beg on the streets. Subsequently, he left Bayan Layi and was fortunate to meet with a Malam who cared about him. His brothers, on the other hand, accepted and followed the doctrines of their Malam and became Shiites as they needed to survive.

In addition, the concept of 'Almajiri' is similar to the boarding house system of education in Nigeria, where parents take their children to school and expect them back at the end of a semester. For the almajiri, most of the children go back home once they are done or refuse to go back home and no one asks about them. In *Born on a Tuesday,* the almajiri schooling system is presented from two different dimensions; negative and positive. From the negative dimension, an almajiri becomes a stooge for his Malam as he adheres to his teachings without questioning, as portrayed through Maccido, Hassan and Hussein who became Shiites because their Malam was a Shiite. They are also misused and made to run errands and beg on the streets and in the Mosque. Comparing Sheikh to his first Malam, Dantala narrates that:

> Sheikh is kind. He is different from Malam Junaidu in Bayan Layi, who made us beg even after working on his maize farm. Working on a farm during planting and

harvest season is better than standing by the road, chasing after cars and having people turn away from you like you are a huge mound of shit. It is better than fighting over food and money at the Friday Mosque" (p. 61).

Also, it becomes easy to transfer different ideological perceptions to the students, as there are no parents to checkmate what is being taught. The almajiri system also makes strangers of family members, as there is loss of familial relationship which could also help shape the life of a child, as portrayed through Dantala's relationship with his brothers.

From the positive perspective, through the almajiri system of education, Dantala becomes multi-lingual. He speaks Hausa, Arabic and English. He has the opportunity to meet people from other tribes and learn their ways. The contrast between Malam Junaidu's Islamiyyah and Sheikh's tutorship points to the fact that the almajiri sytem of education is not bad; the events, situations and outcome are determined by the person in charge of it. By becoming a thug, Dantala knows nothing better as he only continued the process he was trained for: begging for alms, albeit in a different method. However, with the Sheikh, he learned the importance of family, responsibility and self-respect.

Elnathan John also alludes to the ideological perception of the Nigerian Boko Haram. Using contrastive characterisation, John presents the religious conceptions. Abdul Nur's Mujahideen's ideology condemns all forms of Western education and Western ideas, an ideology synonymous with that of the Boko Haram group. He sees all forms of education as evil. He beats Jibril, his younger brother for teaching Dantala how to speak and read in English (p. 86) and also encourages all his followers to burn all their books and certificates (p. 189). In contrast, Sheikh encourages different beneficial education. His 'Haqiqiy' ideology supports education and thus his aim to build schools. He openly supports female education. When he preaches to the congregation, he says "let your women study…let them learn how to read or write. The wives of Christians read and write and our wives cannot even read the Quran" (p. 116). He is impressed with Dantala when he realises the latter is learning how to speak in English and encourages him to use his library filled with books and also gives him more intellect-tasking responsibilities (p. 114).

Abdul-Nur's and Sheikh's ideological perceptions on education are captured in their debate in Saudi Arabia. Abdul-Nur argues that "the Europeans,... needing to conquer Muslim people, sought to start by conquering their culture through worthless and sinful education....They came with liberal ideas and education to slowly eat at the root of Islamic civilization and control" (p. 196). He further condemns Islamic Universities, which he sees as having adopted Western parameters of learning. In response, Sheikh asks Abdul-Nur if he had ever visited and knows the curriculum of any of the Islamic Universities to which Abdul-Nur responds in the negative (pp. 197-8). Sheikh emphasises the importance of knowledge by saying that:

> to fight an enemy, you must understand an enemy. How do you struggle against those whose elements you know nothing about? Seek knowledge, the Prophet sallalahu alaihu wasallam, said. Where are the Muslim schools for our children to attend? Have we built them? I have built one school. But of the millions of Muslim children, how many can go to a Muslim school? Should our people remain ignorant and keep being controlled by the same western forces? Give me one hadith or Quranic verse that tells you that English itself is haram, even by analogical deduction.... You cannot choose deliberate ignorance and claim to be fighting for the cause of Islam (p. 198).

From the above, John echoes Gimba by emphasising the importance of education in Islam, which negates the philosophy that education is haram. Sheikh expresses that Abdul-Nur is only a selfish man who only wants to satisfy his selfish ambitions:

> all you want is to give into your lust for power and get Muslims killed unnecessarily in the streets. That is what is ignorance–allowing your feelings to guide you instead of thinking of whether this will be good for Muslims or not. This is a dangerous thing you are preaching and if

you have the interest of the Muslim ummah at heart, you will stop it (p. 199).

The philosophy that education is *haram* is thus only a tool used in controlling others and not for the benefit of others. The selfish ambition to have control over people like "motorcyclists, tea sellers and butchers" who are also ignorant and have no education, is the major reason for its propagation by Abdul-Nur, who ironically is also ignorant and has limited knowledge of the basic teachings of Islam.

In addition, by portraying Abdul-Nur as a man of violence and strict measures, John gives credence to the view that he is power drunk, has no tolerance and lacks basic understanding of Islamic teachings as Dantala was while at Bayan Layi. He publicly mocks other Malams, especially Sheikh, and encourages his followers to 'make trouble' for people (p. 187) even though Islam preaches peace. Also, apart from always hitting Jibril (p. 80) and insulting everyone (p. 86), Abdul-Nur also hits his wife. According to Jibril, "he treats her like a donkey... like an animal he despises. Some days he locks her in her room without any food because his food is cold or there is too much salt or not enough salt. He beats her with a tyre whip. He forces things into..." (p. 149). This seems to contradict his (Abdul-Nur) own belief that Islam is the submission to the will of Allah (p. 84), as he tries to forcefully make everyone submit to his own selfish will and not Allah's.

Another reason for societal menace is poverty and government's irresponsibility, insensitivity to people's plight and deceit. Dantala and his brothers were sent out to be almajiri as a result of poverty. Rather than help settle societal disputes amicably, the government sent in police officers and soldiers who terrify and terrorise innocent men and women. Dantala laments that his fear:

> began with those police uniforms, those guns, those roadblocks. My fear was fed each time by the petrified faces of motorcyclists, afraid of being made to do frog jumps for offences as little as looking too directly into a policeman's eyes. Or being made to roll in the dust while being slapped and kicked (p. 136).

Faced with such brutality, it is thus not surprising that the people defied some group of soldiers and killed a soldier when the latter told them to disperse at a gathering, thus signifying a total change in people's attitude to the uniform men and increasing societal disturbance. An indication of government's insensitivity to people's plight is also seen when they abandoned the people who had Cholera disease and it was only Non-governmental organisations like Sheihk's Haqiqiy who came to the people's aid (p. 182). There are also no provisions of good roads, hospital facilities and water system for the people, all of which accumulates to anger and eventual revolution by the people. In essence, John in *Born on a Tuesday* reveals that lack of understanding, intolerance, ignorance and government's injustice are tantamount to societal conflicts.

Conclusion

This paper critically analysed religious issues in Abubakar Gimba and Elnathan John's *Sacred Apples* and *Born on a Tuesday*, respectively, from a sociological point of view. Without bias as a result of their religious beliefs and ideals, they both portrayed and satirised significant religious interpretations and how society has been affected by them. Their works sought to change society's opinion about various societal issues in Northern Nigeria. Like many radical and emerging Nigerian writers like Obafemi, Osofisan, Abubakar and others, they both indicate that religion is used as a political instrument to deceive the people as a result of their loyalty to their religion. Also using different characters and societal situations, Gimba and John portray that religious interpretations are based on personal interests, thus decimating the major teachings of Islam. The paper thus concludes that many religious conflicts are not as a result of religious obligations, rather, selfish aims and ambitions, coupled with people's ignorance and government's insensitivity to the plight of the people, are the basic determinants of societal unrest in Northern Nigeria.

References

Boer, J. H. Nigeria's decade of blood: 1980-2002. *Studies in Christian-Muslim relation* (Vol. 2). Jos: Stream Christian Publishers.

Ganga Shodh, (2016). The sociology of literature. Retrieved September 4, 2016. From http://www.shodhganga.inflibnet.ac.in/bitstream/10603/36080/8/08_chapter_01.pdf

Gimba, Abubakar. (1994). *Sacred apples.* Ibadan: Evans Brothers Publishers.

John, Elnathan. (2015). *Born on a Tuesday.* Nigeria: Cassava Republic.

Laurenson, D. T., & Swingewood, A. (1972). *The sociology of literature.* London: Paladin Press.

Takaya B. J. (1992). Religion, politics and peace: Resolving the Nigerian dilemma. In J. K. Olupona (Ed.), *Religion, peace and multi-faith* (pp. 109-123). Ile-Ife: Obafemi Awolowo University Press.

ISBN 978-978-54870-0-8

To obtain your copy, please contact:

Kwara State University Press
Kwara State University, Malete
PMB 1530, Ilorin, Kwara State, Nigeria
Email: kwasupress@kwasu.edu.ng; kwasupress@gmail.com

Chapter 10

The Didactic Dimension of Proverbs: A Study of Aliyu Kamal's *Hausa Girl*

Sani Abubakar

Whenever, there is doubt about an accepted pattern of behaviours, whenever there is doubt about a stipulated line of action, whenever traditional norms are threatened, there are always proverbs.... to vouch, illuminate and buttress the wisdom of the traditional code of conduct (Akporobaro, 2006, p. 69).

Introduction

Different societies all over the world have their indigenous ways of socialising even before the system of formal education. Thus, there are specific methods of inculcating moral behaviour that suit a society's traditional code of conduct. This was done through the use of tales, proverbs and other forms of oral expressions. In tales, the younger generation learns from the experiences of the characters involved in the stories, while proverbs are routinely used in everyday speech, rather directly to instantly correct bad behaviour or lapses. In other words, they are used as tools for discipline (Sarbi, 2014). In their different works, scholars like Ruth Nkem Okoh (2008), Isidore Okpewho (1992), Finnegan (2012), Akporobaro (2006) and the like confirm the didactic function of proverbs. This element of the oral tradition is also being exploited by modern writers today in order to justify its relevance in the present time. This paper traces the blending of Hausa proverbs in the narrative of events in Aliyu Kamal's *Hausa Girl*.

Theoretical Framework

Malinowski's functionalist view is used in the discussion of the use of proverbs in this paper for its concern with the role of folklorist materials in his pioneering work, *Myth in Primitive Psychology*. Malinowski asserts that: "...the immense services to primitive culture performed by myth are done in connection with religious ritual, moral influence and sociological principles" (Strenski, 2014, p. 80). In this regard, Bascom in his essay, "Four Functions of Folklore" (1965), notes that Malinowski's study on the function of myth can be applied to other forms of folklore. He demonstrates that "...folklore fills particular functions in various cultures; ...it works to maintain conformity to accepted patterns of behavior" (Brunvand, 1976, p. 27). Thus, proverbs serve as charters for belief as well as models for action. This is supported by Okpewho (1992, p. 173) who states that Functionalism emerged as a method of studying the life and culture of a society by examining the functions or roles performed by anything practiced in the society as well as the ways in which these functions help to ensure the survival of the society. The idea came up when the American cultural anthropologists thought of the contribution of verbal art or expressive literature in the maintenance of social institution, that is, "...how does folklore function in the culture? (Okpewho, 1992, p. 20).

From the above, it is clear that oral traditions like tales, myths, proverbs and the like could also be studied to determine their role in the society that creates and uses them. Malinowski believes that these oral literary expressions are used for a particular reason and at a particular time, hence their context. He further affirms that: "The text, of course, is extremely important, but without the context it remains lifeless (Dundes, 1965, p. 282). In the same vein, Bascom's essay further illuminates these functions. For Bascom, "Malinowski's remarks touch upon the functions of folklore and upon the relations of folklore to culture, as well as upon what I distinguish as the social context of folklore" (Dundes, 1965, p. 282).

According to Bascom, the four functions are: amusement, validating culture, education and maintaining conformity to the accepted patterns of behaviour. He, however, concludes that: "The four functions can be considered as grouped together under the single function of maintaining stability of culture" (Dundes, 1965, p. 297). From the four types of functions, it is apparent that proverbs are used for a particular purpose, among which is the pedagogical and are context-bound, as Okoh (2008) observes thus:

> The speaker who quotes a proverb must be aware of the right context to employ such a proverb. This actually calls up another aspect of proverbs, namely their teaching function...proverbial usage exhibits enormous didactic potential (p. 128).

The context in which Hausa proverbs are used in Kamal's *Hausa Girl* agrees with the above observation. The proverbs are not used in a vacuum, each proverb used is connected with the situation of its usage, as Akporobaro (2006) puts it thus:

> It is important to note [proverbs] do not teach moral lesson in dry abstract manner. They use exciting situation to generate pleasurable imaginative episodes in terms of which moral lessons are carried into the heart and mind... Moral lessons are transformed into exciting image-patterns which touch the heart causing fear, sympathy or love of the good and a hatred of evil (p. 60).

Since literature has a social function or 'use', the above suits the studies on this text. Writers like the late Abubakar Gimba, Zaynab Alkali, Ahmed Yerima, and Kamal, among others, use their works to reveal moral decadence in the Northern Nigerian society. This issue of immorality is also portrayed in Kamal's *Hausa Girl*. According to Umar (2012):

> The novel raises its baleful finger at the Northern Nigeria movie industry, accusing it of portraying Hausa culture in an improper way and instilling bad morals, particularly in the minds of susceptible youth, all as a result of aping the Indian movie culture (p. 249).

To advocate this, writers use different elements of oral tradition that suit their needs. Among these elements are proverbs. There are recent studies on this aspect, Bichi (2014) examines Islamic influence in Hausa proverbs; Sarbi (2014) treats proverbs as tools for discipline, while Kabir (2014) re-affirms the socio-cultural function of proverbs, tales and the like. What follows is the analysis of proverbs and their role in the context of Kamal's *Hausa Girl*.

The Concept of Proverbs

Proverbs are wise sayings that offer practical wisdom about life. They also contain morals and other traditional views in a metaphorical form. These features are captured in different definitions and explanations of proverbs by different scholars thus:

> Proverbs are short and witty traditional expressions that arise as part of everyday discourse as well as in more highly structured situation of education and judicial proceedings (Dorson, 1972, p. 119).

Proverbs in Africa are effective in a whole range of ways in life and in literature…Now proverbs often imply some general comment on the way people do, or should, or should not behave (Finnegan, 2012, p. 410).

> Proverb … has been and remains a most powerful and affective instrument for the transmission of culture, social morality, manner and ideas of people from one generation to another. Proverbs…give a penetrating picture of the people's way of life, their philosophy, their criticism of life, moral truth and social values (Akporobaro, 2006, p. 69).

These are enough justifications that proverbs have a didactic dimension, though they have also been studied from their aesthetic point of view, which is the essence of literary studies. It is also believed that aesthetics are used to achieve certain objectives, among which is the effects of the aesthetics expression on the listener / reader or as characters employ them in their conversation. Okoh (2008) observes that: "Proverbs can be addressed from, among others, a utilitarian perspective" (p. 125). Therefore, this paper specifically demonstrates that most of the proverbs used in Kamal's *Hausa Girl* achieve their didactic purpose. It is obvious that the non-adherence to the wisdom expressed in the various maxims leads to the doom of especially the central character of the novel, on one hand, and on the other, adherence to the teachings of these proverbs by characters like Nana, Gaji and even Fatahiyya leads them to a harmonious marriage life. This is supported by Akporoboro's belief that:

> more significantly, there is an implicit progressive... attitude to life, belief in the possibility that any condition of man can be altered for the better through the proper application of common sense, self-discipline and by adherence to the natural wisdom inherited from the forefathers and enshrined in the proverbs and wisdom of the people (2006:72).

This gives a clear picture of the condition of both Hajjo as well as Hanne, the actress in the film: 'Hausa Girl', who fail because they do not adhere to the wisdom and advice embedded in proverbs as related to them in the text.

Hausa Proverbs

Proverbs have the same functions in every society. Hausa proverbs are used alongside Islamic ethos in *Hausa Girl*. This justifies the worth of Akporobaro's observation that "... much of the proverbs of Hausa people reveal the influence of Mohammedan [sic] religion ..." (1960, p. 72). This is further affirmed in Bichi (2015, p. 39) that: "proverbs are used among the Hausa for social, educational, religious and political functions." The author, Kamal, is a Northern Nigerian writer influenced by his religion (Islam), as well as his cultural traditions. Hence, the use of proverbs in his text (Hausa Girl) is influenced by his religious and societal traditions.

The use of proverbs in Achebe's *Things Fall Apart*, for instance, is described "... as sometime direct and sometime indirect ... [and also] ... as profound pronouncement on 'life' and maxims as ordinary observations about life (Gangopadhyay, 2012, p. 151). This is why this paper specifically considers the use of proverbs in the text as a societal resurgence. Okpewho (2007, p. 83) has it that: "... traditional African culture is not obsolete but relevant in the articulation of contemporary needs and goals."

Synopsis of the Text

Hausa Girl is the story of an over-ambitious girl, Hajjo Gano, who completes her secondary education with poor grades in all subjects. However, she is an avid reader of Hausa romantic novels and as well as a Hausa home-video fan. These are hobbies that influence her career choice of acting. Unlike her friends who dream of marriage, Hajjo achieves her objectives in life despite all the warnings from her parents and relatives. This she does with the aid of SK, a notorious film director.

Hajjo takes part in a film titled: 'The Girl' as well as a music video titled: 'Hausa Girl'. This results in her setting her apart from her family and her suitor (also a film director), Kabiru Badayi. The novel, *Hausa Girl,* is described by Abdullahi (2012) as:

> *Hausa Girl* unveils the cultural and religious value of the Muslim north. As socio-political and moral ideas of people are embodied in their literature, it is then not astonishing that the immoral acts of the heroine of the novel, Hajjo Gano, and the male principal character, SK, invite severe fury in the novel... Cultural and religious fury is expressed through the generation of the old and wiser people represented by uncle Ilu and his wife, Bala Gano –Hajjo's father, Mullah Amin and Dala. These people symbolize high moral principles and traditional values (p. 251).

It is against this backdrop that Functionalism as a method of examining the oral literary expressions is used in this paper to reassert the didactic dimension of the Hausa proverbs.

Proverbs in Kamal's *Hausa Girl*

There are twenty-five proverbs used at different times by the narrator and the characters in the text. These proverbs can be put into different categories, as Sarbi (2014) opines, which are obedience, dedication, preparation, endurance/perseverance and unity. These functions could be expressed as direct statements, questions, command and warning. However, they may function depending on 'how' and/or 'why' the narrator/characters prefer them. This paper analyses the proverbs based on the context of their usage in the novel. Most of the proverbs take the form of warnings, others seem to stress obedience and dedication and few are on the portrayal of the consequences in the future or an indication of regret and so on. The discussion is based on the above functions but first the list of the proverbs in the text.

Category 1: Proverbs that warn
- Borrowed clothes do not cover your thighs (p. 24/250).
- The wily bird is often caught when it comes down to feed (p. 38).
- If the youth catch you easing yourself out in the open you simply sit on it (p. 70).
- The younger person can't see what the older person sees even if he climbs the mountain (p. 91).
- While one eases himself, if he catches the sight of youths, he should sit down flat on hisexcrement (p. 147).
- The young burn up even before they come to the boil (p. 70).
- Every calabash has a matching pair (p. 108).
- The one who taunts water is the one it will heavily drench (p. 146).
- He who eats alone dies alone (p. 176).
- He who loves you tells you the truth (p. 193).
- A needle unearths a garma hoe (p. 195).
- Biting and blowing is all there is in life (p. 240).
- Whoever takes the tip of the leper must give him a shave (p. 66).
- A tree is bent while it is still a sapling (p. 79).
- Leaving food to cool raises the possibility of someone else having a share of it (p. 110).

Category 2: Proverbs on obedience and dedication
- A boy can join elders to meal by washing his hands (p. 90).
- One knows the depth of a river by looking at those who wade in first (p. 109).
- One doesn't know the glutton of tuwo until the soup runs out (p. 139).
- You hear the news from the mouth of fools (p. 178)?
- Owning your tiny axe excels the plea to be lent another (p. 195).

Category 3: Proverb on regret
- One bears a child but is after all not responsible for its disposition (p. 6).
- "Eye, who do you hold in contempt? "And it answers," Those I see every day."(p. 140).
- Beating is a Warner to the body (p. 16).

Category 4: Proverb on unity
- Wash-my-back-and-I-wash-yours (p. 16)

Category 5: Proverb that expresses impossibility.
- -it may turn out to be strenuous for her, for a woman cripple to marry far away from home (p. 58).

Discussion

The discussion starts with Herzog's remark that: "[An] important function of the proverb is to smooth the social friction and dissatisfaction and to ease the individual in his effort to adjust himself in his setting and fate" (cited in Kamal, 2012, p. 296).The above is in line with Uncle Ilu's traditional way of instilling discipline in his children. Hajjo, the central character in the novel, is among them. The narrator uses the expression "*Beating is a warner to the body*" (p. 16), as it instils the certainty of punishment in the children's mind, so they must, as much as they can, obey the rules. Hajjo's awareness of Uncle Ilu's effort in training them is obvious in the text, but she has already chosen her direction in life, as she always deviates from her uncle's warnings. She also fully understands grandmother's adage when she refers to Hajjo's father, Bala Gano, as she says: *"One bears a child but is after all not responsible for its disposition"* (p. 6). This coincides with Hajjo's proverb that: *"The young burn up even before they come to the boil"* (p. 70), as they challenge each other (with Fatahiyya) on the meaning of proverbs. Hajjo and Fatahiyya's conversation here justifies that the youths are aware of the implication of non-adherence to these wise sayings, as they take them for granted. Hajjo's inability to stand by her uncle's principles of morality initially in the text marks the beginning of the bad turn out of her plight. In the end, Uncle Ilu's *'Beating is a warner to the body'* is justified.

Hajjo's wayward behavior increases as she pre-occupies herself with reading Hausa romantic texts and watching Hausa video films at Fatahiyya's house. She cherishes Hausa movies to the extent that she argues in their support in her encounter with Kabiru Badayi. Gradually, her disrespect or contempt for everyone becomes explicit. This is seen as she exhibits her indecent manners on Gaji's visitors (Gaji's sisters-in-law). Mother shows her intolerance thus:

> What came over you, Hajjo? I am deeply disappointed at your show of bad manners… It has never occurred to me that a child brought up in this house will go so far as to behave disrespectfully to visitors. *A tree is bent while it is still a sapling.* We did all that for you and Gaji (Kamal, 2012, p. 79).

On one hand, this clearly reveals the optimism that, as far as children are well trained, it is assumed or believed that they would behave respectfully. On the other, it reveals the disappointment parents go through after trying hard in cultivating good behaviour and one in the family goes astray. The proverb above means that Hajjo's behaviour defies all the socialising missions of all the agents of socialization.

Hajjo thinks that she has come of age as she, misinterpreting the proverbs: *"a boy can join elders to a meal by washing his hands* and *a boy with money is a travelling companion to men,"* reveals her vanity and confirms her arrogance. This is why Fatahiyya cuts in with *"The younger person can't see what the older person sees even if he climbs a mountain"* in an effort to dissuade Hajjo from the belief that her elder sisters (Nana and Gaji) have nothing to show in terms of maturity. She says, "None of them is sharper than me," (p. 91). Eventually, the relationship between Hajjo and Fatahiyya comes to a climax when they agree to play 'husband and wife' between Hajjo and Fatahiyya's husband. The incident leads to a fight between the two friends and Hajjo is severely punished by Uncle Ilu. As she loses a friend, Hajjo creates another fresh relationship with her sister, Nana when she pays her early morning visits. The narrator reminds us that Hajjo has always been mischievous right from childhood; only Mother could put up with her naughtiness and sauciness of tongue (p. 108).This is why as they get on well with Gaji, Nana remarks thus: *"Every calabash has a matching pair"* (p. 108). And also giving some advice, Nana says: *"…The young must defer to the older person, who may nonetheless choose to rub the head of the younger."* She follows it with *"…One knows the depth of a river by looking at those who waded in first"* (p. 108).

All these proverbs are employed because they "… function effectively in Hausa society, and form a vital and potent element of the culture they interpret" (Bichi, 2015, p. 39). The fourth function of proverbs in Bascom's essay is precisely what both the narrator and characters in this text use their proverbs for, that is, they warn the dissatisfied or the over-ambitious individual to be content with his lot, to accept the world as it is and his place in it and thus to conform to the accepted patterns (Kamal, 2012, p. 296). Hajjo can be described as over-ambitions, a girl that is not contented with her place in the society. These lead her to avoid all forms of social relationship, which further leads her to solitude in her father's house after her secondary education. She becomes an idler and in her search for a companion, she meets SK (Sankowa), who offers her a job as an actress. She acts in his film 'The Girl,' despite her father's warning as well as KB's dissuasions. KB uses a proverb as he advices her on the issue thus: "My strongest advice is this. Never have anything to do with him [SK]. As the Hausa people say, *He who loves you tells you the truth.* So why draw the water for your own broiling?" (p. 193).

Chapter Thirty-two of the novel summarises the film in which Hajjo Gano appears as Hanne Garba. In the end of it, she only benefits by appearing on the film poster and magazine. SK also persuades her to dance in his music video, 'Hausa Girl'. The little she gets from this is used in the renovation of her father's house and the purchase of other items that pleases him in spite of his disapproval. She later realises the extent to which the 'Hausa Girl' video has brought her hatred in a religious society. This is not all as in the end, there is a fight between Bala Gano and SK, which results in the murder of her father. The police chase SK for the illegal release of the music video as well as for homicide. Eventually, the police kill SK for his ferocious attack against them. The irony is that Hajjo still mourns him and KB will not marry her. Her situation is captured in her words thus: "No father. No SK. Where do I turn now?" (p. 249). KB urges her to seek Allah's forgiveness and reminds her of the Hausa proverb *"Borrowed clothing doesn't cover your thighs."* (p. 250). This pedagogical function of the proverb can best be concluded in Bascom words thus:

> [A proverb] is used to inculcate the customs and ethical standards in the young, and as an adult to reward him with praise when he conforms, to punish him with ridicule or criticism when he deviates, to provide him with rationalizations when the institution and conventions are challenged or questioned, to suggest that he be content with things as they are, and to provide him with a compensatory escape from '' the hardships, the inequalities, the injustices'' of everyday life (Kamal, 2012, p. 298).

Conclusion

The paper specifically illustrates the didactic dimension of Hausa proverbs in Aliyu Kamal's *Hausa Girl.* From the analysis, it is justifiable that Hajjo's non-adherence to the truth and her contempt for the wisdom expressed in the proverbs lead to the situation (as explained above) she finds herself at the end of the story. Finally, this justifies that proverbs, especially those that uphold dedication and obedience, are used alongside Islamic ethos to inculcate moral lessons in the typical Northern Nigeria setting. However, despite the impact of foreign culture, the indigenous system of teaching morality is still relevant.

References

Abrahams, R. D. (1972). Proverbs and proverbial expression. In R. M. Dorson (Ed.), *Folklore and folklife: An introduction* (pp. 117 -128). London: University of Chicago Press.

Akporobaro, F. B. O. (2006). *Introduction to African oral literature: A literary-descriptive approach.* Lagos: Princeton Publishing Company.

Bascom, W. R. (1965). Four functions of folklore (pp. 279-298). In A. Dundes, *The study of folklore.* Englewood Cliffs: N.J. Prentice Hall.

Bichi, A.Y. (2015). Evidence of Islamic influence in Hausa proverbs: A preliminary survey. In S. Sani et al. (Eds.), *Harsunan Nijeriya: Journal of Nigerian Languages and Folklore, 24,* 38-46.

Brunvand, J. H. (1976). *Folklore: A study and research guide.* New York: ST. Martin's Press.

Dorson, R.M. (Ed.). (1972). *Folklore and folklife: An introduction.* London: University of Chicago Press.

Dundes, A. (1965). *The study of folklore.* Englewood Cliffs: N. J. Prentice Hall.

Finnegan, R. (2012). *Oral literature in Africa.* Cambridge: Open Books Publishers.

Gangopadhyay, A.K. (2012). Time and the self: On the use of proverbs in Chinua Achebe's *Things fall apart* (pp. 138-154). In C. Anyadike & K. A. Ayoola (Eds.), *Blazing the path: Fifty years of things fall apart.* Ibadan: HEBN publishers.

Kamal, A. (2012) *Hausa girl.* Zaria: ABU Press.

Okoh, N. (2008). *Preface to oral literature.* Onitsha: Africana first publishers.

Okpewho, I. (1992) *African oral literature: Backgrounds, character and continuity.* Bloomington: Indiana University Press.

Okpewho, I. (2007). Oral Literature and modern African literature (pp. 83-91). In T. Olaniyan & A. Quayson (Eds.), *African literature: An anthology of criticism and theory*. Oxford: Blackwell.

Sarbi, S.A. (2014). The Hausa proverbs as tools for discipline. In A. Rasheed & S. A. Aliyu (Eds.), *Folklore, integration and national development in Nigeria* (pp. 135-151). Zaria: ABU Pres.

Strenski, I. (Ed.). (2014). *Malinowski and the Work of Myth*. Princeton: Princeton University Press.

Umar, A. N. (2012). Cultural and religious consternation in Northern Nigeria literature: Reading Aliyu Kamal's *Hausa Girl*. *Katsina Journal of Linguistics and Literary Study, 1*(1), 249-262.

Kabir, A. U. (2014). The Umbilical Cord that refuses to be severed: Evaluating the socio-cultural functions of folklore in 21st century Nigeria. In A. Rasheed & S. A. Aliyu (Eds.), *Current perspectives on African folklore* (pp. 120-131). Zaria: ABU Press.

ISSN 2315-5523

To obtain your copy, please contact:

Kwara State University Press
Kwara State University, Malete
PMB 1530, Ilorin, Kwara State, Nigeria
Email: kwasupress@kwasu.edu.ng; kwasupress@gmail.com

Chapter 11

The True Images of Northern Nigeria in Kamal's *Hausaland*

Hasheem Abdullahi Tanko

Introduction

It is against the background of the alleged silence within the Literature of Northern Nigeria that a lot have been said and written about the region by writers from other regions of Nigeria. While others have attempted to represent the north, it is important to explore representations from a writer from that region; equipped with the cultural understanding of the subject. This is why many consider the images and representation of the region as works of misconceptions cum distortions of the reality of the real north. Writers from Northern Nigeria have responded with the most renowned among, Zaynab Alkali in *Virtuous Woman*, Abubakar Gimba in many of his works, and Ahmed Yarima in *Attahiru*. However, among those constructing identity of Hausa land, Kamal stands out with clear imagery in his novel *Hausaland*. This article examines these images depicted in *Hausaland*. To give the analysis some clarity, we provide a brief history of the Kamal. The work also reads the text from the New-Historicist perspective. This affords an in depth scrutiny of the novel as an object of history which presents past and present realities in order to understand it.

Biography of Aliyu Kamal

Aliyu Kamal was born in the Northern Nigerian city of Kano. A professor of English who has written, at least, nine (9) novels, Kamal lectures in Bayero University in Kano at the Department of English and Linguistics. He was the Head of Department of English and French in the same University in 2009.

Kamal's years in the ancient city of Kano and its environs affords him considerable experiences about the Hausa and Fulani cultures and challenges. Kano and its surroundings is a hub of the Hausa people, and predominantly features as settings in many of Kamal's novels. He is also a critical scholar who has published in Hausa, also. In a professorial lecture, Kamal claims to be writing Islamic novels which, he argues differ in thematic treatments from English novel.

Most of his writings are exploration and exposition of the Hausa culture, people, beliefs and land. Each of his 9 novels has the word 'Hausa' attached to each of the titles: *Hausaland* (2003), *Hausa Girl* (2010) and *Hausa Boy* (2011).

As an insider, Kamal's fictions are windows through which a reader could understand the mixed societies of Northern Nigeria. Just as his fictions reflect the climate, perspective, heritage, language, wisdom, and economy of the region, they also reflect both historical and contemporary aspects of the region. In 2005, his *Fire in My Backyard* received an award from ANA/Chevron.

Theoretical Framework

This work attempts a new-historicist analysis of Aliyu Kamal's *Hausaland*. Historicism predates New Historicism; Historicism is the theory that seeks to situate literature within the context of history. New Historicism emerged as a later development and seeks to understand a literary piece by considering the work within an understanding of the prevailing ideas and assumptions of its historical era. It is "a mode of critical interpretation which privileges power relations as the most important context for texts of all kinds...it treats literary texts as a space where power relations are made visible' (Brannigan, cited in Carter, 2006, p. 9).

For this work, New Historicists views are the most suitable because it is through the contexts history and societal ideals that we seek to explicate the selected text.

This approach will help to reveal the uniqueness of the region through its heritage, culture, her people and challenges as depicted in the novel *Hausaland*.

Synopsis of *Hausaland*

Kamal's debut English novel *Hausaland* was first published by Myrrh Kano in 2003. The novel is a historical and adventurous story with elements of mythology and folk tales. It alludes to the emergence of an interwoven history of intertwined Hausa and Fulani societies through the fictionalization of 19th Century events, especially those of the last phase of Usmanu Danfodio's Jihad.

Hausaland tells much about the shared land in the core Northern Nigeria, between Hausa and Fulani. Although Kamal does not suggest the title to cover both tribes, this does not in any way suggest that there are issues of dominance of Hausa people over their Fulani neighbours and vice versa. In spite of the fact that the Fulani culture does not feature in the book's title, the exposition of the Fulani people's culture and bravery is prominent. This is probably why Fillo (a corrupted version of *Fullo*) is the main character.

Hausaland portrays Northern Nigerian people as historically literate. It depicts images of the Hausa people from the perspectives of Fulani and Fulani's from the Hausa people's point of view.

It is an adventure story with encounters with Nkam (Yoruba) and Nyam (Igbo) tribes seen through the experiences of Fillo. He recalls the story as a first person narrator. Fillo undertakes his journey to the said tribes to discover the mystery he heard in a particular myth. Being a Fulani, Fillo first meets Kado who is also called a son of Kado. He later realises that Kado is an Ngausa (Hausa) man through his physique and countenance. They become friends and set off for a town where Queen Dauzar rules seven towns (legendary Hausa Bakwai). The Queen symbolises both Daurama and Amina, the two legendary Hausa Queens of Daura and Zaria towns respectively. Her name even derived from those Hausa towns the Queens ruled in history, Daura and Zaria. Should you put the initial three letters of Daura and Zaria together it will give Dauzar coinage. Moreover, Dauzar alone in the story covers the attributes of both historic Hausa queens; with the arrival of Kado, he shows bravery by killing the snake dwelling in the only public well. The Queen is attracted to Fillo because of his handsomeness. Kado is brought to Queen for his act of valour and is amazed to see Fillo already at palace. Fillo and Kado are honoured though Fillo decides to flee because of the threats to his life. The Queen is known to kill off her lovers when she finishes with them because she does not share men with other women especially, her subjects. Fillo flees and meets a thigh and a dog in a hut within the heart of the forest. Thigh speaks by repeated uniform clicking sounds and the dog interprets them as the directives given to Kado by which merely following they mysteriously feed Fillo and gives him eggs to crack on some conditions on when he should break. By complying he cracks and a herd of cattle appears from the egg mysteriously which delights him. He thus, continues the journey delightfully.

Fillo recalls his background. He is from the polygamous family. He recalls the rivalry among the women within the family and how after the death of his father the oldest brother, Buba, a son of a Hausa woman ran away with the herd. For these reasons, Fillo harbours revenge in his heart.

Traversing the land, Fillo meets a banished old woman suspected to be a witch. Fillo joins the woman to her dwelling hut. Outing together in search of herbs, they find a discarded bone which, out of old woman's powers turns mysteriously into an ox. King Lamba hears the story of the old woman's huge ox through Kado who discovers the ox when he disguises as a food beggar boy in her house. The King confiscates and slaughters the ox. After butchering it, only the bunch of entrails goes to the old woman-owner and the entrails turn mysteriously into virgin girls from which Takitse (fat made) is the most beautiful with whom Fillo falls in love with. Just to try her in-depth bashfulness *kunya/Fulaaku*, one day, Fillo tries holding all the entrail girls' dresses when they undress and swim. They all, one by one, call him by name so collect their dresses but, Takitse refuses calling him by name and repeated calling him by 'someone' until she nearly drowns. To rescue her, Fillo dives in so drown together unfortunately, into what the Hausa people believed 'Water World'. In the Water World, they experience wonders in the lives of the water people before they finally return to land.

King Lamba snatches Takitse, again, and forcefully marries her and she joins his other three wives but as favoured one, because of her beauty and youth. Out of rivalry, when the King is away for a war, other king's wives insist Takitse should cook for the house as they do. Being exposed to the bare cooking fire, Takitse who cannot endure heat pressure melts into liquid. The king punishes other three wives ruthlessly by beheading them so that their heads, put together, should be used as fire place stones. Only the old woman revives Takitse into life.

King Lamba is being conquered by King Korar. Firstly, during the war, King Lamba was winning because, Kado was the head warrior of King Lamba but, only defeated by the time Kado betrayed him for opponent, King Korar. Kado is reunited with Fillo and, only now recounts how he escapes Dauzar's execution, too.

In another encounter, a monster abducts Takitse from the old woman's house. Fillo outsmarts the monster so, saves Takitse and escape together.

Kado meets Hamman, a banished son of a Fulani leader/*Ardo* because of his refusal to take care of the home cattle. Hamman hires Fillo for his father so that he takes care of the cattle for him. Since, Fulani are diverse in class, in Kano alone, Abdullahi Nasidi Umaru (2008) says there are up to 11 clans of *Fulanin Soro* tribes thus, Fillo now being a contractor for a while is accustomed to his hosts' different ways though Fulani like him, helping the reader to know more about other Fulani people like *Soro/Shadi* competition and its revenge; the rivalry over Ardo leadership tussle between two brothers which, is largely determined by the higher number of cattle one owns; migration to south in search of pasture and moisture *Bangul*. There has been an encounter between cattle keepers and *Jangali* tax collectors. They, by law, take a cow out of certain number counted. Ardo, therefore, outsmarts them by giving them emaciated ones. Some Fulani cattle keepers decide to flee as Baffa who is a brother to Ardo leads them. Yet, they all never escape but caught and subsequently, lose huge cows to *Jangali* tax collectors as a result.

Hamman, the son of Ardo now challenges Ja'e in the contest of Sharo while Fillo challenges Gabdo in the same contest.

Since the novel is meant to symbolise the entire north, Kamal lets Fillo traverses from the assumed beginning of the north, Kanwa/Tadabo (Kano) to the edge, Lorin (Ilorin) where the war (symbolic Jihad) concludes. Obviously it is beyond the assumed orthodox Hausa land in order to allow the reader to see more about the north and other tribes. Thus, as the story advances, the barbaric Nyar people feature who in the novel symbolise *Maguzawa* (the Hausa pagans and traditionalists) and all other pagan northern minorities so collectively like one.

Chief Boring treats Hausa and Fulani highhandedly. They refuse to pay tax and prepare for war seeking help from King Tudu, the symbolic Sultan who fights and wins the prince warrior.

Fillo advances towards southern Nyam people where he meets wailing outcasts first, *osu*, he then realises them as a people living under lethal laws. Fillo finds every simple fault a native committed is punitive by either suicide or execution ironically, as part and parcel of their cultural laws. Amidst them, Fillo claims to be a charmer-herbalist who promises to cure their ailing female chief. He, inadvertently, saves the Nyam people's chief charmer friend from committing suicide simply because he failed to cure the ailing Chief. He realises this when he follows the chief to the sea shore to find the cure of the ailment of the Female chief. He finally finds out that she (the Chief) is at risk of committing suicide. There is tradition of evil magic man who spreads disease by hitting his victim. Fillo, too, is hit by a magic man and a disease spreader also, but fortunately though unusually recovers and never included among the wailing outcasts as the usual practice. It is in the Nyam people's land Fillo sees a boy and a man inflicted by a disease with their bellies swollen on whom bellies subsequently, snakes come out. By this incidence, the mission of Fillo accomplished. Finally, Fillo reunites with Kado at home, again. Kado gets married at home.

Portrayal of the Northern Nigerian Civilization in the Novel

Edward and Ayokhai (2013) identify that there was once a cultural civilisation in Northern Nigeria in Hausa States in particular:

They were centres of scholarship and intellectualism, and such development was rapid and the people could appreciate. The form of knowledge passed down was pragmatic and practical. It was geared towards building a society for self-propelling development and self-sufficiency in terms of production and consumption capacities. It was geared towards building a society for self-propelling development and self-sufficiency in terms of production and consumption capacities. To ensure this prospect, the younger ones were given opportunities to choose between trades to learn and the experts in their endeavour of choice were always willing to teach. The devotion of the trainees to the trainers was great. In the process of learning, emphasis was placed on character and learning. Excellence was celebrated and encouraged by the people. The reason was to ensure that they become profitable for themselves and for their respective societies (p. 4).

Culture is the entire way of life of a society. It is through culture that the identity of any society can be understood and recognised because, some cultural aspects, out of many, are unique and peculiar. In this novel, Kamal displays the cultures of a diverse north. The diversity that entails critiquing by portraying various aspects of lives in the Northern Nigeria but seen through the main symbols of the north Fillo and Kado characters, the Fulani and Hausa man respectively, who Kamal aptly employs and lets them, as vagabonds, meander in the adventure especially that of the Fillo that traverses the land up South so we glimpse different tribes on the dual characters' trips full of branch-making. The music and entertainment constitute culture thus, *Dudandu*, the Fulani flute is first seen blown in order to refresh the memories of the cattle and curb their imminent trespass out of the grazing ranch (p. 2) in the beginning and *Kalangu* drumming for young girl dancers in the middle (p. 158).

Kamal exposes shared practices among the Hausa and Fulani such as moonlight story telling traditions: "...we didn't visit her in the night, as the Wiseman would then insist we recite our verses from memory. Instead, we mostly visited her on Thursdays and Fridays when we didn't go to school so that she could play her elongated *shantu* gourd for us" (p. 32).

Submissiveness in Religion: No marriage no sex is Muslim practice so accepted by Hausa-Fulani northern Muslims as in (p. 49) when escaped from the Hausa fabulous Water World, Fillo remarks: "I wasn't surprised Takitse had left. She didn't want to spend the night with me because we were not married."

In the same vein, Fillo recalls the practice of purdah in his early days: The Wiseman allowed only very young students like us into his house. "All of women is a genital," as he said, "divided into many parts." Mairo's uncovered hair could not be seen by anyone beyond the age of puberty, talk less of her slender calves, which she used to play for us (pp. 32-33).

Submissiveness to God can be seen as in Fillo/narrator who says: "what a cold day!" I hailed someone standing near a wall "that's how Allah wants it to be," said someone suffering from cold. He pressed down one nostril, lifted his head and blew through the other..."

In page 73, Fillo meditates Islamically: "A full moon glowed from the centre of the sky. A few stars called *hen-and-chicks* clung together like a bunch of grapes. They were beautiful; I wished I knew more about them. I looked out sharply for the shooting star, whose spark used to frighten evil spirits eavesdropping in the heavens."

In page 90, Fillo and Ardo warn Leko about shirking tax payment, and for that, we are brought to see a one pillar of Islam that is always considered an obligation, the *Zakat*:

> if they catch you," I said, "they will force you to pay all the debt you owe them" "is it a debt?" "of course it is," Ardo said "it is like paying the poor due, (Zakat) which is religious obligation."

In page 100, "husbands like devoted wives more than troublemakers. Hager advised Prophet Abraham to marry Sarah, why not Laure? Hager and Sarah stayed peacefully without beating the other out of the house. Why not Laure and Sarai?" These similar God submissiveness indicants can be located in pages (178,179,199,243,244,246).

Symbolism: Fillo and Kado, the main characters themselves are the main symbols of the Hausa land if not Northern Nigeria. Baobab tree is another symbol of the Northern Nigeria. It is also seen through (p. 69) when Fillo saves Takitse and escapes from a chasing monster into a large cave:

"At last, we came upon a giant baobab tree. I quickly pushed Takitse into the hole at the bottom of the tree and crawled in after her. It was cool inside because the heat had not penetrated the thick bark…"

Speaking further on the terrain, the kind and admirable climates of the Northern Nigeria are also not skipped by Kamal, as in this dialogue between Fillo and his boss, Ardo, a Fulani settlement leader:

> I know of only two seasons." "there are five. First, there is the wet season, which immediately followed by the hot. The third season is the harmattan period. The fourth comes after the lifting of the harmattan dust, while the fifth is the stormy windy one, which leads us back to the rain.

Conclusion

Kamal writes a different story which can be described as a combination of history, fable, folklore, legend, myth, and a culture. As a Northern Nigerian, readers would find his own point of view of the north more interesting. After a thorough scrutiny from the analysis of the novel, it is obvious that Northern Nigerians especially, the literates begin to respond comprehensively. It is imperative that other northerners should put more effort to attain universal recognition through producing more elegant and credible literatures which could speak for them. On the region's perceived reluctance in Literature, it will be beneficial if state governments in the north organise competitions on literary, even non-literary writings in search of voices from/for the region. Being the mirror of any society, the people of the north should bear in mind Literature is also an identity-maker.

References

Carter, D. (2006). *Literary theory.* Herpenden: Pocket Essentials.

Kamal, A. (2003). *Hausaland* (2007 ed.). Kano, Nigeria: Myrrh.

Kamal, A. (2004). *Fire in my backyard* (2009 ed.). Kano, Nigeria: Myrrh.

Kamal, A. (2010). *Hausa girl* (2015 ed.). Zaria, Nigeria: Ahmadu Bello University Press Limited.

Kamal, A. (2011). *Hausa boy* (2013 ed.). Zaria, Kaduna, Nigeria: Ahmadu Bello University Press Limited, Zaria.

Lenshie, N. E., & Ayokhai, F. E. F. (2013) Rethinking pre-colonial state formation and ethno-religious identity transformation in Hausaland under the Sokoto caliphate. *Global Journal of Human Social Science, 13*(4), 1-10.

Umaru, A. N. (2008). *Daular Fulani a Kano 1806-2002.* Kano, Nigeria: Benchmark Publishers Limited.

Chapter 12

Transforming the Society Through Indigenous Practices: The "Iyawo-Ile" Institution in Okunland as a Case Study

Olushola Ayodeji Akanmode

Preamble

Every community in Okunland tries to link her origin with either Ile Ife or Oyo kingdom. A plausible reason could be because they speak variants of the Yoruba language. Okunland is located inland on the right side of the bank of River Niger above and below the confluence. Its inhabitants include the Abinu, Ikiri, Ijumu, Owe and Yagba. They are presently found in five Local Government Areas in Kogi State, North-Central Nigeria, which include Ijumu, Kabba/Bunu, Mopamuro, East Yagba and West Yagba. For administrative convenience, they were governed in the northern region by the former colonial masters and were formerly referred to as Northern Yoruba. Generally though, the people of Okunland refer to themselves as Okun people and the word "Okun" is derived from their common mode of greetings. "Their economy is generally agrarian, though they engage in trading and are also found in white collar jobs" (Lewu, 2003, p. 70). This paper will examine the roles and activities of selected groups of 'iyawo ile' in Okunland as they affect the socio-economic transformation in their community in order to accord the cultural practice of the institution recognition in other communities in Nigeria.

Aim and Objectives

The aim of this paper is to observe and examine the activities of the 'iyawo-ile' institution in Okunland and its relevance to socio-economic and moral transformation in the society. The objectives are to:

i. Project the 'iyawo-ile' institution and showcase its relevance in a traditional wedding ceremony in Okunland; and
ii. Examine and project the aspects of the cultural practice of the 'iyawo ile' institution that are relevant to the socio-economic and moral transformation of the society

Research Questions

This paper attempts to answer the following questions:

i. What are the meaning and significance of the 'iyawo-ile' institution at a traditional wedding ceremony in Okunland?
ii. What constitutes cultural practices in the 'iyawo-ile' institution and what is its relevance to Nigerian society?

Research Methodology

This paper employs the relevant aspect of the sociological functionalist mode of Bronislaw Malinowski, which pays particular attention to the elements, structure, functions and the cognition of local practices and sees beyond all aggregates that the cultural contexts prevail over the meanings and functions attached to local tales, magic, myths and rituals. The motivation for this contention is strengthened by Malinowski's (1926) submission which is based on: the principle that in every type of civilization, every custom, material object, idea and belief fulfils some vital function, has some task to accomplish, represents an indispensable part within a working whole.

The expression of this approach is akin to the cultural practice of 'iyawo-ile' institutions and their impact in the society.

The methods of research adopted for this work through which the activities and performances of the 'iyawo-ile' institution in Okunland will be unveiled are observation of live performances of selected institutions, oral interviews of selected members of the institution and consultation of relevant materials.

Women's Roles in Okunland

A group of people that have not been given enough recognition in Okunland are the women. Women constitute a larger percentage of the people in the world and they are an indispensable group in the development of any community and the nation as a whole. Against this backdrop, it would be unjust to leave them out of the scheme of things. Observation of what obtains presently indicates that women have limited access to socio-economic rights and privileges and do not enjoy high social status.

Okun women play significant roles in the domestic responsibilities in their various settlements. Such roles include preparation of food, improving the nutritional content of family meals, cleanliness of the surrounding, improving better home care and nursing of children. Aside from these, the women also take up white collar jobs (particularly the educated ones) or engage in trading in order to generate income for the upkeep of the family and themselves.

In the rural Okun setting, farming is the main occupation, but the women are less involved in cutting, hoeing, planting and weeding. "They mainly contribute to the last stages of farm work like harvesting, processing for final consumption. Products meant for consumption and sale are carried to the market, villages or towns by women and children" (Ogidan: unpublished article)

Over time, there are some Okun women who have developed themselves by acquiring good education that has enabled them to obtain the highest qualification i.e. the Ph.D. and even to be placed in significant positions in the society. However, the percentage of women in this category is still relatively low when compared to their men counterpart.

The 'Iyawo Ile' Institution in Okunland

This is a group that comprises strictly of women only and they play important roles in traditional wedding ceremonies that cannot be overlooked, hence the purpose of this study – to project and make relevant this noble institution that is not given enough attention and recognition. The make-up of a community is a collection of different families, therefore, when it comes to the issue of marriage in Okunland, it is not just the nuclear family that supports a 'son' in marrying a wife or giving out a 'daughter' in marriage. Members of the entire extended family are also expected to be a part of the process. Among those that constitute members of the extended family is a group of women popularly referred to in Okunland and, even, Yoruba land in general, as 'iyawo ile'. A group of 'iyawo ile' refers to a group of women who are wives to different men from the same family and lineage irrespective of the women's age, race and creed. They are a minority whose roles in the activities involved in a traditional wedding ceremony cannot be over emphasised. Except in 'Iya Gbedde' that has variances in little ways, the activities and roles of a group of 'iyawo ile' are similar all over Okunland.

For a woman to be fully recognised as 'iyawo ile', she must be formally married to her husband, i.e. both of them must have gone through all necessary marriage rites. Those who became 'wives' as a result of getting pregnant outside wedlock will not be well respected by the family members of her 'husband' until they formalise their union by going through the customary process of a traditional wedding ceremony. Although such a woman who becomes part of the extended family as a result of getting pregnant outside wedlock is still considered to be an 'iyawo ile', she will continue to be taunted until she is formally wedded into the family. It was not a common thing in the olden days to have a situation such as this, i.e. premarital sex leading to a child/ children outside wedlock and thereby becoming 'iyawo ile' informally. These days, it has become so rampant and those involved seem not to be bothered about it.

All 'iyawo ile' of the same family usually come together formally to form an institution where they carry out their activities in an orderly manner. The coming together creates a forum to know one another better, especially in the order of hierarchy and to also discuss important family issues. They usually hold meetings once a week (preferably Sundays), especially those in the village. Those that reside in towns or cities can do likewise if they so desire, but those in villages adhere strictly to this arrangement.

Prerequisites to Engaging Services of 'Iyawo-ile' Institution

The fact that the intending couple's mothers are members of 'iyawo-ile' institution in their respective families does not mean that they will automatically enjoy the services of members of the institution when the need arises. The institution has to be formally invited if the bride's or groom's mother desires its participation, involvement and services, especially for the reason of observing tradition and to also add colour to the traditional wedding ceremony.

The invitation is usually done in a traditional way. One or two weeks before the traditional wedding day, the mother of the intending bride or groom will send presents (usually delivered in a native bowl) comprising fifty 'obi abata' (kolanuts), some biscuits or sweets and the sum of one thousand Naira to the 'iyawo-ile' institution. This form of invitation is more recognised than an invitation card. The sum of money paid in the olden days was 'toro' (three pence) or 'sisi' (six pence) and thereafter it was increased to two hundred Naira. Subsequently, in line with the increase in the economic standard and high cost of average living in the country, it was increased to one thousand Naira. Although the intending family could give more than this, giving less will never be acceptable. As a matter of fact, the amount given from one thousand and above will determine the quality of dishes ('igba') the institution will purchase as gifts to the bride or bridegroom's wife if it is their son that is involved. If the amount is high, the dishes will equally be of high quality but if it is low, so also will the dishes be of low quality. The dishes are usually presented to the bride when she is taken to her husband's house after the wedding ceremony.

However, it should be noted that not all the money given to them as invitation present would be used in buying dishes. Part of it will be kept in the institution's savings for future use. The institution, however, does not keep its savings in the bank, simply because they see no need for it. Their savings also include contributions from each member of the institution at their weekly meetings. It is mandatory for each of them to contribute any fixed convenient amount. Defaulting will not be tolerated and it was discovered during this research that the institution enjoys the cooperation of all members in this regard.

Pre-Traditional Wedding Activities

After the 'iyawo ile' institution has received the invitation, it is mandatory for it to identify with the intending couple's family and to demonstrate its acceptance of the invitation. This is done by each member of the institution individually collecting an impressive load of firewood and taking it to the intending couple's family house, about four days before the wedding. It is compulsory for all members of the group (young and old) to carry a load of firewood each. Old ones amongst them who do not have enough strength can assign the duty to their children. Scanty load of firewood will not be accepted and defaulters will be fined.

The firewood carrying ceremony is usually associated with a lot of pomp and pageantry. All members of the 'iyawo ile' institution will dress in the 'aso ebi' (ceremonial uniform) they had earlier agreed on. There will also be a lot of singing and dancing. In 'Iya Gbedde', the traditional musical instrument called 'opele' is used as an accompaniment to the native songs rendered repeatedly as the group proceeds to deliver the firewood. Such songs include:

Song 1:

Iya oko gha pewa ade
Awa ko le sai debi ayo

Meaning

Our sister-in-law (bride) has called upon us and we are here, we cannot ignore a call of joy.

Song 2:

Call...Ori lo mo ohun te da le
Response...Ori lo mo ohun te da l'ese...

Meaning

Man's destiny will determine what he/she will become in life.

On the day the loads of firewood are presented, it is the duty of the bride's or groom's mother to cook and hold a feast for all members of the institution, numbering up to fifty or more in most cases. Also, she must present gifts to them, which they will share among themselves after leaving the bride's or groom's house. The gifts usually include a bag of salt, tubers of yam, some dry fish, 'orunla' (dry ground okro) and all soup condiments like dry pepper, iru (locust beans). To all these is also added a reasonable amount of money, depending on their number or as demanded by them. Part of the money will be shared among them and the rest goes to their kitty.

A family that is buoyant enough to kill a cow for the wedding gives the neck of the cow to the group of 'iyawo ile' to share as custom demands. However, the quantity of items given to the group varies, depending on the financial status of the intending couple's families. Giving them these items, aside from being customary, is very important so that the group will be at peace with the bride or groom. Being at peace with the couple will attract the institution's genuine prayers and blessing. As a matter of fact, they believe that it is their right to receive all these items and denying them could lead to bitterness and discontentment on their part. To avoid these, the intending couple's family (especially mothers) will see to the group's fulfilment and satisfaction. All these items are thereafter cooked and each member of the institution brings bowls to receive her share. Even the old ones who could not be present during the activities will have their own share sent to them. However, if the items are not substantial enough to be worthy of cooking, a knife will be used to divide the items into small portions, even to the smallest item like seasoning cubes and each person will be given her share. This is done for the purpose of transparency and fairness. By so doing, none of them would feel cheated.

A day or two before the wedding, the institution will assemble at the family house of the bride or groom in order to render assistance in carrying out domestic chores like cooking, sweeping, washing of dishes etc. On the groom's side, it is expected that they clean properly the matrimonial house of the bride.

Traditional Wedding Day Activities

On the wedding day, the group, dressed in 'aso ebi' (ceremonial uniform), sings and dances to the bride's or groom's house very early in the morning. They sit with the bride's or groom's mother in order to be readily available to carry out domestic chores. As they work, they sing along, thereby making the atmosphere to be lively. Such songs include:

Song 3: (for the bride):	Meaning:
Iyoko ti gha mei re'le oko o 2x	Our sister-in-law is on her way to her husband's house
E pa'ghulele e ru gege	Make loud ululations
Omo'leja mei re'le oko.	For a worthy daughter is getting married today.

The bride's oriki (ancestral praise) could also be included. For instance, a bride from 'Omolodu' clan in Aiyetoro Gbedde could be eulogised thus:

Song 4:	Meaning:
Akosun hungi mei re'le oko o	One who uses yam to roast firewood is on her way to her husband's house
Iye 'molodu mei re'le oko	One of our family members is on her way to her husband's house
E pa'ghu lele e ru gege	Make a joyful noise
Iyoko gha mei re'le oko.	Our sister-in-law is on her way to her husband's house.

Song 5 (for the groom):	Meaning:
Baba oko gha me seun da gha orun	Our brother –in-law has done
O seun o da gha orun.	something that we are pleased with.

They continue with their activities until the actual wedding ceremony begins. It is their duty to stay with the bride or her mother until the time comes for them to escort the bride outside to join her husband who is already seated at the venue of the ceremony. A veil is usually used to cover her face in order to prevent everyone from seeing her face until her husband or his parents removes the veil and she is led out, amidst a lot of singing and dancing. The songs include:

Song 6:	Meaning
Onitemi mere'le oko oju mi me ro	My dear is going to her husband's house, I am missing her already
Oyere yere ye ge	I am missing her already Oyere yere ye ge (has no particular meaning other than adding melody to the song)
Bayi kase seun gha.	This is how we do our thing.
Song 7:	**Meaning:**
Oluwa mi mehi to'rin	Walk gently my beloved
Edera to'rin, to'rin	Select your steps carefully
Iyoko mi mehi to'rin	Walk gently my sister-in-law
Edera to'rin, to'rin.	Select your steps carefully.
They also chant:	
Iye oko gha mehi bo o, eme yena	Our sister-in-law is coming
Ohi ee, ohi hun,	Clear the way
Ohi kekere aki ke.	Ohi he, ohi hun, ohi kekere akike (has no particular meaning).

Before releasing the bride, leaders of the group of 'iyawo-ile' will spread small wrappers on the bride's path or present bowls to receive money from the groom's family and friends. If the group is not satisfied with the amount of money placed on the wrappers or in the bowls, they would adamantly refuse to release the bride and sing thus:

Song 8:	Meaning
Omi mo kun, e yan ni n gha ko'gha 2x	The road is flooded, send help to get us
Igbo mo di, e yan ni n ngha ko'gha	the road is bushy, send help to get us please

They liken the situation of not releasing the bride because of their dissatisfaction with the amount of money given by the groom's family, to a helpless situation such as being in an overflowing river where assistance is needed to cross over.

Song 9:	Meaning:
Oko iyawo me gungun komi	The groom gave me bone
Esi, me moghi s'aja re	Why is that? I am not your dog
Oko iyawo me gungun komi	The groom gave me bone
Esi, loki me saja re?	Why is that when I am not your dog?

The unacceptable amount of money is likened to being offered a piece of bone by the groom instead of meat.

The group could really go beyond a reasonable limit with this aspect of the wedding ceremony, especially if the groom's family is wealthy and they are aware of it. After placing the wrapper on the bride's path and receiving money, they could go further to place another small wrapper on her chair so as to collect more money from the groom's family and friends before she would be allowed to sit down. They reason that the groom would be displeased with his bride standing up instead of being comfortably seated and therefore would be compelled to give out more money. After releasing the bride, the group has no more avenues by which it can enforce the groom, his family and friends to pay more money, except when the engagement items are brought in and they are displeased with one or two things.

In the past, it was customary for the group to initially present a 'fake 'bride,' i.e. someone different from the real bride, in order to deceive the groom. The person could be the bride's sister or an aged woman from the bride's family. The presentation would be done one or two time(s) before the real bride is eventually brought forward. The 'fake' bride's head and face is usually covered, which makes it easy for the groom to be deceived until he removes the veil. This tradition has, however, been eroded by modernization and religion, except in very rare cases.

The activities of the 'iyawo ile' institution on the groom's side are not as elaborate as those of their counterpart from the bride's family. The issue of taxing the bride's family for whatever reason does not arise. Their major source of gratification is from the groom's mother, who gives out gifts to them in cash and food items. Nevertheless, they still play very important roles such as sitting with the groom's mother, assisting in domestic chores and serving food to guests and visitors. Other very important roles they play are escorting the groom to enter the bride's compound, which in most cases, is also the venue of the ceremony, with singing and dancing, carrying the engagement items for presentation to the bride's family and receiving the bride after the whole ceremony. In some cases, the youngest in the group is mandated to pour water on the new bride's feet before she (bride) enters her husband's house for the first time after marriage. This aspect is also fading away, as it is deemed unnecessary, archaic and unholy.

While carrying the engagement items to the bride's family, they sing:

Song 10:	Meaning:
Ile oko gha li le owo emo s'egan	With no gainsaying, our husband's house is a house of riches
Ewo kamu s'otita ijoko li le oko gha	In our husband's house, the material that our stool is made of is money.

Here, the wives create an impression of the groom's family being very wealthy in order to impress the bride's family.

After bringing in all the engagement items, it is the duty of the group of 'iyawo ile' from the bride's family to inspect them so as to ascertain that all the items demanded are included. If it is discovered that the items are incomplete or any of them is damaged or broken, for instance a broken tuber of yam, there would be a protest. The group would refuse bluntly to accept the items until amendment is made to the error made by the groom's family. Such an amendment entails replacing the damaged item or providing the missing one. Inability to do so would amount to the group estimating the cost of the missing or damaged item and taking its equivalent in cash. Their reason for being so adamant is that in as much as no part of the bride's body is missing or damaged, i.e. she is not handicapped, therefore the items must be complete just as the bride is complete. There is usually jubilation and rejoicing when eventually all the items are certified to be acceptable.

An important item to the group among the engagement items is the envelope containing the money meant for 'iyawo ile' and it is addressed as such. The amount could be two thousand naira or more, as demanded by them. The amount is usually determined by the number of wives in the group. At the end of the ceremony, the envelope would be handed over to the leader of the group and part of it would be shared equally among all of them, while the rest would be kept in their savings.

The final and equally important role by the group is performed when it is time for the bride to leave for her husband's house. While escorting her they sing:

Song 11:	Meaning:
Onihun mo gbahun re, irasese *Mogbahun re, ira sese*	The owner has taken what belongs to him (Note: 'ira sese has no significant meaning. It is just an added melody to the song
Song 12:	**Meaning:**
Ododo kan....... A gba hun aree	The only 'flower' we have has been taken away from us (Here, the 'flower' represents the bride).

Post-Traditional Wedding Day Activities

In the past, it was the duty of the 'iyawo ile' institution from the groom's family to bring the bride from her house to her husband's house after the traditional wedding ceremony. Nowadays, the common practice is for the couple to go straight to the groom's house after the wedding reception. Nevertheless, the 'iyawo-ile' institution from the groom's family would still be on ground to receive the new 'iyawo' (wife) formally into their fold. As they do this, they sing in appreciation to the bride's family for releasing their daughter to become part of their own family. The usual song is:

Song 13:	Meaning:
Omo kan ghan ghun gha, eseun 2x	We have been given a child, thank you
Ahoroho omu, eseun	One who is beautifully endowed, thank you
Awojo wojo awo, eseun	She will live long
Ilolo tinu omo, eseun	She will bear many children for us.
Aghunnomo watojo	
A s'egbon s'aburo	
Aghun nomo walala.	

Integration of Moral Values

Another very important role the institution performs before and during the course of the wedding ceremony is giving out advice to the couple, particularly the bride, in form of songs. The songs mainly centre on the need for good morals that aid peaceful living with her husband's family, friends, neighbours etc. and guide against broken homes and dispute in marriages. They emphasise on the following for the bride:

- Importance of patience
- Shunning of quarrels, fights and bickering
- Ability to command respect
- Upholding dignity and honour

- Embracing the spirit of obedience
- The need to be hospitable, accommodating, loving and caring
- Ability to maintain peace
- Eschewing pride and arrogance etc.

Advice for the groom:

- To avoid quarrelling and fighting with his wife
- Have the ability to settle disputes amicably
- Restrain from reporting his wife to her family members
- Possess and sustain love and care for his wife etc.

Some of the moral advisory songs are:

Song 14:	Meaning:
Oko be ki iwo, were njo	When your husband calls on you
Wo se were o, were njo	Hasten to heed his call
Ewa were o, were njo	Go quickly
Ewa were omo, were njo.	You go quickly.

Song 15:	Meaning:
Wo ba dele oko re	When you are in your husband's house
Momo ya papara	Do not be stubborn and difficult
Wo baya papara	Otherwise your children will behave likewise to you.
Omo aya papara ghi wo o.	

Song 16:	Meaning:
Ewi ghon oba mi pe mode o	Tell my husband that I have come
Elenini ghon ghin layin mi o e.	Detractors, get behind me.

Song 17:	Meaning:
Eni to ba gbe, eni t'oba hin	Whoever was not properly wedded
	Whoever did not have the traditional musical instrument

Eni t'oba fo pele gbe rele okore	opele) played when going to her husband's house
Abe mongoro l'ogbe soyun	Definitely got pregnant under the mango tree
Oforu salo o.	And ran away in the middle of the night.
Song 18:	**Meaning:**
Gbigbe lagbe	We have performed the wedding rites
Iyawo gha mewule roju	Our wife do not be unhappy
Gbigbe lagbe 'yare rele.	Your mother equally went through the same process.

The Economic Relevance of the Institution

Aside from the money given to the group at various instances cited earlier such as invitation to participate in wedding activities, after delivery of firewood, releasing of bride, envelope among engagement items and voluntary cash gift from the couple's parents, the group also raises fund through weekly contributions by each member. The money is usually collected during their weekly meetings which, in most cases, hold on Sundays.

Another means of generating income is through fine. This is applicable to absentees from meetings and anyone who defaults in bringing her load of firewood. Interestingly, it was discovered during the course of this research that the group hardly ever lacks fund. Surprisingly too, it was gathered that they do not lodge or save their money in the bank. The usual practice after the end of their activities at a traditional wedding ceremony is to count the money realised, then part of it is shared among all the members, while the remainder is kept as savings with the group's treasurer. The sharing of the money is usually done with all sincerity. Everyone gets her own share, including old and frail members who can longer participate in any of the activities and are forced to stay behind at home.

It is important to add that many of the wives have regular jobs where they earn a living and it is not that they rely solely on what they get from their activities at a wedding ceremony. Such jobs include teaching, farming, trading, tailoring, hair dressing, weaving etc. This explains how they are able to pay for the group's 'aso ebi', contribute money at meetings and even pay any fine. Invitation for the group's involvement at traditional wedding ceremonies does not come on regular basis, therefore, it is not an occupation but just a pastime they engaged in mainly for the sustainability of tradition.

Aside from sharing part of the money realised among members of the group, part of the remaining money that is kept in the group's savings is used to purchase gifts for the bride's or groom's parents. Part of it could also be used to offset loan incurred by any member who could not afford the mandatory load of firewood and had to borrow in order to meet up. The concerned member would be expected to pay back the loan at an agreed time.

Concerning the weekly contributions made at meetings, the usual practice is to share a large portion of the accumulated income among members at the end of the year, while the rest is reserved for running expenses. In addition, a larger percentage of the money saved by the group is given out as petty business loan to any interested member. It is expected that the beneficiary of the loan would trade with it, in as much as the group is in support of the choice of trade. Thereafter, she is expected to pay back the loan at the end of the year with interest. The interest is calculated based on the profit she realises from the sales. Here, the group functions as a cooperative society even though it is not registered. Part of the proceeds from this type of transaction is shared as usual, while the remaining is.

Income generated by the group is also expended individually. Each member uses out of whatever share comes to her to supplement her regular income and whatever comes(if it does) from her husband as housekeeping allowance, for taking care of the family and herself. Top on the list of her priority in most cases are the children and this is crucial because no doubt, a child well taken care of will most likely turn out to be productive in the society. An individual can also use her own share of the proceeds to contribute to community development such as building of a town hall.

Political Involvement

Members of the institution usually participate actively in any political obligation in their community as the need arises, provided they are duly recognised and informed. In most cases they respond positively to any political party/figure that seeks their involvement and support, especially in the areas of campaigning and voting.

The Social Relevance of the Institution

This can be portrayed through the following themes:

Unity: The coming together of this group of women and their collective performances show not only that they are organised, but that they are also united.

Peace: The group takes it upon itself to settle any dispute between/ among two or more members. Their advice to the bride on the need for a peaceful co-existence with family members, friends, in-laws, neighbours also indicate the need for peace in our society.

Solidarity: This is clearly demonstrated among members of the group and with the couple's family members. The group agrees together on any decision/ action taken. For instance, when they agree to wear a particular ceremonial uniform (aso ebi), no member violates the instruction. In the same vein, collecting money from the groom's family requires solidarity effort from the group of 'iyawo ile' from the bride's family. Other members of the group are usually in support of one or two members assigned to speak on their behalf.

Fairness: This is demonstrated through the group's method of sharing things given to them. Food items and money given to them are shared equally without any form of insincerity. Old ones and even widows still receive their share.

Hard work: Aside from the domestic chores they engage in, carrying an impressive load of firewood from the place of gathering or purchase all the way to the bride's house requires a lot of hard work.

Industry: Many of the women are quite industrious, as they engage in one business or the other in order to make ends meet.

Love: Taking it upon themselves to buy gifts for the couple, presentation of loads of firewood, helping with cooking and other domestic chores etc. are all show of love and care for the couple and their families.

Dignity and Pride: The group of 'Iyawo Ile' from the bride's family's act of rejecting any substandard amount given to them by the groom's family implies that they have a sense of dignity and pride. This stance will erode the thoughts of 'a beggar has no choice' from the mind of the groom's family in whom the group has high expectation of gratification.

Findings

This study has been able to make the following findings:

Songs, Music and Dance Aesthetics: There is a resourceful use of songs, music and dance as metaphors by the 'iyawo-ile' institution. The three elements serve as means through which the institution not only adds colour and entertainment at the wedding ceremonies, but also means of expression to the couple and their families.

Eroding culture: The interests to engage the activities of the institution is waning gradually among the new generation couples and, in some cases, even their parents, mostly because of religious beliefs and modernisation. It is common these days for the bride or the groom to have preference for their friend's services instead of the 'Iyawo Ile' institution. The fear expressed by a few members of an 'iyawo-ile' institution interviewed is that the culture could go into extinction if it is not preserved.

Non-participation of Urban women: Many 'okun' wives who reside in urban areas do not identify with the institution. They do not attend meetings even when they visit their native land, neither do they make any contributions, nor purchase 'aso ebi' etc. Such women are not likely to enjoy the services of the group whenever the need arises.

Financial Handicap: Some members of the group, especially those with no regular source of income, cannot meet up with contributions and other financial commitments to the group. This invariably results in shortage of fund for the group.

Education: Many of these women are not educated at all, while some are only partially educated. This shortcoming could retard their contributions to the socio- economic development of their community. Related to this also is their low level of skills acquisition- proper acquisition of skills can enhance their income.

This study is also able to find out that the group lacks adequate knowledge on business management and investment. Improper management of business can lead to loss of income and resources. The group's savings could also be invested or kept in a savings account so that it could generate more income instead of rendering it redundant at home.

Conclusion and Recommendation

The indigenous practice of the 'iyawo ile' institution in Okunland goes beyond just adding colour to a traditional wedding ceremony. The salient values derived from this practice in their own way contribute to the socio-economic development of their community. These contributions, which range from their activities at the small nucleus family level to the larger community, no doubt have brought delight to many homes and communities. The messages embedded in their songs and activities are directed at achieving, among other things, peaceful co-existence, good morals, sense of responsibility, hard work, mutual respect, love, good neighbourliness, promotion of development through industry, elimination of conflict and violence, dignity and fair partnership. These values are very relevant and essential to be integrated and imbibed by any community that desires genuine socio-economic development. This study recommends that scholars, researchers, critics, community and national leaders should explore and imbibe the values inherent in cultural practices in different Nigerian communities as a means of transforming our deplorable nation.

References

Lewu, M. A. Y. (2003). The contributions of the Roman mission to the development of formal education in Okunland, Nigeria, 1920-76. *Journal of Arabic and Religious Studies, 17*, 69-80.

Malinowski, B. K. (1926). *Myth in primitive society*. London: Kegan Paul.

Unpublished Oral Interview
Deacs. Araiyetan. Oral interview. 15 Feb. 2013.
Mrs. Owolabi. Oral interview. 15 Feb.2013.
Mrs. Olorunmaiye. Oral interview. 18 Feb. 2013.
Michael, Abigael. Oral interview. 19 Feb. 2013.
Elebiyo, Abigael. Oral interview. 19 Feb. 2013.
Tolohunlomo, Lydia. Oral interview. 19 Feb. 2013.
Imikaiye, Abigael. Oral interview. 19 Feb. 2013.

Chapter 13

National Integration in Jamil Abdullahi's *Idfa' Billati Hiya Ahsan*

Abdulrazaq M. Katibi

Introduction

Recent events in the socio–political history of Nigeria indicate a risk to the attainment of a united Nigeria, a situation that if left uncared for, may lead to a total eclipse of the much desired goal and objectives of building a vibrant and egalitarian society as stated by the Nigerian constitution. Therefore, the vision and mission of becoming one of the twenty leading countries of the world may be unrealisable. A peep into the Nigerian society reveals a lot of anti-social behaviour like corruption, kidnapping, thuggery, tribalism, secession treats, political deceit, erosion of indigenous languages and religious riots which are like cancer, and, if left untreated may consume the Nigerian project. In an effort to redeem this problem by the past and the present Nigerian leadership, many policies and programmes have been provided and executed to further entrench national unity among Nigerians. These efforts include certain constitutional provisions such as Federal Character, National Youth Service Scheme, Federal and State Educational Institutions, National Agencies, among others.

The struggle to integrate all strata of the Nigerian society is also championed by literary artists who show commitment through their writings and performances. These literary works are written and performed in the many diverse languages and also in English language. Notable among these literary writers and artists in this respect include Hubert Ogunde, Wole Soyinka, Dan Mairaya, Oliver De Coque, Chinua Achebe, Haruna Ishola, Gabriel Okara and many others.

These works contribute immensely towards the attainment of national integration among Nigerians. However, as old as Arabic and Arabic literature are in Nigeria, little is known about the contributions of these Arabic literatures, especially towards the entrenchment of national unity and cohesion among ordinary Nigerians. Therefore, this paper intends to highlight the efforts of Arabic literary writers in the struggle to build a strong united Nigeria based on mutual understanding, cultural transformation and linguistic diversity, especially as expressed by Jamil Abdullahi in his novel, *Idfa' billati Hiya Ahsan*.

Integration and the Nigerian Literary Source

Integration plays a pivotal role in human society. *The Oxford Advanced Learner's Dictionary* (2010) defines it is the act or process of mixing people who have previously been separated, usually because of colour, race, religion, etc

From this definition, some facts are extracted, which include: integration must be in human society. It is an act of bringing different parts together as one. It always takes place in an environment where conflicts exist. It is also a process that consumes time and in different stages and it must also involve consent of the rival groups.

In any human environment, it is often believed that a man can never be an island unto himself, that is, no human society can progress or develop without having contact with another. This integration can take the form of regional, cultural, religious, social, political, economy, among others. In fact, it is worthy to note that all empires, nations and super powers known to man are products of integration where cross-fertilisation of human and material resources are allowed to prevail.

Nigeria became a political entity when the three regions (North, East and West) were amalgamated, which resulted into regional integration, an action that indicates a clear departure from communal and tribal interaction. The process of this regional interaction ended when the British colonial government and the leaders of the three regions signed and sealed the agreement, which was known as the Amalgamation, in 1914.

Followed by this process is the political and social integration which the government of the day believed will bring about social and cultural integration. Unfortunately, these social and cultural integrations were incomplete because the process was truncated by difference in political ideology and loyalty of the political elders to their ethnic and tribal groups. Thus, this has a devastating and catastrophic effect on the process of building a Nigerian Nation.

The Nigerian society today is characterised by the effect of ethno-religious conflicts which have permeated all its strata. These include religious riots, kidnapping/abduction, insurgency, militancy, corruption, conflict between herd-men and farmers, etc, although, concerted efforts are being made by the government to reconcile and integrate all conflicting factors. Despite this, many anti-social norms still persist in many parts of Nigeria. This ugly trend prevailing over the Nigerian society will not take the country and the people to the promised land if pragmatic actions are not taken by all and sundry.

It is our indisputable fact that literature reflects the society. Therefore, all actions and inactions of the people in the society are captured using all the literary genres and techniques. Literature has, among other functions and responsibilities, the revival of cultural and linguistic heritage of the society, social integration, discussing of National issues, psycho-mental development of the people and educating the populace etc as explained by Katibi (2013).

In response to the clarion call to defend and protect Nigeria against imminent collapse and ascendant attacks by different groups, many literary artistes have put up works to portray the Nigerian peoples, cultures, values and norms either to the Nigerians themselves or to the international community. Wole Soyinka, in the book titled *Poems of Black Africa* (1981) collected a large number of poems written by Africans on different issues. Nigerian poets captured in the anthology include J.P. Clark and Wole Soyinka. Also, Nwoga (1985) in his *West African Verse* listed some Nigerian poets who had written on the Nigerian culture. Among them are Osadebay's *Song of Hope*, Okara's *One Night at Victoria Beach*, and Wonodi's *August Break*.

Prose and Drama play an important role in the integration process in Nigeria. Issues related to National development are raised and discussed literarily. There is a long list of Nigerian prose writers who take upon themselves the act and art of projecting the cultures in different forms and enlightening other people on other cultures. Some of these prose writings are done either in English, Arabic or indigenous languages in Nigeria. Notable among them are Chinua Achebe, Wole Soyinka, T.M. Aluko, Halimah Sekula, Zainab Alkali and many more. In drama, writers like Ahmed Yerima, Olu Obafemi and many more are fully committed to the unity of Nigeria through writing. It is worthy to note that these literary writers chose different themes to write about, only that a critical look at their works reflects undiluted and unshaken commitment to the projection of Nigerian diverse culture. They never call for disintegration or acrimony by any means.

Arabic literature is fast becoming one of the major forces in the Nigerian literary market today. This is because of the position of Arabic language in the country and its strong relationship with socio-political, religious and linguistic developments of Nigeria. Most importantly, Arabic readers cut across the geo-political zones of Nigeria, thereby making issues raised in any literary work a national issue just like any other Nigerian. Literary writers in Arabic language are Nationalists working for the unity and progress of the country.

In order not to divert the intention and attention of this paper, we shall briefly list some of the literary artists who have written and discussed National integration either directly or indirectly. In poetry, poets like al-Ilori, Issa, Tijani Adekilekun and many more, raised many questions on unity and cultural integration among the people. Other issues like national identity and national holidays are always discussed in their poetic presentations, Likewise, national issues, especially cultural and religious harmony, are often preached in prose writings of Arabic expression. Examples of such include Mai-Ungwar's *Limadha Yakrahunana* (2006), Jemilu Abdullahi's *Idfa' Billati Hiya Ahsan (*2004), al-Hijriy's *Khadimul-Watan* (2008) and al-Haqiqi's *Rihlatu Zahrah* (2012). Apart from these Arabic prose works, there are other translated stories from Nigerian languages into Arabic. Some of these translated works are *Ireke Onibudo* written by D. O. Fagunwa and translated by A. S. Abdulsalam (1994) and *(Ogboju Ode Ninu Igbo Irumale)* also written by Fagunwa and translated by M. M. Jimba (2002) and *Ote Nibo* written by Olu Owolabi and translated by Lawal I. Abdur-Raheem (2009). It also includes a collection of *Afenmai* stories from (Edo) translated into Arabic *Qisas Khattil Istiwaaᶜi* by Z.I. Oseni (1999). All these translated works also portray Nigeria's multi-cultural and ethnic diversity and the need to integrate. Arabic drama also plays an important role in the over-all development of Nigeria, especially in the areas of socio-cultural and religious integration of Nigerian people. Some of these works are Z. I. Oseni's *al-Amid al-Mubajjal* (The Honourable Dean) (1994) and *al-Attabaqatul Ulyah* (The Upper Class) (2010). Others are Alabi (2012) *Gharat Nujum* and many others. These dramas by their theme, plots and characters, reflect the Nigerian society and its cultural diversity, problems associated with it and solutions.

Review of the Book

Here, we shall briefly highlight some major events emanating from the novel. This will give us an insight into what to expect regarding our major topic, which is integration.

1. Posting of graduating students: The story is aimed at expressing emotional and socio – cultural experience of Bashir, a young graduate from Bayero University, Kano in accordance with the Federal Government Policy He was posted to Oyo State (Ibadan) for the compulsory National Youth Service to scheme which he obliged (Abdullahi, 2004, pp. 2-3).

2. Agony of Departure: Meanwhile, Bashir, who is the main character of the story, had already expressed his love and possible marriage to Sarah before he completed his degree and there seems to be no qualms between them along the line. The reason that brings about high emotional feelings between the two, especially when the former came to bid the latter farewell. Sarah stood motionlessly and appeared as if she was lifeless in reaction to the shocking news of the

departure of her fiancé to a strange land, which she was not ready for, although Bashir assured her of his commitment to her and that the future is going to be brighter for them on his return safely (pp. 9-12).

3. Bashir's South - West experience: On getting to Ibadan, Bashir was received by his father's old friend, Alhaji AbdulKarim, in his house where he was introduced to Yoruba people, culture, important places and socio – cultural events in Ibadan during his stay. He took time to visit the Premier University (University of Ibadan), Mapo Hall, Cocoa House, Gbagi Market among others. Bashir was fascinated with all the socio – cultural activities and places he had seen most especially the climatic condition which is quite different from what it is in the North. Bashir was not done with what he had seen in Ibadan, he was later taken to Lagos by Ghali, a relative of Alhaji AbdulKarim, where he saw many other important places in the then Federal Capital City. Among the places he went to was Festac at Iganmu and Apapa areas (pp. 52-104).

4. In the course of Bashir's visit to many places in Ibadan, he was accidentally taken to Ghali's friend's house where they met Nabilah and he later married her (pp. 36 – 40).

5. Betrayal of Sarah: Back at home in Kano, Sarah had already reconsidered Bashir and denounced him as her future husband for the reason not stated in the story but which may be unconnected with the absence of Bashir for a long period of time. Surprisingly, it was Tajudeen, one of Bashir's friends that Sarah later married. The message got to Bashir through his friend, Ali, by telephone call. Of course, Bashir felt betrayed and became disgusted.

6. Bashir engages Nabilah: This occurrence led to Bashir to take a drastic move by connecting with Nabilah with the intention of proposing her for marriage. His proposal was successful. Bashir did not feel cheated by losing Sarah, but instead, was fulfilled by engaging Nabillah (pp. 83–84).

7. Bashir reconciled with Sarah and Tajudeen: Another surprising part of the story is the reconciliatory move by Bashir while he visited Tajudeen's family purposely to deliver a message to the family and more importantly to diffuse the tension in the mind of Tajudeen and his family; the matter was later resolved.

This is what brings about the title *Idfa' Billati Hiya Ahsan* (pay with what is better), that is, Bashir did not pay evil with evil. Bashir later goes to Ibadan to conduct the marriage ceremony with Nabilah, while Alhaji Abdul Karim represents the groom's father (pp. 97-106).

Themes of Integration in Abdullahi's *Idfa' Billati Hiya Ahsan*

At this juncture, we shall extract some texts which discuss and express integration, analyse them, especially as they reflect geographical, social, religious and cultural integration and finally make some comments.

1. *Regional Integration:* By this, we mean where the writer expresses different geographical experiences that are felt either by an individual or group of people, directly or indirectly. As we all know, Nigeria is a country that has different climatic conditions due to the geographical parameters that characterise each region. For example, Northern region is known for hot weather and harmattan because of its proximity to the Sahara region of Africa; whereas, the South is known for heavy rainfall and thick forest. The writer, in his effort to integrate the geographical and climatic conditions between the North and the South places a northerner in the south and describes how he (Bashir) adapts to the weather; clearly explaining how Bashir is feeling in his new environment.

كان اليوم أحدا، الجو معتدل نسبيًّا، وإن كانت السحابة الكثيفة تغري بهطول وشيك للأمطار، مناخ بدأ بشير يعتاده كان فى الأيام الأولى حليف مظلة. أنى ذهب (p. 42).

The day was a Sunday and the weather was partially moderate even though the cloud was thick, threatening and ready to rain. A weather that Bashir begins to familiarise with, unlike the past when he used to move around with umbrella.

From the above, the writer explained some climatic conditions which Bashir had enjoyed in Ibadan: moderate weather condition, cloudy sky, heavy rain and thunderstorm. This is a clear departure away from the harsh climatic condition and little rainfall in the North. With this, Bashir will be able to differentiate and appreciate the different climatic conditions of the North and South regions. However, it may be wrong to perceive that a climatic condition of a particular region is better than the other because each has its own peculiarity and its usefulness which may not be found in other.

2. *Social Integration:* Social interaction is a key factor in the overall development of any human society. It is a process which allows each and every sector or society to interact, pick-and-drop the ideology and way of life for the purpose of forming an entity. Education is one of the essential tools in which social integration is perfected.

Jamilu Abdullahi, in his book, narrates and practised the importance of social integration. He gives accounts of how Bashir (an Hausa man from the North) got himself educated and informed about Yoruba people in Ibadan and Lagos by visiting selected social, educational and cultural centres despite the bad assumption and believe he had for the people of the western region. Among his feelings include:

إن ما يقلقني هو ابتعادى عن الشمال، وكم سمعنا بحوادث اضطرابات وبمجاوز عدوانية ، وخاصة فى الجنوب الغربي مما جعل الناس يعتبرون المنطقة قنبلة موقوتة، قابلة للإنفجار كل لحظة (p. 6).

> What disturbs me is my distance from the North. We have heard several incidences of riots and unjustified violence, especially in the South – West region, which makes people (from the north) believe that the region is a time – bomb ready to explode anytime.

Bashir raises fear of leaving the North for the far South especially because of what he heard about incessant riots and hostility, especially in the South-West. But his visit to places like Mapo hall, Koko House and University of Ibadan changes his perception (pp. 26-29).

He also took time to visit Lagos to familiarise himself with places like the National Theatre, Tafawa Balewa Square, Muritala

Mohammed Airport, Lagos Central Mosque and National Stadium (p. 48).

After the completion of the service year, Bashir and his friend Ghali go to Lagos, Bashir gets a total psycho-social reversal of his feelings to the people and the entire Western region. He becomes proud to be a Nigerian. All his negative feelings about the region have completely vanished and evaporated.

3. *Cultural Integration:* Culture entails norms, values, languages and religion of a particular group of people. In other to avoid total domination of a particular culture over the others in a particular region, there must be "cultural integration". Among the features of cultural integration are cultural exchange and retaining of one's belief and practices.

No doubt, the culture of the people of the North where Bashir came from is quite different from the culture of the people in the South-West. Islam and Hausa dominate the North, whereas Yoruba and the presence of traditional worshippers are found in the West, even though, Islam remains an important element in the area. According to the story book, the writer presents a number of cases where Bashir had contacts with Yoruba culture, even though he was eager to have the feelings and experience. His friend had challenged him to acquire Yoruba language to the extent of writing a letter using Yoruba language. Not only did Bashir accept the challenge, but he added that he was not afraid to be addressed as *"Kabiyesi"*, a special way of greeting Yoruba rulers (p. 16). In another development, Bashir found time to further integrate himself with Yoruba culture by making a conscious and cautious visit to Liberty Stadium Ibadan where he witnessed cultural parade of Yoruba. Among the interested displays he saw were *"Egungun"* (Masquerade), *Angere* (masquerade on stunts), Yoruba drums and dances. This cultural visit also took him to the museum where he saw and captured Ife Bronze, one of the Yoruba identities. Bashir was so captivated by the cultural treasure of Yoruba culture and commented; thus:

إن يوربا-والحق يقال-لشعب ثريّ بتقاليده وفلكلوراته العالمية الشهيرة.

Yoruba people are indeed rich with culture and popular folklore.

This comment summarises Bashir's impression and total conviction that Nigeria has a lot of potentials to be discovered among its people irrespective of regional, social, religious and cultural differences. It is the responsibility of the government and its agencies to further explore all possible means to allow Nigerians to understand one another's culture.

Another aspect where cultural integration was fully practiced, was when Alhaji Abdulkarim (an Ibadan based businessman) was asked to represent Bashir's family to ask for Nabilah's hand for marriage from her family in Ibadan (p. 85). This scenario, in fact, is the ultimate result expected from all Nigeria citizen's after the completion of full integration of all strata of society where regional, social, religious, cultural and linguistic barriers will not be impediments for our private and national lives.

Conclusion

In this paper we have been able to introduce and explain the concept of National integration, its importance and the efforts of the stake holders to further re - integrate all segments of Nigeria, especially when the country is experiencing political, economic and cultural decay. Past efforts of literary writers in Arabic language and English Language to express unity and understanding among Nigerians are briefly relayed. One of the works written on this aspect, especially national integration, is a story written by Jamil Abdullahi Titled *"Idfa' Billah Hiya Ahsan"*. The writer was able to highlight how the main character, Bashir (an Hausa man from Kano) was able to use his Youth Service scheme to further understand and appreciate the diverse culture of the people, language, social and religious aspects of the people of Ibadan and Lagos in the western part of the country. Apart from these beautiful experiences, Bashir also came home with a Yoruba girl (Nabilah) to replace his former confused and naïve fiancée from Kano, his hometown.

The paper is also able to conclude that literature is an important instrument to repair damages and mend all fences that may have caused some misunderstanding among Nigerians. And Arabic prose writers are shown to have also contributed their own quota in this respect. We also realised the need to encourage literary writers to portray the positive aspects of the Nigerian culture for the purpose of understanding one another. It is also discovered that Arabic literature could be an alternative for English literature in the discussion of National issues and affairs in the country.

References

Abdullahi, Jamilu. (2004). *Idfa' billati hiya ahsan*. Kano: *Darul-Ummah* Printing Agency.

Abdulsalam, Ahmad. S. (1994). *Qosbul mukhayyam*. Ijebu-Ode: Shebi Otiman, Printing Press.

Abdur-Raheem, I. Lawal. (2009). *Al-intikhab muamarah*. Lagos: Razanson Enterprise Company.

Alabi, A. A. (2012). *Gharat nujum*. Ilorin: Al-Mudif Printing Press.

Al-Haqiqi, Muritado. A. (2012). *Rihlat-zahrah*. N.p.: N.p.

Al-Hijri, Hamid. M. (2008). *Khadimul-watan*. Ilorin: Alabi Printing Press.

Jimba, Mashood. M. (2002). *As-soyyad jarihi fi-gabati afarit*. Ilorin: Al-mus Poly-Consult.

Katibi, Abdul Razaq. M. (2013). Functions of literature in the human society. *Addad: Journal of Arabic Language, Literature and Culture*, 2(1).

Mai-Ungwar, Salisu. D. (2006). *Limadha yakrahunana*. Kano: Sambushi Printing and Publishing House.

Nnwoga, Donathus. I. (1985). *West Africa verse*. Singapore: Longman Group Limited.

Oseni, Z. I. (1994). *Al-'amīd al-mubajjal*. Auchi: Darul Nur.

Oseni, Z. I. (1999). *Qisas-khattil istwai*. Auch: Darul-Nur.

Oseni, Z. I. (2010). *Attabaqatul ulyah*. Auchi: Darul Nur.

Oxford Advanced Learners Dictionary. (2010). New-York: Oxford University Press.

Soyinka, Wole. (1981). *Poem of Africa.* London, Ibadan: Heimann Educational Books Limited.

Chapter 14

Ideologies in Conflict: A Critical Discourse Analysis of Auwalu Yusufu Hamza's "Cheating Destiny"

Rabi Abdulsalam Ibrahim

Introduction

Ideology as a concept has several meanings depending on the perspective from which it is defined. Generally, it is said to be the beliefs which influence people's behavior, actions, reactions and interpretation of events in their lives. All texts are influenced by ideology arising from the author, the society and other experiential factors. Thus the study of texts from a critical discourse approach tries to 'unveil' the ideology embedded in a text. This paper examines 'ideology' in the context of Hausa society depicted in the short story, 'Cheating Destiny', by Auwalu Yusufu Hamza. The setting in the story is a Hausa society and thus this concept is investigated against the backdrop of a shared ideology among the Hausa people. The story is selected because it portrays Hausa people in Hausa communities and the modern challenges they face. Hamza's depiction of contemporary thinking about social issues is examined. The ideology behind the basic assumptions that determine the choices made by people in the Hausa society is studied against the background of a dynamic society. The main objectives of the paper are to: i. investigate the devices that the author uses to portray Hausa people's ideology; ii. explore how the story depicts conflicting ideologies in the society, and iii. explain how the author challenges existing ideologies in the Hausa society. It is usual to find that in Northern Nigerian novels, a dominant Hausa ideology is used to justify patriarchy, misogynist tendencies, polygamy, women subjugation, denial of girl-child education and domestic violence (Usman, 2007; Abdu, 2007). This paper, however, demonstrates how a dominant ideology is in conflict with another competing ideology.

Plot-Summary of 'Cheating Destiny'

Told from an omniscient narrator, the story is about a democratically elected Governor who attends a school's essay competition. The students were asked to write essays on their perception of *almajirai* (children who come to cities to learn the Qur'an but end up becoming beggars) in the society. At the event, they were asked to individually read aloud their essays. The competition is won by a little girl whose essay explains the sad plight of *almajirai* in the society, showing that if the society wants to help them, it has to address the way they (*almajirai*) think of themselves. To demonstrate her compassion for *almajirai*, she gives away her cash prize to some beggars- *almajirai*- at the venue of the competition.

The Author

Auwalu Yusufu Hamza is a relatively new writer who has published collections of short stories. He was born in Nguru, Yobe State of Nigeria and his parents are from Kano. Hamza obtained a Bachelor Degree in Anthropology from City University, New York. He also has a Professional Diploma in Mass Communication. He worked at the Kano State History and Cultural Bureau and the Centre for Research and Documentation, Kano. He writes in both Hausa and English. 'Cheating Destiny' was published in his collection of short stories, *Citizen's Parade and Other Short Stories* (2006).

Theoretical Framework

The theoretical framework used in this paper is Critical Discourse Analysis (henceforth CDA). CDA is a multidisciplinary approach to the study of, both spoken and written discourse. It shares interests with diverse disciplines such as linguistics, cognitive psychology, sociolinguistics, anthropology, sociology, ethnography and ethnomethodology. In fact, Bloor and Bloor explain that the term 'Critical Discourse Analysis' is used because of the several influences from different areas of study and not just linguistics (Bloor & Bloor, 2007, p. 2). CDA examines "practices and customs in society both to discover and describe how they work and also to provide a critique of those practices" (Bloor & Bloor, 2007, p. 3). CDA is a rapidly developing area which objectives include but are not restricted to: "analyse discourse practices that reflect or construct social problems; to investigate how ideologies can become frozen in language and find ways to break the ice; and to investigate how meaning is created in context; and investigate the role of speaker/writer, *purpose* and authorial *stance* in the construction of discourse" (Bloor & Bloor, 2007, pp. 12-13). In CDA, language is examined, bearing in mind several contextual influences such as gender, politics, racism, economy and people's attitude. Furthermore, linguistic items in different genres are studied in CDA because their use in texts and discourse triggers a desired concept (Bloor & Bloor, 2007, p. 77). Treadgold (1989, p. 107, cited in Paltridge, 2006) explains that spoken and written genres are not just linguistic categories but "among the very processes, by which dominant ideologies are reproduced, transmitted and potentially changed." Paltridge (2006, p. 45) citing Clark (1995) explains a number of ways in which ideology might be explained in a text:

> The analysis may start by looking at textual features in the text and move from there to explanation and interpretation of the analysis. This may include tracing underlying ideologies from linguistic features of a text, unpacking particular biases and ideological presuppositions underlying the text and relating the text to other texts, and to readers' and speakers' own experiences and beliefs (Paltridge, 2006, p. 45).

Some concepts that CDA uses in examining texts include framing, foregrounding, and presupposition. *Framing* of a text refers to the angle from which a writer or speaker talks about an issue (Gee, 1999;

Blommaert, 2005). Framing deals with how the text is presented and the perspective taken by a writer or speaker. By analysing the word choice of a text, a researcher can bring out the latent ideology that contributes to the production of the text. Bloor and Bloor point out that framing is important in CDA "because the way we view the world carries cultural messages that become normalised and accepted as everyday common sense" (2007, p. 11). *Foregrounding* is the technique of making some linguistic feature or an issue prominent. That is, some things are given prominence more than others. Thus, the researcher is left with the task of identifying what is emphasised and the effect of this emphasis. Closely related to this is *backgrounding,* which is the downplaying of an issue in relation to other issues raised in a text. *Presupposition* is the assumption the writer or speaker makes in the production of discourse. Assumptions made in a text arise from a myriad of social, cultural and political contexts, all of which portray the ideology encoded in it.

Perspectives on Ideology

'Ideology' as a term has a multitude of meanings which stem from a rich historical background. Ideology can be used narrowly to refer to "an explicit set of political beliefs, such as liberal, conservative, or socialist ideologies, usually assumed to be in conflict" (Bennett, Grossberg, & Morris, 2005). It is also used to mean "broader systems of beliefs, ideas, and attitudes that have direct implications for political commitments and actions. In this sense, the Cold War was seen as a battle between communist and capitalist ideologies." (Bennett et al., 2005). Thirdly, ideology is also used in opposition to "fact", "logic", "reason", "philosophy" and even "truth". It is always the other side – and never one's own- that has an ideology" (Bennett et al., 2005). In this sense it is largely a pejorative term. In literary criticism, Kavanagh (1995, p. 310) explains the concept of ideology from Althusser stating that ideology "designates a rich system of representations worked up in specific material practices which help form individuals into social subjects who freely internalise an appropriate picture of their social world and their place in it. Ideology offers the social subject not a set of narrowly "political" ideas but a fundamental framework of assumptions that define the parameters of the real and the self..." (Kavanagh, 1995, p. 310). For many theorists who develop theories of ideology, there is an implicit presupposition that the critic is speaking from the position of truth or making a scientific critique, as is found in the work of Louis Althusser. Consequently, ideology is usually identified as false consciousness or an illusory expression of the actual circumstances of life. Foucault worries about the notion of ideology and gives three reasons why the general perception of ideology is problematic:

> The first is that whether one wants it or not, it is always in virtual opposition to something like the truth.... The second inconvenience is that it refers necessarily ... to something like a subject. Thirdly, ideology is in a secondary relation to something which must function as the infra-structure of economic or material determinant for it (cited in Mills, 2003, p. 11).

This argument holds because there is never a position where a person speaks from no ideological viewpoint. Like the post-structuralist, Pierre Macherey and Loius Althuser, Foucault agrees with the assumption that all knowledge, including theoretical knowledge, is determined not only by the economic base, but by a combination of institutional, social, and discursive pressures. The critic can be critical of certain aspects of knowledge, but there are limits to what can be thought and grouped as "knowable". Foucault claims that the relations between economics, social structure and discourse are complex; they determine what can be thought at particular times but with none having primacy over the other.

Drawing from previous work done on the concept, Bloor and Bloor, who follow a CDA approach, define ideology as "a set of beliefs and attitudes, consciously or unconsciously held by a social group" (2007, p. 174). The point that ideology can be unconscious is emphasised by Paltridge (2006) who notes that "values and ideologies which underlie texts tend to be hidden rather than overly stated" (p. 45), and that texts "are never ideology-free nor are they objective" (p: 45). Indeed, in CDA, Bloor and Bloor point out that beliefs that originate from ideology may not be consciously held by an individual, as they can be "so deeply ingrained in our thought patterns and language that we take them for granted as self-evident." As such, in CDA, analysts need to be aware of this. Furthermore, a person's ideological position may be screened by his choice of words.

Monuments vs. Pits: Contrasting Ideologies in Hausa Society

Presuppositions, as mentioned earlier, form the background assumptions against which discourses are produced. A strong presupposition present in the story is the religious undertones of the general setting of the story. Religion is a complex belief system in which human beings engage with a spiritual reality. This engagement with the sacred is marked by observing certain rituals and spiritual reverence. Language centres on its users and users exist in a society, therefore it is not surprising that language is intertwined with socio-cultural values, of which religion is part. These socio-cultural and religious values are part of ideology. In the story, before the essay competition began, an opening prayer was said, thus marking the place of religion in the society. Also, when the little girl who eventually wins the competition, stood up to read her essay, she "blew her nose in a calm calculated manner, extended salutations and then continued (Hamza, 2006, p. 36). Muslims offer salutation when they sneeze and it is reflected by the writer here to subtly create a character of a girl who was brought up with knowledge of her religion.

A dominant perception in the worldview of Hausa people is the concept of destiny. Hamza, in 'Cheating Destiny', holds up the common ideology of a certain group of people regarding politics and the underlying role of destiny in the lives of people. At the beginning of the story, the Governor arrives at the venue where party enthusiasts awaited him:

> Circumstances! Twist of fate may be. A gift from the above... phrases camouflaged into sermons serve to describe the ascendancy of the Governor; party faithful

> drew a dividing line. On one side, even party thugs sing sermons amidst spells of drug-induced chants of Destiny! Destiny!! Destiny!!! (Hamza, 2006, p. 35).

The framing of the story is the contemporary political arena in Northern Nigeria where everything political is covered with religious undertones. Though this feature of religion-politics is not only found in Northern Nigeria, as Pittin (1991, p. 38) points out, in Nigeria, though a secular country, "the struggle for political control is being played out through increasing reference to and manipulation of religious ideology." This is reflected in 'Cheating Destiny', for the elected Governor in the story is a Governor because of 'a twist of fate'. This belief is influenced by Islamic teachings. Indeed, one of the articles of faith in Islam is the acceptance of fate whether good or bad. This reflects the Hausa people's ideology in which destiny explains away a multitude of events. In the political arena, destiny via religion is used to justify doubtful victories and soothe political failures. Hamza uses short phrases to give his own perspective of contemporary politics: 'Circumstances!', 'Twist of fate may be'. 'A gift from the above' ... 'phrases camouflaged into sermons', 'even party thugs sing sermons amidst spells of drug-induced chants of Destiny! Destiny!! Destiny!!! (2006, p. 35). Hamza uses these short ironical words to show the way some people perceive political issues. More obvious is his use of the phrase 'camouflaged into sermons' to portray a situation where political ideology is wrapped up with layers of deceptive religious phrases. Even though the acceptance is expected from Muslims, Hamza chooses to portray the concept as tainted by political drug addicted hoodlums. It is not unusual in literary-critical discourses to link ideology with politics, however, Kavanagh (1995, p. 312) cautions that ideology is analytically different from, although always related to "politics". Even though ideology may be latent, it is possible to uncover it by critical examination of a text. Hamza never mentions any religious influences in his story, but the whole story is permeated by the influence of (various interpretations of) religious teachings.

Hamza uses a 'little girl' to present a view about *almajirai* that challenges existing social and cultural values: "Then came the third reader; a little girl. The microphone had to be adjusted ... laughs from across the student body accompanied the adjustment of the microphone (Hamza, 2006, p. 36). The writer foregrounds the smallness of the little girl with phrases of emphasis such as *a little girl; microphone had to be adjusted;* and *laughs from across the student body.* By using a little girl to present an insightful essay, Hamza, as a writer, seems to celebrate 'woman' and her intellect, showing that female children have the potential to create change in the society. This challenges existing prejudices about females.

Hamza also uses the little girl's essay to talk about the plight of beggars in the society, and to show two contrasting ideologies that are present in contemporary Hausa society:

> My father tells me a foundation for a monument was laid when I was born. It is the same for every individual, my father confirmed. ... 'When the baby begins to grow, the Monument begins to take shape; socialization for a meaningful life in the community emerges almost automatically. Do this. Don't do this, with religious teachings coming along to stress for recognition of the ultimate source of life and death, riches and prosperity.' This is the way I hope to grow up, thinking of myself as a Monument, looking up to the ultimate source for everything I need (Hamza, 2006, p. 36).

From the above we are given a perspective regarding how a person's life is shaped by how he or she is brought up. The role of people in the society and religion in shaping a person is mentioned. In this view, what a person becomes is determined by how well or not he follows the various norms and values of the community and religion.

However, in the same girl's essay, we come across a different perspective of life:

> *But a bitter reality hit me when each day strings of Almajirai come in and out of my grandmother's house in the old city... Kodankanzo! Kodan dago-dago!!Iyakokonakomiya! These Almajirai were born the way I was... monuments from the start. ...*

> *The other day at the market, one small boy came up to my father with such words...'...yabaku mu samu!' My father shouted at him, saying it was neither Thursday nor Friday, he said the boy should be in school... 'Go and clean up.' My father uttered towards the boy in disgust. But my attention was not with the filth adorning the child, nor the fact that he was not in school, not even the hunger he advertised worried me but the words, '... yabaku mu samu'. These words mean the little boy is not part of the religious lessons that I benefitted from. He is not being helped to develop to become a Monument, but a Pit.*
>
> *Both Monuments and Pits serve humanity in different ways; one is developed in a pleasant way and people associate with it in an estimable kind of way while the other is only fit for waste* (Hamza, 2006, pp. 36-37). (Italics in the original)

The above excerpt draws attention to the different ways of thinking as reflected by the girl and her father. The use of the word *child* (in the second paragraph), creates an image of a young and helpless person, foregrounding the fact that *almajirai* are often sent to the city when they are very young. They are young, dirty and almost always hungry. This is compounded by their poor school attendance. They learn the Qur'an from their *malam* (Qur'anic teacher) every day except for the Islamic non-working days, Thursday and Friday. This is the reason for her father's remark. Thus, here we have her father worried about the appearance of the boy, while the girl is troubled by the latent ideology of the *almajiri*. The little girl, in fact, believes that it is this ideology of the *almajiri* that forms the greatest barrier to success much more than those external 'features' which her father observes only. Hamza, as a writer, then shows us conflicting perspectives to the problem of *almajiranci*: it is not their being dirty, uneducated and hungry that is the problem, but rather how they and some other people (like the girl's father) think about their place in the society.

This Monument vs. Pit analogy presents two contrasting worldviews or, as it were, ideologies. One which upholds the place of man and religion, and the other which upholds the power of man over man. In this seemingly contrasting ideologies, there is an underlying belief in God: Monuments are monuments because they are nurtured and taught to seek everything from God. Pits are pits because they are not shown love and care and above all else, they believe that it is man who collects from God and then gives them (*yabaku mu samu:* translated roughly to mean, May God give you money/ food so that we can get it from you*)*. This belief is one that some groups of people with wealth and power would want entrenched in the minds of *almajirai*. For if the latter believe that they are 'destined' to receive only alms given by the rich, then the coveted position of the rich is secured. In other words, *almajirai* do not pose any threat to them because they will not revolt against them. Ideology creates an 'abstract' situation where, to use Kavanagh's (1995, p. 308) words, "everyone – from dominant and subordinate class alike – understands and perceives the prevailing system of social relations as fundamentally fair on the whole (even if it hasn't done so well by them), and/or better than any possible alternative, and/or as impossible to change anyway." The *almajirai* in Hausa societies are very young children sent to the city to learn the Qur'an. Salamone (1969-70) (though not discussing *almajirai* in particular) explores the psychosocial crisis faced by Hausa children and argues that separation, usually for weaning, from their parents at an early age was a common practice. Salamone and Salamone (1993, p. 372) use Smith's (1969) study to point out that Hausa culture is characterised "as one of patron-client relationships. Factors, including birth-order, family prestige and individual personality, assist the Hausa in determining the patron-client nature of all relationships in their highly stratified society. Socialisation practices active throughout life assist the Hausa in determining whether (s)he should view self as the patron responsible to a client or a client responsible to a patron in a particular relationship." This perhaps explains the unconscious ideology of Hausa people regarding the relationship of *almajirai* with other people in the society. For the *almajirai*, this expectation of 'handouts from the people in the city is part of their *identity* as *almajirai*. They believe that is how things should be; that is, they have to be given the basic necessities of life because they are *'almajirai'*.

Interestingly, both these (Monument vs. Pit) perspectives about life have one thing in common – they all agree that there is an Omniscient God who provides for mankind. In the Monument ideology, God gives to everybody without exception. How a person chooses to use or waste God's gifts is up to him. In the Pit ideology, God gives but only to a select few who may give to those not-so-blessed people of which class the *almajirai* fall into. Even though both ideologies hold the belief that God destines such and such fate upon man, the former acknowledges the role of man in what he becomes, while the latter stresses the unescapable nature of fate. The closing remark by a participant in the school competition after the winner gives her cash prize to the *almajirai*, further expresses this belief:

> Poor girl! She thinks she can cheat destiny by merely distributing cash to *Almajirai*,' a voice uttered from behind the Governor... there was a little sarcastic laugh from those sitting on either sides of the man who made the comment (Hamza, 2006, p. 38).

A close examination of the text reveals that Hamza uses juxtaposition as a device to make the differences between the two ideologies marked. The imagery of the monument is a powerful one, and contrasting it with a pit evokes a picture of striking inequality. The use of juxtaposition is common in Hausa poetry which predates that of Hausa story-writing Sullivan (2009, p. 317) discusses the ideas of Furniss, stating that "one of the most common poetic styles presents ideas in stark opposition for greater effect. The comparison arises: subtle language stylisation employing positively or negatively "value-loaded" terms, but is often illustrated by opposing human prototypes as this way, the poet is able to both critique a social problem and point proper mode of behavior as the solution" (Furniss, 1995, pp. 49-50). With regard to Hamza's use of juxtaposition, we find that the girl's view of the *almajirai* is presented as the better of the two ideologies in the essay.

In 'Cheating Destiny', Hamza presents a society where the *Almajirai* are an excluded social group. This is portrayed by the way they are described in the story: the *almajirai* were "peeping from outside the back window [of] the hall' (Hamza, 2006, p. 38). This shows the physical exclusion of the *almajirai* in the story. In the competition, the essays are about *almajirai*. In other words, they are the objects of discourse in the written essays of the students, yet they are not allowed to come inside the venue where the essays are being read. They stand outside looking at the seated guests talking about the plight of *almajirai* as if they were objects. This objectification of the *almajirai* is reinforced by the ideology of exclusion, which explains the relation between the *almajirai* and the people in the society. Again, juxtaposition is used to create a contrast for the reader: the image created is one where there are two groups of people - one group inside the hall, sitting down in comfort, and the other group (*almajirai*) is outside, standing and craning their necks to see what is happening in the hall. From a CDA perspective, these *almajirai* make no effort to come inside, because they themselves believe that 'outside' is where they belong. In other words, their own ideology excludes them from the other people in the society. Looking at the analysis above, we argue that Hamza presents a perspective where the *almajirai* think that their fate is sealed; that they are destined to be always in the disadvantaged position, with a bowl in their hands seeking for crumbs from others. However, by using the Monument and Pit analogy, he offers an alternative way of thinking for and about the *almajirai*.

Conclusion

As a whole, the story mirrors the social identities and ideologies of groups of Hausa people in Northern Nigeria. Using destiny as a concept present in the belief system of the Hausa, he attacks the cultural values which form part of their ideology that allow the continuation of the *almajirai* system of learning. One ideology portrayed is that you are born in a certain status and you cannot 'cheat destiny'. That is, in specific terms, *almajirai* are beggars not because of any religious and social factors, but because they are destined to become so. This underscores the belief that fate decides what or who we become and not anything else or our own efforts. The other view is the belief that God and man together carve out the ways things are in the society. By juxtaposing the two ideologies, Hamza challenges existing cultural practices and at the same time offers another way of 'seeing' the societal issue of *almajirai*.

References

Abdu, B. (2007). Feminism and the Northern Nigerian novel: An appraisal of Zaynab Alkali's The Stillborn and the virtuous woman. In Saleh Abdu & Muhammad O. Bhadmus (eds.), *The novel tradition in Northern Nigeria: Proceedings of the 4th conference on literature in Northern Nigeria* (pp. 160 -168).

Bennett, T., Grossberg, L., & Morris M. (2005). *New keywords: A revised vocabulary of culture and society.* Malden, MA: Blackwell.

Blommaert, J. (2005). *Discourse.* Cambridge: CUP.

Bloor, M. & Bloor, T. (2007). *The practice of critical discourse analysis: An introduction.* London: Hodder Education

Clark, R. (1995). Developing critical reading practices. *Prospect, 10,* 65-80.

Furniss, G. (1995). *Ideology in practice: Hausa poetry as exposition of values and viewpoints.* Köln: Rüdiger Köppe Verlag.

Gee, J. (1999). *An introduction to discourse analysis: Theory and method.* London: Routledge.

Hamza, A. Y. (2006). Cheating destiny. In A. Y. Hamza (Ed.), *Citizen's parade and other stories.* Kaduna: A.J Publishers.

Kavanagh, J. H. (1995). Ideology. In F. Lentricchia, & T. McLaughlin (Eds.), *Critical terms for literary study* (pp. 306 -320). Chicago: Chicago University Press.

Mills, S. (2003). *Discourses of difference: An analysis of women's travel writing and colonialism.* London: Routledge.

Paltridge, B. (2006). *Discourse analysis.* London: Continuum

Pittin, R. (1991). Women, work and ideology in Nigeria. *Review of African Political Economy, 18*(52), 38-52.

Salamone, F. A. (1969-70). Further notes on Hausa culture and personality. *International Journal of Social Psychiatry, 16,* 39-44.

Salamone, F. A., & Salamone, V. A. (1993). Kirki: A core value of Hausa culture. *Africa: Rivistatrimestrale di studi e documentazionedell'Istitu toitalianoperl'Africa e l'Oriente, 48*(3), 359-381.

Smith, M. G. (1969). The Hausa system of social status. *Africa, 29*(3), 239-254.

Sullivan, J. (2009). From poetry to prose: The modern Hausa novel. *Comparative Literature Studies, 46*(2), 311-337.

Treadgold, T. (1989). Talking about genre: Ideology and incompatible discourses. *Cultural Studies, 3,* 101-137.

Usman, A. K. (2007). Unveiling the faces behind the mask: Women Participants in Contemporary Hausa Movies in Northern Nigeria. In Saleh Abdu, & Muhammad O. Bhadmus (Eds.), *The novel tradition in Northern Nigeria: Proceedings of the 4th conference on literature in Northern Nigeria* (pp. 145-159).

Chapter 15

Re-Thinking the Woman in Northern Nigerian Literature

Abubakar Othman and *Razinat Mohammed*

Introduction

Northern Nigeria, in spite of its vast land mass and demographic diversity, stands out among the other regions of Nigeria as the most homogeneous entity. Despite the divisive influence of religion fragmenting the region into Muslims, Christians and Traditionalists, and the plethora of tribes variegating its demographic landscape, the people of Northern Nigeria are, nonetheless, very much similar in cultural outlook, social attitude, and physical traits, with the Hausa language serving as a unifying lingua-franca. The language is spoken and in almost all the ethnic communities that make up the region. With language being an effective instrument of cultural transmission and transformation, the Hausa language has engendered cultural unity, social harmony, economic prosperity, and ethnic integration among the diverse people of Northern Nigeria.

There may however be pertinent issues of construct and consciousness within the entity we refer to as Northern Nigeria and especially its literature. Clergy and scholar, Bishop Mathew Hassan Kukah (2013) captures this thus:

> I must confess that the terms "Northern Nigeria" and "literature" are wrapped in ambiguity and controversy. We continue to use the term "northern Nigeria" despite the creation of 19 independent states out of this former

region. As if in defiance, despite the creation of the 36 states and 6 zones in Nigeria, these states still continue to hold together and define themselves as Northern Nigeria (p. 32).

What culture or ideological thread holds these diverse people with different cultures, languages, together to qualify as united? This conceptual ambiguity, therefore, creates difficulty in defining the term 'Northern literature'. "What does Northern Nigerian literature mean and what should it look like?" asks Bishop Kukah (2013). He suggests possible solutions to the confusion by asking some leading questions:

> Is it in the Poetry, Songs, Dances, or Writings of peoples of the north speaking about themselves in Northern Nigeria, or the writings of peoples from the areas speaking about Northern Nigeria? ... What medium of communication can be referred to as Northern literature? (p. 32).

Indeed, Northern Nigeria has a unique literary identity created by the early writers of the region such as Abubakar Imam, Abubakar Tafawa Balewa, Mohammed Bello, and Mohammed Gwarzo, among others. These writers wrote in the Hausa language and were read and understood throughout the region. Their themes and styles were largely influenced by the Islamic world view and literary imagination. One prominent aspect of this world view is the image of women in the society.

The common image of the woman created by the early writers was that of a home maker, saddled with the natural responsibility of child bearing and up-bringing, in addition to her domestic responsibilities of cooking, cleaning, and providing emotional satisfaction to the man as husband. As a predominantly feudal and patriarchal society, women in northern Nigeria share common experiences of social oppression, economic exploitation, political marginalisation, and cultural subjugation. Hence, literature being a creative reflection of the society in which it is produced depicts women in that stereotyped image. Northern Nigerian writers portray women in from this society as weak, subordinate to men, and incapable of independent action and initiative.

The thesis of this paper, therefore, is that women in the north have always been strong and capable characters in the society, but patriarchy and male prejudice conspired to project the woman as weak, subordinate and incomplete without the man. Unfortunately, the women themselves unwittingly subscribe to this subverted image and begin to see the situation as both natural and unalterable. We conclude that, the influence of globalisation and the dismantling of socio-cultural barricades between societies, there is the emergence of a new woman not only in northern Nigeria but Africa as a whole. There is a growing realisation of women's potentials as brilliant and powerful, at par with their male counterpart. However, there is also a parallel misconstruction of this emerging woman as rebel and libertine who jettisons her past and ignores her present place in society, to embrace the whirlwind of globalisation in the pursuit of her dreams.

Theoretical Orientation

Studies have shown that women have tremendous power and are able to use such powers to change their homes and, indeed, the society. In this respect this paper deviates from the popular feminist theories and ideology that asserts that gender is the fundamental division in society and the major determinant of power relations between the sexes (Lovenduski & Randall, 1993, p. 5). While feminist theories are necessary to some extent, the premise of this research requires an examination of other theories of popular women's movements. These are the Masculinist theory propagated by Chinweizu, and others which we refer to in this study as the Matriarchist theory.

The Masculinist theory of Chinweizu (1990) stresses that women have power. In his analogy, he compares the nature of the much talked about men's power and concludes that "in human society, it is not male power but female power which is supreme" because "men may rule the World but women rule the men who rule the world" (pp. 4-5).

Chinweizu's view-point is of particular relevance to this study in that it reaffirms the 'hidden' but obvious powers of women which he observes is the invisible six-seventh of an iceberg compared to the visible one-seventh which is the men's. Also supportive of the fact that women have immense power over men is the Trinidad Calypso singer, Denyse Plummer, quoted in Chinweizu 1990, who proclaims that "woman is boss" and Patti Boulaye, the Nigerian expatriate actress, who believes that "most men are controlled by women" (Chinweizu, 1990, p. 9).

The matriarchist theory is based on the premise that women can exert their power not only on men but also on other women with the sole purpose of dominating and oppressing their desired targets. In other words, the oppression of women in a matriarchal enclave is no more strange than their when they are oppressed by men in a patriarchal society.

A matriarchal society though strictly none existent does not negate the existence of matriarchal activities spearheaded by powerful matrons "who dominate family groups or clans, who are patriarchs in all but their gender' (Chinweizu, 1990, p. 9). To back-up this argument, Omolara Ogundipe-Leslie (1987) identified the many statuses of African women. She states that "women's roles within kinship systems are not always determined by their sex. A woman can be codified as husband to her mother, her own siblings, and women married into her patrilineage" (pp. 8-14).

Literature Review

Thinking about the woman, most often, either begins from, or leads us to the premise that she is a subordinate and marginal being. Hence, she is considered a mere tangential issue in matters relating to a male dominated society. The English language in its lexicology portrays our subject as *wo*man, *fe*male or *s*he, using suffixes which annexe her to the man. In myths and histories, the woman is portrayed as resourceful but requiring the compliment of a man (hero) to realise her potentials. In Greek mythology, for instance, Pandora is a strong and stoic character who carries the burden of society. But she is manipulated and portrayed as a *femme fatale* and made liable for society's miseries. Similarly, Helene of Troy, a great woman whose enigmatic beauty launched a thousand ships (of war) and burnt the topless towers of Illium would not be celebrated for her strength but be parodied as the epitome of evil in English literature.

In Nigeria, women of yore were great political leaders and war commanders but who, nevertheless, were incomplete without men. Queen Amina of Zazzau, for instance, was a great leader who nevertheless, had to dress like a man to command her 'Queendom'. Similarly, Queen Daurama of Daura, in spite of her leadership qualities and strong power over her 'Queendom', ends up ultimately, not worth more than a mere prize for a man who demonstrated a singular feat of bravery.

African literature is replete with stereotypes of women as docile, weak, willingly subservient and passive. These stereotypes, according to Davies and Graves (1986), whether from the negritude movement with its romanticisation of women, or from the more recent years in which she is depicted with greater fidelity, the images (of African women) are ... less than whole (p. 25). Chikwenye Okonjo Ogunyemi (as cited in Ogunbiyi, 1988) describes Nigerian literature as 'Phallic' dominated as it is by male writers and male critics who deal almost exclusively with male characters and male concerns. She submits that in much of Nigerian literature, male writers regaled the reading public with stereotypes of female characters: the witch, the faithless woman, the prostitute, the femme fatale, the virago, and those male writers with a romantic disposition dangled women as goddesses or helpless victims (pp. 60-61).

However, the myth of female subordination has come to be challenged recently by women writers who, according to Austin-Peters (1994, p. 33) "have brought new angles and insights into fiction, rejecting portrayals of women as self-effacing, docile and passive observers in the world of men." In the same vein, Chinyere Grace Okafor asserts that Chinua Achebe's and Cyprian Ekwensi's constructions of women's experience as tangential to the masculine world have been challenged in the novels of Flora Nwapa and Buchi Emecheta, whose heroines are vital and viable individuals, engaging in a world shared with men, defining their own spaces and contributing to the social reality of the world (p. 81). Helen Chukuma (1994), writing on the feminist dilemma in African literature, observes that the female character in African fiction is a "fucile lackluster human being , the quiet member of a household, content only to bear children, unfulfilled if she does not, and handicapped if she bears only daughters" (p. 215). Similarly, Razinat Mohammed (2008b) states that early male writers like Tutuola and Achebe are guilty of gender partiality in their representation:

> the society had no time to waste with the women folk whose significant contributions to communal matters centred on singing and dancing during ceremonies. The women did not fit much into the heroic cadre of the society at the time and, therefore, were not subjects of literary imagination or creativity (p. 92).

Razinat is also quick to fault the assumption that only earlier male writers are guilty of stereotyping women. She contrasts their works with those of later generation and states that the novels of Flora Nwapa, Nigeria's first published female novelist, and the plays of Zulu Sofola, set women as backbones of families, by actively engaging in commerce and agriculture "…women as the stabilising force in men's lives" (pp. 92-94).

The adoption and reflection of Marxist ideology in African literature, spear-headed by writers such as Bode Sowande, Femi Osofisan, Sembene Ousmane, and Ngugi Wa Thiong'O among others, and the impetus given to women by the Nigerian civil war, promoted a better and more creative understanding of the place of women in the society in the works of Nigerian writers of the 1980s and the early 1990s.

Femi Osofisan in *Morontodun,* Bode Sowande in *Farewell to Babylon*, and Fred Agbeyegbe in *The King must Dance Nake* not only redeemed the image of the woman in literature, but also gave credence to the efforts of earlier female writers such as Zolu Sofola and Flora Nwapa in disagreeing with the patriarchal bias and myopia of earlier African writers. In so doing, a new trend is set in motion for writers and critics to re-think the image of the woman. Iniobong I. Uko (2006) gives a more vivid description of these new trends thus:

> These trends involve such features as Iconoclasm, the deliberate repudiation of all arch symbols of traditionalism and orthodoxy, as well as women's prescient critique of

female subjugation, psychological brutality, individual inferiorisation and exclusion on gender lines (p. 82).

The Depiction of Women in Northern Nigerian Literature

Northern Nigerian literature is in many ways unique among the literature of other parts of the country. Coming out of a long tradition of storytelling dominated by women who teach morals, virtuous conduct, the beauty of nature, and the sanctify of life, the literature is, therefore, more inclined to philosophical postulations, psychological introspection and meditation about the universe and man.

Although like any other literature in the country, northern Nigerian writers write about their local culture and tradition, most of them are substantially influenced by Arabic and Islamic tradition and literacy. According to Sabi'a B. H. (1994, p. 2) before the advent of western education in northern Nigeria, literature had existed for centuries in the form of Arabic and Arabic-based languages such as Ajami. Therefore, the literature of the region derives its characteristics not mainly from western tradition as in the other parts of the country, but basically from the Islamic culture that greatly permeated the socio-cultural life of the region.

The depiction of women in northern Nigerian literature is, therefore, a reflection of the Islamic orientation and cross cultures of the people of the region. The form and content of northern Nigerian literature is also a reflection of the degree of influence the Islamic culture has on the people. While Ajami provides them with the orthography with which to transmit the local language, the copious borrowing and code mixing from Arabic to Hausa also helped the integration of the ethno-religions peoples of the north where the Hausa language is widely used.

Irrespective of religion or ethnicity, the perception of women is common to virtually all northern Nigerian writers. However, their style and subject matter differ according to their ethno- religious background, gender, and ideological orientations. Among the earliest writers in northern Nigeria who wrote in the English language, Zaynab Alkali, Labo Yari, Hauwa Ali, and Abubaker Gimba are outstanding in their depiction of women. Although each has a distinct perspective to the matter, nevertheless they are united in their inclination towards the stereotyped image of the woman. These stereotypes however come under serious objections and redefinition by contemporary women writers. This is consequent upon the current globalisation of culture, gender issues and the diffusion of ideologies such as feminism. The novels of Yari, especially his earliest work, *Climate of Corruption* (1978) and his book of short stories, *A house in the Dark* are good illustrations of the traditional perception of the woman as subordinate to man. Yari's depiction of the woman in *Climate of Corruption* is both gender biased and stereotypical.

In the novel, Maimuna is presented as a prostitute in spite of her natural attributes of beauty and good manners, and, the writer does not give any convincing reason for Maimuna's lifestyle as a woman of easy virtue. She is a woman of enviable qualities which makes the narrator describe her as a Jinni. Ideally, these qualities could be used to project her in a good light. While it is not obligatory for the writer to toe the line of moral didacticism, nevertheless, it would have served a more useful purpose if Yari were to extract those positive qualities of Maimuna from her debased lifestyle as a whore, and used them to redeem her image and develop her into a wholesome woman. Instead, Yari takes her out of her hotel room draped in debauchery, straight to the asphalt road and kills her.

Similarly, in a "Cavalier of the plain", one of the short stories in *A House in the Dark,* Safiya, the main character, is depicted as a pawn in the hands of both men and women. She is divorced by her husband but still remains at his mercy. Her husband may decide at a short notice to reabsorb her into the marriage as if all her life depends on it. However, she falls in love with another man, the cavalier prince of the plains, who also sees her as an object of pleasure not treasure. He also compares the pleasure of her company in bed with the pleasure he derives from galloping on his stallion. In her docility and subservience, she also becomes a pawn in the hands of her uncle's wives who involve her in lesbianism.

In both stories, the women end up tragically, dying ignominiously without self fulfilment and redemption. Safiya hangs herself because the Cavalier lover deserts her, and Maimuna dies in a car accident on a shameful journey following a man to Kaduna. These are hardly charitable ways to depict the quintessential women of northern Nigerian society.

Zaynab Alkali's depiction of the woman in her novels is hardly better than that of Lari, in spite of the fact that Alkali is female. In her earliest novel, *The Stillborn* (1984) the heroine of the novel, Li and her childhood friend Faku have a common dream of marrying men of their choice. To actualise their dream, they rebel against the strangulating life of the village and escape to the city. However, Li's sister, Awa does not approve of their action, even though she also desires the good things of life and a happy marriage. Awa therefore remains in the village in passive acceptance of her fate, hoping that whatever comfort and opportunities the city offers its inhabitants would one day also come to the village for her to realise her dreams, Li and Faku do not however find fulfilment in the city.

This passivity creates the impression that women lack initiative for a meaningful life, hence the only thing easy for them to do is prostitution. In *The Stillborn,* Faku engages in prostitution to ease her life of misery. Alkali seems to say that there is a good reason why a woman can engage in prostitution, and more often, they do so as victims of the ubiquitous patriarchy, as Kassam (Newell, 1997, p. 118) hastily concludes on Faku. But it is actually the problem of stereotype bedevilling northern writers who portray women in such a negative form as passive and fatalistic. Alkali's portrayal of Li as a resourceful woman who can make it in life without depending on the protection and privileges of marriage is a good thesis in re-thinking the woman in northern Nigerian literature. However, it appears like an antithesis to the thesis, when Alkali, in the later part of the novel, transforms Li into an overbearing and power conscious domestic partner who, because of her economic status, sees herself as the man of the house. Li would have served as a good example of the image of the woman, who is an integrating factor, a stabilising force, and symbol of the resourcefulness, doggedness and economic strength of women, if Li had used her opportunity to hold together, not to reverse, the family hierarchy.

Abubakar Gimba's novels, *Sacred Apples* (1994) and *Witnesses to Tears* (1986) are slightly more introspective in their depiction of the woman in northern Nigerian literature. Both Zahrah and Hussaina, heroines of the two novels respectively, are presented as educated women *ab-initio*. However, like the heroines of Alkali's and Yari's works, Zahrah and Hussaina are also embroiled in matrimonial quagmire. Gimba uses their faithfulness to Islamic injunctions about marriage to portray them as docile and passive thereby reiterating the stereotyped image of the woman. But it is also here that Gimba begins to differ from the other writers by re-thinking the image of the woman. After subjecting Zahrah to all the frustrations, pains and agony of marriage which leaves her distraught and disgusted with the institution, Gimba equips her with alternative strength to forge ahead in life. Zahrah picks up her certificates and walks into the labour market where she finds gainful employment. However, rather than make her a rebel against marriage, Gimba uses the wisdom and experience of Zahrah's grandmother and brother to bring her back into marriage. She marries into Nousah's house where she encounters the problem of polygamy in her relation with Nousah's two wives, Salmah and Aalimah. While she becomes completely submerged in her gory experience of jealousy, suspicions and threats to her life, she does not succumb to fate and accept the problems passively as most writers do. Instead, Zahrah uses her education and experience of an earlier marriage to set an agenda and develop her manifesto for the re-ordering of society's thinking about the woman and awakening the consciousness of women about their place and purpose in the society and in life generally.

The thinking here differs from the mythical or chivalric notion that the woman is always a victim, and weak requiring a man to salvage her. Zahrah's eventual self-development from victim and weak, requiring a man to salvage her to eventual self-development is Gimba's thesis in re-thinking the woman as capable of triumph over societal impediments. Similarly, in *Witnesses to Tears* (1986), Gimba weaves the stories skilfully into a treatise on marriage with the thesis that there is no substitute to the woman in the home. Therefore, as an indispensable factor in the family, the woman must not be made a pawn, a victim or a subordinate in marriage.

Mr Anas, father of Hussaina the main character of the novel, is a monogamous husband. When his wife dies suddenly leaving him with the little child, he is left with a huge responsibility to play the roles that are often the responsibilities of women and mothers. The father may be strict in discipline but does not have the tricks the mother has in ensuring moral discipline in bringing up the girl-child. Hence, Hussaina grows up under her father as an indulgent child lacking the know-how of a woman. She falls victim to lust and deceit resulting in a pregnancy and a hurried marriage to a near stranger. Gimba seems to say here, that were it not for the absence of a mother this may not have happened.

Globalisation and the New Woman in Northern Nigerian Literature

Globalisation with its attendant 'think locally and communicate globally' ideology, greatly affected the form and content of creative writing in Nigeria. In northern Nigeria especially, the primordial ideals of feudalism and patriarchy that used to hold the woman down, and the obscurantic dogmata of culture and religion that hitherto defined and differentiated people by their gender are now faced by new challenges introduced by globalisation. Women liberation movements, feminist ideologies, human rights and political rights activism, new democratic ideals, the politics of terrorism, corruption and economy, and all other issues of our modern society, greatly impacted on the woman in Africa, which also, by cause and effect, impacted on the quality of our literature.

With women now serving as Chief Executives of financial institutions, business enterprises, ministerial and ambassadorial responsibilities, and especially the legitimate illegality of the existence of the office of the so-called First Ladies in our democratic governance, women have come to assume too much powers that as First Ladies they can even hold government to ransom through their husbands.

This new woman in Africa makes it imperative for our writers to re-think the way she is perceived and depicted in literature.

In northern Nigeria, certain aspects of the new woman may be unthinkable; ideas such as lesbianism, polyandry, gay marriage, and single parenthood are obvious anathema to the moral high ground on which the north stands tall. Accordingly, however, the stereotyped image of the woman as a domestic servant, an object of pleasure not treasure, an unacknowledged producer of wealth, a weak, docile, and subordinate person, may equally be unthinkable to ascribe to the new woman in northern Nigerian literature. Although the new image of the new woman was perceived much earlier by contemporary northern writers such as Ahmed Yerima, B.M. Dzukogi, E.E. Sule, Abubakar Othman, Idris Amali, and Ahmed Maiwada, among others, their vision of the new woman was at best, euphemistic. Writing in the Alter-Native tradition of their generation, they indeed provided an alternative image of the woman but without re-thinking her powers as leader and decision maker. It was not until the emergence of Helon Habila on the literary scene that there was a serious re-think of the statue of the woman in our literature. The writings of Helon Habila, therefore, mark the beginning of the post Alter-Native tradition. Other writers of this tradition in the north include Razinat Mohammed, Idris Okpanachi, Angela Miri, Halima Usman, Abubakar Adam Ibrahim, Aisha Nana Ahmed, Aliyu Kamal, Tukur Garba, Hadiza Aliyu Saulawa, Ummi Kaltume Abdullahi, and Patricia Bondima among many others.

Among these writers, however, Razinat Mohammed is the most vibrant and outspoken on the issue of women in northern Nigerian literature. Her three works *A Love like a woman's, Habiba,* and *The Travails of a First wife* are seminal on the new woman in northern Nigeria. Closely following her is the poetry of Angela Miri with her rebellion against marriage. Mohammed's short stories, *A Love like a Woman's* (2008a) is far removed from the monotonous theme of the woman as a subordinate creature. It is a bold look at gender issues where the woman is portrayed as an oppressor and victimiser too, just as she is also an exemplary character in matters of love and human relationship. In the various pictures that make up the story, Mohammed seems to say that the plight of the woman in the north should be blamed not only on the overbearing attitude of men but also on the thoughtlessness and wickedness of women towards their fellow women.

Human relationship is the common thread that binds the stories together, and which the author uses to gauge society's sensibility as human beings. In one story there are female and male characters acting together, tackling the same problem differently and arriving at the same solution eventually. For instance, "Something to Live for", which is the first story in the collection, is essentially about the plight of a woman called Afi who finds herself under the heart-breaking tutelage of a husband. However, rather than bore her readers with the issue of oppression, subordination and helplessness of the woman, Mohammed skilfully interlaces the woman's plight with that of a man, a total stranger to her called Efida. Their chanced encounter in the jungle is not only auspicious but also, in critical term, a dues-ex machina for Afi and a rite of passage for Efida. In their mutual reaction to each other they discover something to live for. Ordinarily, in the tradition of stereotype and common place feminism, it would have been the story of a woman who is a daughter of an inconsiderate father and wife of a heartless husband who will not give her freedom even after giving him a child willy-nilly, for the simple reason that 'he claims to have given my father a lot of money on my head' (p. 12). Afi's attempted suicide would have become a major feminist manifesto using stereotype plot structure of an oppressed woman in a male controlled society who suffers passively and dies in the hands of men. However, as a skilful writer who is uninterested in stereotypes, Mohammed resolves Afi's problem creativity without making her groan under the claims of subordination and fatalism.

Angela Miri's *Running Waters and other Poems* (2006) is a significant contribution to northern Nigeria poetry. Written like a figurative diary about a woman's love life, Miri uses the poetic techniques of metaphor and irony to launch a polemical attack not on patriarchy, but specifically on the time-honoured institution of marriage Divided into two parts, and subtitled "streams" and "rivers" respectively, *Running Waters...* meanders through streams of imagery and cleft valleys of irony to a confluence of rivers of metaphor bubbling with lucid thoughts and spacious ideas. In the first part, encounter "Streams" of emotion, passion, and suppressed feelings which keep the woman "deep down the abyss". In part two we find the streams burst into "rivers" of anger, fear, and hate which eventually flow belligerently into a seamless sea of freedom for the new woman in northern Nigeria.

But what type of freedom does Miri find for the woman in the north? It is a freedom that sets her free from all moral restraints and emboldens her to see the revered institution of marriage as a supermarket where you go shopping, not for life time partner but for mere objects of fancy for keeps. She thus comes to discover the surliness of men who say 'I love you' when actually they mean, 'I curse you'. Therefore, Miri admonishes her fellow women not to labour in vain over the worn-out phrase because, if it were worthy of joy 'I could have jostled the feasting bottles/ in celebration of 'I love you' (p. 4). But while she harbours disgust for her man (Supposedly the husband) who never shows her how much 'I love you', her desire for love is however, 'Strengthened by privileged knowledge of someone who cares' and therefore 'I will weep no more' (p. 5).

At this point Miri introduces an antithesis to her thesis of freedom for the woman by extending this freedom to include the choice to be faithful or unfaithful in marriage. Hence the rest of the poems are nothing but praises of her past lover now hovering over her matrimonial life and whom she says is more deserving of respect than her legal man. Thus the free woman in Miri's new world is the one who is a rebel against moral restraints, a maverick against conventions, a libertine, and an iconoclast against religion and tradition. This is hardly an enviable image for the new woman in northern Nigerian literature.

Conclusion

While women are underrepresented and stereotyped in literature, and in as much as these are works that reflect the society in which it is produced, it is incumbent upon us as creative and critical writers to give restorative representation of the women in contemporary society. There is the need to explore and bring to the fore women's hidden strengths and latent powers hitherto circumvented by tradition. However, in doing so care must be taken not to be misled by the rudderless ship of globalisation sailing adrift on the high seas of modern society. While it is bad enough to always project the woman as weak, subordinate, and whose ultimate goal is to become a domestic wife or a prostitute, it is certainly problematic to depict women as rebels of reasonable tradition; women whose ideal of civilisation and individual freedom is to indulge in lesbianism, single parenthood, gay marriage, and disrespect to societal norms and values.

References

Alkali, Z. (1984). *The stillborn.* London: Heinemann.

Austen – Peterse, O. (1994), Feminism in post-independence West Africa. *Journal of the Modern Languages Association of Nigeria, 2.*

Chinweizu. (1990). *Anatomy of female power: A masculinist dissection of matriarch.* Pero Press.

Chukwuma, H. (1994). *Feminism in African literature: Essays on criticism.* New Generation Books.

Davies, C. B., & Graves, A. A. (Eds.). (1986). *Ngambika: Studies of women in African literature.* Trento African World Press.

Gimba, A. (1986) *Witnesses to tears.* Ibadan: Malthouse.

Gimba, A. (1994). *Sacred apples.* Ibadan: Evans Brothers.

Kukah, M. H. (2013, June 30). Some thoughts on multimedia and northern Nigerian literature. *Sunday Trust,* p. 32.

Lovenduski, J., & Randall, V. (1993). *Contemporary feminist politics: Women and power in Britain.* New York: Oxford University Press.

Miri, A. (2006). *Running waters and other poems.* Lagos: Malt house.

Mohammed, R. T. (2008a). *A love like a woman's and other stories.* Ibadan: Kraft Books.

Mohammed, R. T. (2008b). Foremost writers, gender partial. *Unimaid Journal of Women Studies, 1.*

Newell, S. (Ed.). (1997). *Writing African women: Gender popular culture in West Africa.* London: Zed Books.

Ogunbiyi, Y. (Ed.). (1988). *Perspectives on Nigerian literature* (Volume One). Lagos: Guardian Books.

Ogundipe-Leslie, M. (1987). The female writer and her commitment. In E. Jones D. (Ed.), *African literature today* (No 15) (pp. 5-13). London: James Curry.

Sabi'a, B.H. (1994). *A study of the theme of religion and culture: The fiction of Ibrahim Tahir and Zaynab Alkali* (Unpublished M.A. Thesis), A.B.U., Zaria.

Uko, I. I. (2006). Transcending the margins: New directions in women's writing. In E. N. Emenyonu (Ed.), *New directions in African literature: A review* (pp. 82-93). Oxford: James Currey Publishers.

Yari, L. (1978). *Climate of corruption*. Zaria: A.B.U. Press.

Chapter 16

Theatre for Development and Women Empowerment in Northern Nigeria: A Study of 2015 *Kuyambana* Development Communication Field Experience

Jubril Abdullahi and *Habeeb Adebayo Salaudeen*

Introduction

The crusade for women empowerment in socio-political and economic activities has been at the forefront of global agenda. Discourse about gender equality, equity and mainstreaming are nomenclatures used to connote women empowerment. Countries of the world, International agencies and corporate bodies like the United Nations Women, International Trade Centre, the World Bank, among others, have formulated policies, strategies, organised summits, conferences, workshops and campaigns towards mitigating the menace of women segregation and create space for women empowerment through participation and inclusiveness in social, economic, structural and political development intervention.

In developed countries, women empowerment has shifted from mere inclusion in development intervention to empowered participation in the socio-economic realm of the society. The reverse is the case in the African continent, as we are still groping within the shores of women inclusion. This and the lack of cultural sensitivity are largely responsible for the huge failure recorded in many development projects, as several interactive and participatory communication tools used in the failed efforts seem complicated, too formal, full of numerical data and technicalities which might not be appealing to the rural people. TfD as participatory communication methodology pitches its tent within the people's cultural milieu. Equally, TfD has joined the league of advocates for women empowerment and participation and it's playing crucial roles in Nigeria. Though greater success have been recorded in some regions like Benue TfD workshop, Niger TfD intervention, salient cases of women exclusion are in operation in the core rural Northern regions due to some cultural and dogmatic practices that are inimical to development.

Despite these challenges, some ground breaking successes have been recorded through the use of TfD as methodology and there is a resounding hope that those cultural practices that deter women participation are chameleonically going into extinction. In view of this, the 2015 Kuyambana Development Communication Field Experience is indeed a new voice in the campaign towards women empowerment.

Women Empowerment

The word empowerment seems to be over -flogged in the global arena in relation to achieving sustainable development. Though, in recent times, the idea of empowerment has been relatively focused on the women. Rahman (2013) posits that, long before the word empowerment became popular, women were speaking about gaining control over their lives and participating in making the decisions that affect them in the home and community. This is true of the situation of the African and Nigerian women in particular. In other words, the achievement of sustainable development cannot be said to be absolute if women were to be sidelined. Empowerment refers to those resources, such as ideas, knowledge and skills, that become available to the community as a result of collaboration with the project. Such resources are the cornerstone of social capital because they build self-confidence in people as they explore new ways of seeing and acting. Adams points to the limitations of any single definition of 'empowerment', and the danger that academic or specialist definitions might take away the word and the connected practices from the very people they are supposed to belong to. Still, he offers a minimal definition of the term 'Empowerment' as "the capacity of individuals, groups and/or communities to take control of their circumstances, exercise power and achieve their own goals, and the process by which, individually and collectively, they are able to help themselves and others to maximise the quality of their lives."

Women Empowerment refers to strengthening the social, economic and educational powers of women. It refers to an environment without gender bias and everyone has equal rights. Kate opines that "empowerment enables women to take control of their own lives, set their own agenda, organise to help each other and make demands on the state for support and on the society itself for change." This means that improving the status of women enhances their decision-making capacity at all levels, especially in the area of education. The issue of women empowerment is currently reigning supreme in development/ global discourse. Kishor submits that:

> Empowerment denotes women's increased control over their lives, bodies, and environments. In discussion of women empowerment, emphasis is often placed on women's decision-making roles, their economic self-reliance, and their legal rights to equal treatment, inheritance and protection against all forms of discrimination, in addition to the elimination of barriers to access such resources as education and information.

Based on this statement, one pertinent thing to note when discussing women empowerment is the issue of women's rights. These rights have been identified in Universal Declaration of Human Rights held in Beijing, China, 1995. The Charter stated that:

> The inalienable rights of all members of the human family is the foundation of freedom, justice and peace in the world... in the dignity and worth of the human person and in the equal rights of men and women and have determined to promote social progress and better standards of life in larger freedom.

More specifically, an aspect of the universal declaration of human rights that dwell on women is the Convention on the Elimination of all forms of Discrimination against Women (CEDAW). The statement says in part that discrimination against women violates the principles of equality of rights and respect for human dignity, it is an obstacle to the participation of women' on equal terms, with men in political, social, economic and cultural life of their countries, it hampers the growth of the prosperity of society and the family and makes more difficult the full development of the potentialities of women in the service of their countries for employment and other needs (CEDAW, 1995).

The critical section or constitutional principle which tallies with the core goals of CEDAW is that of achieving equality of rights, obligations and opportunities before the law for women through the application of the anti-discriminatory clause that stipulates that: "All citizens without discrimination on any group whatsoever have the opportunity for securing adequate means of livelihood as well as adequate opportunity to secure suitable employment."

Past governments have made several efforts to scale up women related empowerment programmes in various areas, particularly in education. Abiola (as cited in Undiyaundeye, 2013) identified these efforts when she says:

> Government at all levels and other stakeholders in Nigeria's educational sector have attempted to address gender inequalities. For example, the universal primary education (UPE) and the blue print on women education developed by the Federal Ministry of Education in 1990 when UPE collapsed in 1984 were attempts at addressing gender inequality in access to education (p. 10).

In clear terms, the national gender policy focused on the pursuance of legal equality for women and men and the removal of all obstacles to the social, economic and political empowerment of women. Terms like women empowerment, gender mainstreaming, gender equality, among other nomenclatures, are geared towards women inclusion and participation in development efforts to achieve sustainable development.

Northern Nigeria and Cultural Realities

Historically, Northern Nigeria was an autonomous division within Nigeria, distinctly different from the southern part of the country; it had independent customs, foreign relations and security structures. The region is uniquely drier than the southern half, stretching north from the capital Abuja across the Sahel to the Niger border.

Culture plays a significant role in any development discourse. There cannot be sustainable human development in any society without serious consideration of the critical role of culture in development because it refers to the totality of a people's way of life ... how they work, play, love, marry and interact among themselves. Development experts and communicators must never forget that culture is not static; rather, it is dynamic.

In Nigeria and Africa, cultural values, beliefs, norms, mores and so on are so close to the people's lives that any attempt to neglect or underplay them in any development plan or scenario will be disastrous and of no effects. Closely related to culture is religion. People take their religion so serious that anything, including development efforts or philosophies that run counter to their religious beliefs or practices, are strongly rejected. The implications of this cultural reality for development experts and development communicators are quite obvious.

Failures in development efforts are greatly tied to the fact that development communication scholars have not been able to distinctively sieve out the difference between cultural and religious practices.

Before the emergence of the contemporary northern Nigeria, the north had produced women who stood for other voiceless women. Queen Amina of Zazzau, a legendary female ruler known for her territorial expansion and ingenuity in architectural defence the famoua Nana Asma'u, sister of Sultan Usman Dan Fodio was at the heart of a movement promoting women's literacy and agency across the north in the 19th Century Sokoto Caliphate and Haija Gambo Sawaba who in the mid to late 20th Century was a beacon of strident, uncompromising women's voices everywhere.

Furthermore, Ibrahim Sheme (2010) stressed that "the notion many people have - ironically (including Muslim men), about the Muslim woman is not true. Women in Islam are not the proverbial "second best" but equal parts of the whole. They are not, as many erroneously believe, the spare tyres of the human wheel, but partners in progress who must not be relegated."

Islam as a religion does not restrict women from participating in serious development issues therefore; the avoidance of women participation in development discourse is basically culturally inclined.

Therefore, there is the need for development workers to interrogate the core and essence of certain cultural and religious practices, and harness them in fostering gender mainstreaming for sustainable development.

TfD and Women Empowerment

Theatre for Development, popular theatre, theatre for transformation among other nomenclatures attached to it, is an alternative form of theatre different from the conventional trend, it recognises the creative potentialities of the rural masses and seeks to activate those potentialities for the good of the community. It is a form of theatre that celebrates the human person as a being capable of using his/her cultural forms to transform him/herself, therefore his society, for the better (Ifatimehin, 2013, p. 106). TfD is one of the interactive tools with which to liberate the citizens. A renowned TfD scholar, Abah (2003, p. 122), declares that:

> Theatre for development is the theatre practice addressing itself to the issues and concerns of the marginalized urban and rural poor. It has increasingly started to be used not only to talk about the marginalized but also to talk to authority and policy makers to sensitize them to the implications of policy decision. .... TfD has become a strong research as well as development communication tool all over Africa... TfD is a theatre of action whose outputs results from participation.

This means that TfD is a people oriented medium through which their voices can be heard. It does not only address the ruled but also send signals of warning to the rulers and it creates awareness through the participation of all members of the society (male and female) in a rehearsal towards changing their deplorable condition for the better. Such participation is what is called empowerment. Reinforcing the empowerment capacity of TfD, Okwori (2002, p. 161) writes:

> Empowerment involves developing power with and within the people. This power emanates from awareness, from the knowledge of one's capacities, resources, limitations and challenges. Once people gain power, they are able to resist and destroy the conditions that dis-empower them. Empowerment is, however, achievable through certain processes which are imbued with popular participation. Popular theatre may be one of such processes.

Supporting this, Abah (2002, p. 70) argues that empowerment leads to liberation. He maintains that:

> In popular theatre, liberation may be gauged by the extent to which empowerment has been caused....through freer discussion of issues (eg gender).... Empowerment however is a middle point in the procedural destination of Popular Theatre which is concrete to change in the community.

From the foregoing, it is apparent that if TfD as Popular Theatre, is at the centre stage of discussing societal issues through participation, empowerment and awareness which will now lead to liberation, then Women empowerment is one of those issues.

In Northern Nigeria, TfD has been the most potent tool for enhancing women empowerment and participation. Several women empowerment interventions have been carried out but because of some cultural issues, especially women exclusion from participating in development process, fewer setbacks have been recorded. However, since cultural sensitivity is core in development intervention, TfD practitioners in northern Nigeria has continued to mitigate such exclusion through the use of female facilitators for the women behind curtains. Increasingly, the situation is not as intense as it was because, women in some regions, now openly participate in development discourse alongside with men. Women from the Christian dominated areas greatly participate in open discussion on issues bothering them. We can therefore infer that TfD is at the heart of women empowerment.

The Kuyambana Field Experience

Kuyambana is a very large territory, consisting of several villages like, Kuyambana, Zululu, Garmade, Tudun Wada, Madam, Galadima and the Fulani settlement known as Mogo, dispersed around the Kuyambana Hill. Historically, they were living on the mountain in their different clans during which their fore fathers occasionally came down the mountain for farming purposes. This ritual took place for a very long time before the era of slave trade in the 18th century when African Kings sold their people in exchange for the white man's gift. The Kuyambanaking, named Katuri, also sold his people in like manner. This ugly experience made the Kuyambana people to migrate from the mountain to occupy various landmarks. Shortly after the abolition of slave trade, the government of the Late Sir Ahmadu Bello asked the Kuyambana people to re-unite so that government can assist them, therefore, the people of Kuyambana all came together to constitute the villages in Rumayya, Sabondaji, Garkuta, Kuban, all speaking the same language – Rumayya,- under the leadership of a central District Head (Hakimi). Today, Kuyambana, a Christian dominated village, is found in Kauru Local Government of Kaduna State. They are a loving and accommodating people. One surprising thing among the people of Kuyambana is that they accommodate everybody irrespective of your ethnicity and religion. The major occupation of the people as expected is farming for both males and females.

Engagement with the People

The Kuyambana 2015 Field Experience of the Masters Students of Theatre Arts and Development Communication, under the Department of Theatre and Performing Arts, Ahmadu Bello University, Zaria, took place for about nine days, starting on the 21st of January, 2015 at Kuyambana, Kauru Local Government of Kaduna State. For the Theatre Art major, it was a TfD Field Experience but for the Development Communication (Dev.Com) Students, it was a Dev.Com Field Experience simply because, TfD is just one of the participatory tools in Development Communication. On getting to the community, we were welcomed by the Hakimi (District Head), his cabinet and the entire community who gave us the part of their home as accommodation and even fed us throughout the nine days. The field work started with a transect walk with the help of the Community Based Organisations (CBO's) which were readily available to help us. They took us around the community and freely interacted with us. From our own observations, we noticed several challenges, but we pretended as if we didn't, hoping that the people will identify those challenges by themselves. Based on Abah's concept of Methodological Conversation, several participatory tools of engagements were used, such as the Theatre for Development (TfD), Participatory Learning and Action (PLA), Participatory Video (PV) and Photography (PP), Community Viewing (CV) as Mirroring and Behaviour Change Communication models (BCC) tools to tease out and prioritise the problems of the Community, through the use of Pair Wise Ranking and the Problem Tree. On a market day when all the men had gone to the market, the women took the centre stage and made vital contributions that were acknowledged by the men. However, the problems common to the six villages were similar, and they include:

> Lack of good roads and electricity;
> Lack of primary healthcare centres;
> Health challenge;
> Lack of safe drinking water;
> Inadequate classrooms;
> Lack of fertilisers;
> Insufficient land for animal grazing, among others.

After the problems prioritisation, health became the most pressing need that should be addressed. One key issue that was prominent was open defecation, but this seems not to be a problem to the people. During the analysis of the health problem using the problem tree to identify cause and effect of health challenges, the issues raised include, the prevalence of Malaria, typhoid, and Cholera attack. They were able to make connections between open defecation and other diseases as the root cause of the health problem. The community people, especially the women, also realised that, even if the healthcare facilities were to be on ground, they will keep treating the illness forever. Therefore, we made community action plan with the people so that strategies and efforts to eradicate open defecation will start almost immediately. Fundamentally, the women singlehandedly volunteered to support their husbands by providing the roofing sheet, cement, bricks and the toilet heads and added that the men should do the construction. Indeed, the most tasking responsibility have been taken care of by the women who massively participated throughout the process.

At the end of the field work, the Sarkis (Village Heads) and townspeople gathered at Zululu, the Village of the district head and there was communal celebration. On this day, several traditional gestural and oral art forms were performed in celebration of our engagements, which further strengthened the ties between the Kuyambana people and the ABU community. It is a form of Corporate Social Responsibility or community service as part of the University's contribution to the development of her host community.

After the celebration, a set of improved banana and palm-kernels trees were donated to the community women based on their impressive participation by the Department of Theatre and Performing Arts. Also, a teak and palm-kernel tree, also donated by the Masters Students were given to each of the six villages. At our departure, some of the women shed tears claiming they would miss our company.

Follow-up

Between the 12th and 15th of March, 2015 was the follow-up of the field work. Prior to the follow-up, there were contacts between the Theatre Department and the community through the District Head over a bigger communal celebration. The essence of communal celebration is for the community people to invite well - to - do sons and daughters of the land and the Chairman of the local government to witness the progress made in the community through collaboration with the University community and to further assist in solving some other identified problems in the community. The communal celebration, to a larger extent, helped the community to raise fund and further scale up their voice to the world towards attracting donor agencies' attention. Also, among the Masters students were journalists, and communication experts who also aired important findings and breakthroughs from the students' engagements with the people. These, among others, helped to bring the attention of the government to the ongoing intervention in Kuyambana community. Some of the success indicators include:

i. Most of the households had started digging soak-away pits for their toilets;
ii. Some formerly uncovered wells were now covered;
iii. Some of the villages have met and deliberated on how to reconstruct a primary healthcare centre.
iv. The women's banana and palm kernel plantation was growing well. e.t.c.

The Palm Tree and Banana Plantation as Economic Empowerment

Though not so huge, the women's palm trees and banana trees donated by the Department of Theatre and Performing Arts are a form of economic empowerment. During the follow- up exercise, the women representative made a public commendation of the University community for their benevolent effort. They howevers ubmited that they would nurture the plants and when they start yielding fruits, they would be using the money for a developmental project that would benefit all. This, suggests that the Kuyambana women in the nearest future will have resources to solve little social problems.

Women Participation as Empowerment

Based on cultural reality in the core rural settlement in Northern Nigeria, it is hardly possible for women to participate in development discourse. This exclusion of women in public activities is seen by many as a form of religious obligation, but on a fair note, Islam, as a religion, does not restrict women from coming out to express their views on issues that affect them but sternly cautions against unnecessary mingling among the opposite sex. For instance, in 2011 Likoro Community Theatre Experience, the women were not allowed to come out and participate, but a group of female facilitators went into the inner sitting room to engage them in discussion. The fact that these women were not allowed to come out boldly to discuss their issues in the public for the development of their community poses greater challenge to the sustainability of any development effort in their community. Women are the most affected by any development challenge at the grassroots level, therefore, any form of exclusion is a threat to their right.

Unlike our earlier field experience in Likoro 2011, in Kuyambana women's participation greatly contributed to the outcome of the field work. They were able to participate due to the fact that they are predominantly Christians.

Women participation in development discourse can be termed as a form of empowerment because it gives them a free space to express themselves by voicing out their deplorable condition. Generally, the positive outcome of the field experience was largely hinged on the reactions and participation of the women and that is why development experts and frontiers of knowledge are advocating for women inclusion without which real development cannot exist. Spectacular among the villages were Tudun Wada and Kuyambana Women's participation in serious debates through interaction and cultural performances.

Fig. 1: *Tudun-Wada women in a traditional dance section.*

Fig. 2: Kuyambana women in a drama skit

Our involvement with these women has shown beyond doubt that women still hold paramount position in making change and development happen because they are the most affected. The empowered participation of the women birthed several outcomes:

- In Tudun Wada, the women performed various songs in their dialect, which further invoked the spirit of participation. Before this dramatic experience, some of the women were noticed to be cautious and within their comfort zones, but, however, they became more open, interesting and entertaining after the singing session. 'When people are allowed to express themselves in their own language which they understand, the best output is achieved' (Emphasis self).
- In Tudun Wada, Health challenges like typhoid fever, malaria, cholera, hepatitis etc., became a major discourse and the women through the problem tree analysis, were able to identify the root cause and effect of these aforementioned diseases. Apparently, the women, through their own analysis, realised that all these diseases are connected to open wells and open defecation due to lack of proper toilet. Although, they agreed that lack of functional health clinic in the community is a problem, they realised that through their collaborative effort, the root causes such as open well, poor sanitation and lack of toilet, if contained will significantly reduce the effect of these diseases and thereby minimise need for a clinic.

- One of the participants, Mrs. Abigail, when asked of her occupation, said its farming. We further asked that when any of her children has a cholera attack, who stays at home to take care of the child and what happened to their farm at that point? She responded that, "I am the only one left to take care of the child, the farm will become bushy and it will affect the productivity rate." They all however agreed to provide covers for their wells, and showed readiness by producing materials like cement, water and sand for the building as a form of support to their husbands.
- There was a consensus among the women to form a steering committee to achieve the aim of meeting these two demands of covering the wells and building of toilets. They also suggested the need to have a larger forum that will involve both men and women and thereto strategise and conceptualise the modalities of bringing them to reality. The concept of participation is hinged on the involvement of all the stakeholders in a community and this was vividly demonstrated by the women in their expressions and actions.
- In Kuyambana, women showed through their drama skit, the challenges they face when helping a pregnant woman to the hospital as a result of bad roads and lack of functional nearby primary healthcare centre.

Conclusion

This paper x-rayed the concept of women empowerment and gender policy in Nigeria. It reviews literature on gender mainstreaming and sustainable development, taking into consideration the Northern Nigerian society and her cultural realities and how TfD can foster women empowerment. The paper has proven that women empowerment is at the heart of Development Communication through the use of TfD, PLA and other participatory tools. It also presents women empowerment in Northern Nigeria at the level of participation and economic empowerment. One major weakness in this intervention is that there was no documentation of other problems identified and this might cause any development worker who is interested in carrying out an intervention in like manner to start all over again. As we left the community, we left with their outlined problems, leaving them with memories of their yet unsolved problems.

Recommendations

Every development effort is a work in progress due to its cyclical nature Therefore, the following recommendations are hereby outlined:

- The use of Community Information Board (CIB) to document community problems because if they wake up every day to realise that just one out of these problems has been solved, they will feel the need to act rather than fold their arms and waiting for government.
- Development workers should always factor in gender mainstreaming to achieve real and sustainable development.
- Modalities should be devised to get across to the women behind doors through female facilitators or dense probing skills that will provoke the men to get their wives to the public places to speak of their plight.
- Solutions to several social vices cannot be met if women are not given free space to participate in such discourse.
- The peoples' cultural forms should be a starting point for community engagement for greater output.
- TfD workers are encouraged to deploy several participatory communication methodologies for effective and memorable field experience.

References

Abah, O. S. (2002). The dynamics of intervention in community theatre for development. *Contemporary Theatre Review*, *12*(1-2), 59-77.

Abah, O. S. (2003). Methodological conversations in researching citizenship: Drama and participatory learning and action in encountering citizens. In O. S. Abah (Ed.), *The Geographies of Citizenship in Nigeria*. Zaria. Tamaza Publishing Company Limited.

Ifatimehin, O. O. (2013). Theatre for development and the growing need for inclusiveness. Kafewo, S. A. Iorapuu, T. J., & S. E. Dandaura (Eds.), *Theatre unbound: Reflections on theatre for development and social change. A festschrift in honour of oga Steve Abah.* Zaria: Ahmadu Bello University Press.

Okwori, J. Z. (2002) Popular Tteatre, popular participation and empowerment. *Contemporary Theatre Review, 12*(1-2), 161-170.

Rahman, Md. Aminur. (2013) Women empowerment: Concept and beyond. *Global Journal of Human Social Science, Sociology and Culture, 13*(6), 8-13.

Sheme, I. (2010). Breaking out time for women in Northern Nigeria. Retrived from http://ibrahim-sheme.blogspot.com.ng/2010/10/breaking-out-time-for-women-in-northern.html

Undiyaundeye, F. (2013). The challenges of women empowerment for sustainable development in Nigeria. *Academic Journal of Interdisciplinary Studies, 2*(11), 9-14.

Chapter 17

Language and Cultural Values: The African Socio-Perception to Greetings

Anne Omotayo Alaiyemola

Introduction

In linguistic environments, people are conditioned to be sensitive to, and appreciative of, certain cultural values that govern interpersonal interactions. Greeting, a universal sociolinguistic act is described by Firth (1972, p. 1) as facilitating "the recognition of an encounter with another person as socially acceptable." Grimshaw (1981, p. 208) defines an encounter as occurring when an individual is socially recognised by another individual or set of individuals. The implication of which is that greeting is a joint acknowledgement of encounters.

The specifics of greeting is culturally determined. Societies that are more culture conscious attribute more significance to this linguistic act. In African societies as in most others, greeting incorporates both linguistic and paralinguistic elements which facilitate as means of entrenching love and brotherliness, fostering unity and tranquillity in the human interactions.

This paper aims to highlight the forms and functions of greetings. However, as universal as the phenomenon may be are there universal sociolinguistic functions to greeting? What are the variables of greeting? To what extent is greeting an obligatory element in human behaviour? And what are the linguistic and paralinguistic features of greeting? Answering these questions is not to limit the work to dual level of greeting, that is greeting between two individuals at a time but it will also include greeting between an individual and a group. Formal interviews of different cultural settings were conducted. The normal casual and informal forms of greeting between speakers on various occasions were observed. The study is based on the following hypotheses/ assumptions:

1. That greeting is a universal sociolinguistic phenomenon.
2. That greeting is a mandatory strategy of politeness.
3. That the value placed on in Africanssocietiesis culturally prescribed.
4. That greeting is expressed via linguistic and paralinguistic media, and;
5. That people's attitude to greeting is culturally determined.

That humans communicate through language is the key distinguishing factor among other animal species. The growth of sociolinguistics attests to the importance of social realities in the art and act of communication. Trudgill (1974, p. 32) describes language as not simply a means of communicating information but also a very important means of establishing and maintaining relationship with other people by saying things socially acceptable.

Sotiloye (1992, p. 134) sees sociolinguistics as a field of study which relates societal problems to linguistic or language problems. It tends to answer the questions, who says what? To whom? Where?When?How and Why? From this definition and questions posed, this paper is an attempt to examine who says what, to whom, (an individual or a group), where, when, and why in the exchange of greetings.

Our ideas and attitude and generally all other things about us help others to formulate opinion about us. No one is an island and whether we like it or not, we come in contact with other people every day and saying socially or otherwise. This is in view of the opinion that greeting is essentially an aspect of politeness phenomenon and Lakoff (1973, p. 53) says that "to be polite is saying the socially correct thing." However, it is not the 'saying' but the 'doing' in greeting, in most cases that determines acceptability of the saying. This brings us to the para-linguistic features that accompany greeting.

Paralinguistic Features of Greetings

Many verbal expressions point to the importance of non-verbal communication. Wright (1989, p. 18) believes that "we communicate more through actions than words." This agrees with the adage that says "actions speak louder than words" or "face to face is better than a hundred letters." In spite of these clichés, non-verbal communication remains an area of study to be fully developed. Campbell and Hepler (1965, p. 159) are of the opinion that "a good deal of non-verbal communication goes on around us and it is so important because we make decisions based on it."

The above explanation is to show that paralinguistic features which are the non-verbal communication that take place in greeting cannot be over-emphasised. Paralinguistic features differ from culture to culture. Grimshaw (1981, p. 127) stresses the fact that "certain social relationships occur but are manifested differently in all societies." That is because these differences depend on the environment or setting for their meaning. In Nigeria for instance, using the left hand to gesticulate or point to someone or thing is a sign of disrespect and a way of saying 'I am not interested in greeting you'. Adeoye (1997, p. 19) records that "a slow handclap is an expression of disgust in Britain, to the Greek, shaking of the head from side to side in a rocking motion means "yes or I agree." Despite these culture induced differences in the interpretation of paralinguistic features, there are still many universal features that convey the same meaning regardless of culture. Paralinguistic features are necessary accompaniment in greetings. This is because they occur alongside, interact with and produce together with greeting a complete and meaningful speech act. Therefore, for greeting to be appreciated and for it to produce the desired result or functions it must not exclude the use of appropriate paralinguistic features.

Corner and Hawthorn (1993, p. 28) and Alaiyemola (2017, p. 13) analyse different kinds of paralinguistic features which include:

gestures, head-nods, facial expression, kinesics, voice qualities, proxemics, posture, haptics, etc. These paralinguistic features deal in the main with this study topic, greeting and each will be highlighted below.

Facial Expression

Goffman (1967, p. 5) states that "every person lives in a world of social encounter involving him either in face to face or mediated contact with other participants." He therefore defines face "as the positive social value a person effectively claims for himself by the line others assume he has taken during a particular contact." This analysis of the paralinguistic feature of the facial expression in greeting is very important because man, wherever he finds himself and especially in the midst of others tends to project a good image of or about himself. Facial expression therefore works better as a way of providing feedback on the greeting of one person to another. Closely related is Kinesics.

Kinesics

This is the study of facial expression, eye movements which convey meaning. Kinesics consists of illustrators, regulators, emblems, affect displays, adapters and posture. All these border on communicating with parts of body to evoke meaning and communicate sense. This also holds a lot of potentials for greetings and those involved in it. Greetings that are not complemented with gestures and gesticulations, eyes movement and facial expression are often boring and lack genuineness to observers.

Gestures

According to Corner and Hawthon (1993, p. 31) "gestures are movements of hands, feet or other parts of the body." In greeting therefore gestures can communicate the emotional states of the interlocutors. It can also complete the meaning of utterances and replace speech. This feature is well articulated where speech is impossible for one reason or the other. Head nods are also a special kind of gesture. Across all cultures, head nods are used to beckon, show direction and in salutation. In salutation (greeting) which is our concern, it can be used to reinforce or support greeting or even to encourage the speaker to continue a conversation.

Voice Qualities

These include pitch range, degree of voice hoarseness, sharp or smooth transition in pitch, articulation, control, resonance and tempo. The implication of these is that interlocutors are supposed to project and articulate ideas appropriately to one another. Without appropriate voice qualities and vocalization strategies, many greetings will not be fully appreciated

Posture

This is the way one sits, stands, kneels, bends, prostrates or walks. Identifying various postures and imparting their meanings to people when one greets ultimately assist their appreciation. Communication is dynamic: the manner of greeting will project one's cultural/moral background. Greeting sluggishly, smartly, haughtily (i.e. not kneeling or prostrating) etc. have a way of projecting one's attitude to life and culture, generally.

Haptics

This is the touching behaviour or the use of touch to communicate. Shaking of hands, embracing, holding arms, patting backs in greetings have a way of assuring and reassuring people of your good intentions. This touching behaviour will be limited to certain areas of the functional – professional type, not the love – intimacy, sexual – arousal etc. types (see O'Hair et al., 1995). To touch or hold people indiscriminately, especially the opposite sex, is tantamount to moral/cultural debauchery on the part of whoever the guilty one is, not 'haptics' any longer!

Proxemics

This is the use of distance or space to communicate. It is generally noted that closeness means intimacy and friendliness while detachment or distance suggests hostility or lack of concern. When greeting, draw the line so as to bridge the public space. Personal and social space should also be reduced in such a way that people would want to communicate freely with each other or one another as the case may be.

Functions of Greeting

There are different functions that greeting in Africa perform. These can be to open or close a verbal interaction; to show politeness; as a way of socialising; to encourage others; to show concern. Whatever happens, African greeting is meant to meet a need and to function for particular circumstances.

Grimshaw (1981, p. 131) opines that "whatever the exact characterization of the forms and functions of greeting may be, verbal interactions in most societies begin with some sort of greeting and termination are marked by farewell." These are two of the major things learners learn first in any language. The most systematic examinations of greeting and farewell are those of Goffman (1967) and Firth (1972).

Goffman is able to demonstrate an extremely rich range of functions facilitated by greeting and these are:

a. Presence validation
b. Politeness
c. Threat denial
d. Petition
e. Display and Identity establishment for self and others.

These functions analysed by Goffman do not differ from the functions of greeting postulated by Grimshaw (1981, p. 208) which are:

i. To show respect and/or solidarity
ii. To obtain and to validate presence recognition

iii. To introduce display
iv. To threateningly underline recognition and
v. To identify interlocutors to others

Firth (1964, p. 68) in an attempt to explain the functions of greeting, says; "it is a type of speech in which ties of union are created... or mutual recognition of status and relationship." He further gives some attention to continuity and change in greeting forms and to learning of correct greeting forms as functions of greeting. Both Goffman's and Grimshaw's assessment of the functions of greeting tally in many ways and shall merged thus:

i. *Greeting serves as Politeness Strategy/Showing Respect and/or Solidarity*

Greeting serves as a productive strategy for being polite, showing respect and or solidarity in any community. Being polite has a social acceptability everywhere and this can be reflected through a simple form of greeting and saying the socially correct thing to people politely, showing of respect and solidarity irrespective of age, sex and status is a very important function of greeting.

ii. *Presence Validation/ Obtaining and Validating Presence Recognition*

Obtaining and validating presence or recognition is a function of greeting. In any gathering, it would rather be improper for anybody to just begin addressing a group of people already gathered before his arrival, no matter his position, without first greeting the gathering to validate his person/presence and to make his presence acceptable.

iii. *Identity Establishment for Self or Others/Identifying Interlocutors to others*

Grimshaw (1981, p. 209) is of the opinion that "when encounter between known parties take place, greeting exchanges must occur except under specifiable sets of conditions." It is possible sometimes to have an unknown person or persons in the company of other people. There is need to identify the interlocutors to others which may be initiated by greeting exchanges. All societies have greeting and its functions must be socially accomplished by its verbal and paralinguistic accompaniment.

Greeting among members of a typical African community is crucially relevant to peaceful co-existence and friendly inter personal relations. Failure to greet could jeopardise peaceful and friendly interpersonal relationship between individuals and even groups.

Greeting among members of typical African communities is crucially relevant to peaceful co-existence and friendly inter personal relations. Failure to greet could jeopardise peaceful and friendly interpersonal relationship between individuals and even groups. Indeed Africans specifically consider greeting as a very important aspect of home training hence, a child who fails to cultivate the habit of greeting is looked down upon as uncouth or spoilt. It is no surprise that when you want to know the mind of Africans about anybody, they will describe that person first by the way he greets. For instance, they can say "oh he/she greets" or "that person does not greet." This is a typical African way of description.

It is therefore obvious that there exists a close relationship and fascinating inter- play in the cultural value of Africans, their greeting forms as well as their attitude to greeting. Wherever an African finds himself, he sees greeting and all it stands for, as a personal asset/property which he must guide by using it effectively both to speakers and non-speakers just to show how proud of the culture he is. Thus the attitude of Africans agrees with the opinion of Firth (1964, p. 66) that: "every man carries his culture and much of his social reality about him wherever he goes."

Greeting as a politeness or solidarity strategy is highly appreciated and is made to occupy a prime place in the socio-cultural value of Africans.

Forms of Greetings

It is clear that African people have different forms of greeting that are stylised for different occasions. Recognising the polarised nature of the society i.e. the class distinction among the people, the dialects makes adequate provision for cementing the relationship between or among members of the society, irrespective of any differences. Thus, we have greeting forms that are exclusively meant for pregnant woman, marketers, travellers, the sick and the appropriate repertoire of greeting for whoever he comes across.

One significant observation may be made here concerning these forms of greeting in Africa. It could be noticed that a few of these forms of greeting cannot be translated literally to English. For example "Ekule" in Yoruba language and "ina wuni" in Hausa has no direct translation in English. This shows that Yoruba and Hausa people like many African people are more greeting conscious than other parts of the world.

Participants

The different forms of greeting have different participants taking part in the greeting. Sometimes the participants may be an individual to another i.e. between any two people or an individual to a group or a group to another group. The participants depend mostly on the occasion for which the particular form of greeting is being used. For instance, "eku ikunra" which is a greeting form for a pregnant woman cannot be used by everybody that comes across her but "ekaaro" in Yoruba; "inakwana" in Hausa and "nnow" in Igbo (good morning) is a greeting form employed by any respectful person who is polite enough to greet.

Paralinguistic Accompaniments

In Africa generally and Nigeria especially the paralinguistic accompaniment of greeting includes, prostrating or bending by the younger male person to the elderly ones or sometimes bending and kneeling by the younger female person to the elderly people. Hand – shakes are for people of the same age group or status or where an elder initiates the gesture. Facial expression like smiling, frowning, raising the eyebrow to show concern, waving of the hand, embracing and head nods are all the paralinguistic accompaniment of greetings that abound in Africa.

Occasion of Use

The African languages and Nigerian dialects are so rich that anybody who is proficient in any or the different dialects and is accustomed to the peoples' way of life is able to relate well with other speakers without much difficult. Each form of greeting is meant to be used appropriately, for instance, you cannot just meet someone hale and hearty without any visible sign of anything being wrong with him and say "peele" in Yoruba or "kewo" in Okunland (one of Nigeria dialects) and "sunnu" in Hausa which are greeting forms to be used for someone sick or tired. Knowing the appropriate use of each form of greeting goes a long way to easing friction.

Frequency (Complusory or Optional)

It should be understood that most of the forms of greeting are compulsory for every member of Africa society. The few optional ones could be hinged on the fact that the richness of the dialects have made up for them in other forms of greeting. For instance the young little boys and girls in Yoruba may not greet a pregnant woman as "ekuikunra" or "ekuewa", for ladies making their hair, but depending on the time of the day they would greet "ekaro, ekasan or ekale." This could have made up for the most appropriate form of greeting which is impolite for children to utter.

Application and Justification of Hypotheses

This paper aims at applying and justifying the hypotheses presented earlier above. It also suggests what every individual or the society at large stands to gain by regularly observing greeting rituals as a mandatory sociolinguistic behaviour. The five hypotheses proposed in the beginning are based on the observation and interviews on greeting in some African dialects. These observations and interviews cover the various forms of greeting in Africa, the sociolinguistic functions accomplished by greeting in Africa as well as the attitude of African people to greeting. We shall now attempt to validate or invalidate the five hypotheses.

Hypothesis One: That Greeting is a Universal Sociolingistic Phenomenon

Greeting is not only universally applicable, it is obligatory. If members of a speech community especially Africa communities are to co- exist peacefully and are to fully enjoy the potential resources embedded in interpersonal relations, greeting constitutes a gateway to any positive development in any society.

In language acquisition, the first area in which a child or a learner consciously or unconsciously practices is to know how to greet. Greeting is a most important aspect of language through which members of a speech community express social communion.

Hypothesis Two: That Greeting is an Obligatory Strategy of Politeness

Greeting is almost synonymous with politeness in a traditional African setting/ culture, hence, anybody who fails to greet incurs not only a public disapproval of his habit, but also an insult or even a bad name for himself and his family. Greeting is therefore used to demonstrate the virtue of politeness not only to familiar people but also to people that are not familiar and "first impression", it is said "lasts longer."

Hypothesis Three: That African People Value Greetings Because They are Well Cultured

African languages have a sufficient repertoire of greeting out of which appropriate forms are selected for different periods of the day, different occasions, seasons of the year and different classes of people. Greeting forms for each of these cases are quite elaborate. Africa people are well cultured and failures to abide by the norms or rules that guide their socio-cultural values are seriously frowned at.

African greetings are full of idioms, proverbs, praise songs (mostly rendered at the king's palace or when an important personality dies) praise songs/poetry are rendered in praises of past achievements, personality or ancestors. African languages are therefore qualitatively rich and the peoples' manner show they are culturally conscious.

Hypothesis Four: That Greeting is Exprssed via Linguistic and Paralinguitic Features

The Para –linguistic features are not used to serve as substitutes to, but to complement the linguistic features. For instance, when a young girl kneels down without uttering a word of greeting to complement her kneeling down, she will not be answered. Thus in Africa, a young man does not only prostrate or bend and a young lady does not kneel before elders, he/she must also utter some words of greeting. Neither does he/she just utter some words of greeting without complementing these words with the appropriate Para-linguistic features.

Hypothesis Five: That People's Attitude to Greeting is Culturally-Determined

The analysis of greeting in African languages show that language is inter-twined with the culture of its users. It equally serves as a reflection of inter-twined personal relation and socio-cultural and social values. In spite of the fact that greeting is a universal sociolinguistic phenomena people from different linguistic backgrounds have different attitudes to greeting. While an African person may feel slighted and hurt for not being greeted by a familiar person, other people from other cultures may not necessarily feel the same way.

Ordinarily, day-to-day interactions are more informal and relaxed among the African people and this informality invariably reflects in the greeting habits of the people. The root of this informality could be traced to the indigenous language and culture of the people. It is no wonder then that as informal as it seems, greeting rituals are taken very seriously in Africa to the point that anyone who wants to enjoy mutual co-operation and fellowship with other members of the community must adhere strictly to them.

Conclusion

This study has highlighted the sociolinguistic functions of greeting and the various forms of greeting in Nigeria. Greeting essentially performs similar functions in most African languages and dialects but the determinant factors of greeting that is, the various factors which are participants' age, sex, status, occasion of use, Paralinguistic accompaniment, frequency status (compulsory or optional) and its functions are important determinant of greeting in Africa and in most places. Every individual stands to gain public approval and fruitful interpersonal relations by regular observing greeting as a mandatory sociolinguistic behaviour. Members of the society would co-exist peacefully and enjoy the best from one another as greeting plays the important role of oiling the wheel of social interaction.

References

Adeoye, S. (1997). An analysis of the paralinguistic element in selected newspapers obituaries (B.A. long essay). University of Ilorin, Ilorin, Nigeria.

Alaiyemola A. (2017). Non-verbal communication approach to inculcating moral values in tertiary institutions. *English Language, Literature & Culture, 2*(2), 12-16.

Corner, J. & Hawthorn, W.H. (1993). Communication studies: An introductory reader. London: Edward Arnold.

Campbell, J. H., & Hepler H. W. (1965). Dimensions in communication: Readings. California; Wadsworth Publication Company Inc.

Firth, J. R. (1964). On sociological linguistics. In D. Hymes (Ed.), *Language in culture and society: A reader in linguistics and anthropology* (pp. 66-70). New York; Harper and Row

Firth, R. (1972). Verbal and bodily rituals of greeting and parting. In Jean Sybil La Fontaine (Ed.), *The interpretation of ritual: Essays in honour of A. I. Richards* (pp. 1-38). London: Routledge.

Goffman, E. (1967). Interaction rituals: Essays in face-to-face behaviour. Chicago: Aldine Publishing Company.

Grimshaw, A.D. (1981). Language as a social resource: Essays. Stanford, California: Standard University Press.

Lakoff, R. (1973). The logic of politeness: Or, minding your P's and Q's. In C. Corum, T. Cedric Smith-Stark, & A. Weiser (Eds.), Papers from the 9th Regional Meeting of the Chicago Linguistic Society (pp. 292-305). Chicago Linguistic Society.

O' Hair, D. et al. (1995). *Competent communication.* New York: St Martin's Press Inc.

Sotiloye, B. (1992). Sociolinguistics. In Ore Yusuf (Ed.), Introduction to language. Ilorin: Unilorin.

Trudgill, P. (1974). Sociolinguistics: An introduction to language and Society. England: Penguin.

Wright, A. (1989). How to communicate successfully. England; Cambridge University Press.

Chapter 18

War against Terrorism: An Analytical Study of Issa Alabi Abubakar's *Assubaa'iyyat*

Tajudeen Yusuf

الحرب ضد الإرهاب: دراسة تحليلية لقصيدة عيسى أَلَبي أبوبكر

تاج الدين يوسف

Abstract

Ilorin is one of the Northern Nigerian societies where Arabic literature, most especially poetry, is highly valued for giving voice to the deepest feelings and concerns of the people of the nation. Being an Islamic cultural center, some indigenous Arabic scholars, endowed with the art of poetry, have played a central role in the development and integration of the nation irrespective of the cultural diversities in the nation. Presented in three sections in Arabic, this paper examines one of the contemporary Arabic poets named Issa Alabi Abubakar and his contribution to the integration and peaceful co-existence of the nation. A theme addressing terrorism, a tragedy that creates fear in the minds of people and claims the lives of innocent people, has been selected from his collections titled *Assubaa'iyyaat* for study and analysis.

المقدمة

الإرهاب بوصفه بجموعة الأعمال التي تعرض للخطر أرواحاً بشرية بريئة، أو تهدد الحريات الأساسية، أو تنتهك كرامة الإنسان[1] من الظواهر الخطيرة التي يعانيها العالم اليوم، فقد شهد المجتمع البشري ولا يزال يشهد ألواناً من الصراعات في جميع نواحي الحياة، السياسية منها والاجتماعية والثقافية والدينية، فإرهاب بوكو حرام وأمثالها في المجتمع النيجيري من الأمثلة الحية، الدماء تسال كلَّ يوم، وأرواح الأبرياء تُزال، ويترتب على ذلك كله فقدان الإنسانية والروابط الاجتماعية بين أفراد المجتمع في جميع المستويات، ومن هذا المنطلق جاءت فكرة التكامل والاندماج الوطني سبيلا للنهضة الإنسانية لأجل غرس ثقافة التعايش السلمي في المجتمع.

والشاعر ابن بيئته، وابن عصره وما يدور حوله من الحوادث، فقد كان للشعر دور كبير منذ القدم في معالجة قضايا المجتمع، وبما أن الشعر في جميع العصور والبيئات مرآة تنعكس عليها أحوال المجتمع وجميع الأحداث التي يكتنفه إيجابياتها وسلبيات مجتمعهم، فإن شعراء شمال نيجيريا قد أدوا دورهم في جعل شعرهم مرآة يقرأ من خلالها واقع المجتمع، وكانوا الصوت الناطق لما يحدث في المجتمع وما يطرأ عليها من التغيرات والحوادث. وقاموا بالدعوة إلى مكارم الأخلاق والمثل العليا والترابط، ومن فحول الشعراء النيجيريين الذين يشار إليهم في هذا المجال الشاعر عيسى ألبي أبوبكر. وهو من الشعراء النابغين الذين جعلوا للشعر العربي مكانة لا يستهان بها في ديار نيجيريا وخارجها، جعل الشعر وسيلة للتعبير عن الهوية الوطنية. ويعد كتاب "السباعيات" من عيون دواوين ألبي أبي بكر عالج فيها قضايا الحياة المتنوعة.

تهدف هذا المقال إلى دراسة سباعية من سباعيات عيسى ألبي أبو بكر لإبداء دور الشاعر في الدعوة إلى الاندماج الوطني ونشر الحياة المشتركة

بين أبناء المجتمع على اختلاف معتقداتهم وعناصرهم الاجتماعية والثقافية. وتتكون الدراسة من مقدمة، نبذة يسيرة عن الشاعر، وعرض القصيدة، ثم تحليلها، فالخاتمة. وتتبنى الدراسة المنهج الوصفي لتحليل الأبيات الشعرية المختارة لكونه أنسب أنواع مناهج البحث في الآداب.

الشاعر عيسى ألبي أبو بكر

يعد عيسى ألبي أبو بكر أحد أشهر الشعراء الأفارقة ونابغ بين الشعراء النيجيريين في العصر الحديث، وهو من أجمعهم لكثير من المعاني في قليل من الألفاظ، فقد نالت قصائده إعجابًا بين الدارسين داخل نيجيريا وخارجها، ويكفينا دلالة على شاعريته أن معظم أشعاره قد درست في كثير من جامعات نيجيريا، وقد اهتم الدارسون وخاصة في المدارس العليا في نيجيريا وخارجها بقصائد أبي بكر وأولوا اهتماماً خاصاً بالتعرف على دقائقها، ونال احترام الجميع لحكمته ثقافته ونبوغه الشعري ويدور قصيدته هذه حول الدعوة إلى الأمن والأمان والتضامن والاندماج الوطني والدعوة إلى ثقافة التعايش السلمي بين أفراد المجتمع والابتعاد عن كل ما له صلة بالعنف والإرهاب. وتتوّج الحكمة هذا الشعر بهالة من الوقار تعكس شخصية الشاعر الحكيم.

عرض للقصيدة الإرهابيون[2]

قذَفُوا الرعب في قلوب العباد	وأسالوا الدماء في كــلّ واد
كيف تحقيق ما يرومون بالإر	هاب أو هدم سور أمن البلاد
إن ما لا ينال بالسلم قد يصـ	ـعبُ إحراره بغارات عــاد
أيُّ شيء يا قومُ أغلى من النفـ	ـس التي يُرْهِقونها بفســاد؟
أيُّ دين دعا إلى العنف والتمـ	ـثيل بالأبرياء لنيل المـراد؟
قاتَلَ اللهُ من يشجعُ في كُـ	ـلِّ مكان تَشَدُّدَ الأوغــاد
إن إرهابَهم يفيدُ عـدوَّ	اللهِ مِنْ قِبَلِ ضَيْره للعبــاد

التعريف بالقصيدة

هذه القصيدة بعنوان "الإرهابيون" من عيون قصائد دوّنها الشاعر عيسى ألبي أبوبكر في ديوانه الموسوم بـ"السباعيات"، ويعد هذا الكتاب من الدواوين والأعمال الأدبية التي أنتجها أبوبكر ومن روائع الشعر المعاصر في الأدب العربي النيجيري، تميزت القصيدة بالتكامل والانسجام وبجمالية شعرية خاصة، بالإضافة إلى روية فنية شاملة. ففي القصيدة التعبير عن فكرة الشاعر وموقفه ضد عملية العنف والإرهاب والتنكيل الوحشي بالإنساني في المجتمع البشري. يعبر الشاعر عن شعوره ضد تلك الأحداث المؤسفة والنكبات الأليمة التي استولت وبلاتها على العالم معبّرًا عن تلك المأساة التي قد أدت إلى سفك دماء الأبرياء وتشريد الشعوب من أراضيهم وأوطانهم، ويؤكد الشاعر أن تعاليم الأديان السماوية جميعها بريئة كل براءة عن العنف والإرهاب، ويدعو الشاعر الجميع إلى التمسك بكلّ ما يؤدي إلى الأمن والسلام، وأن ما لا يُنال بالسلم يصعب نيله بالعنف والإرهاب، كما دعا إلى التعايش السلمي والذي هو الحياة المشتركة في السلم والأمان في مناخ تسوده المشاركة والصداقة.[3]

تحليل الأبيات

في البيت الأول يقدم لنا الشاعر حقيقة الإرهابيين وأعمالهم الشنيعة والتي من بينها التهديد باستخدام العنف والتخويف والإكراه لتحقيق الغايات والأهداف،[4] وما يترتب عليها من سفك الدماء وتدمير أنظمة المجتمع، ذلك لأن في ظل الأمن والأمان والطمأنينة يؤدي كل فرد من أفراد المجتمع واجبه على الوجه الأكمل، وتؤدي كل جماعة واجبها كأحسن من ما يكون الأداء. في البيت الثاني والثالث عاب الشاعر الإرهابيين الذين يمارسون العنف لنيل مقاصدهم. وإذا كان (الإرهاب) هو التهديد باستعمال عنف غير عادي

لتحقيق غايات سياسية كانت أم دينية أم اجتماعية عند بعض المحللين،[5] فإذا كانت في تعبير سياسيين رمزًا لكسب تعاطف الشعوب لتظل مساندة لحكومتهم أو للقضاء على من يخالف مصلحتهم،[6] فإن شاعرنا يقف موقفًا مخالفًا وسلميًا، ويرى أن (الإرهاب) قولاً كان أم فعلاً لا يجلب إلا البؤس والخسائر في الأرواح والأموال فحسب للمجتمع، بل هو إهدار وخرق فاضح لحقوق الإنسان الأساسية، وتفكيك تماسك نظم المجتمع، وتهديد خطير لعلاقات التعاون بين أفراد المجتمع والشعوب والتعايش بين البشر والسلام والأمن على المستوى الوطني والعالمي. ويرى أن اعتماد مبدأ القوة والعنف وسيلة لتحقيق الغايات يقود المجتمع للهلاك والخراب. ولا شك أن مناهضة الإرهاب لا تكون إلا بالرد الإيجابي، وإزالة الإساءات المثيرة للشعوب، وذلك لأجل استمرار التواصل الإيجابي وبث التعايش السلمي في المجتمع.

ويؤكد الشاعر في الرابع والخامس على خطورة انتشار عملية الإرهاب وما شاكله في المجتمع البشري وما يترتب عليه من سفك الدماء البريئة في الشوارع وأنها من أبشع الجرائم والاعتداء في المجتمع.[7] ويؤكد الشاعر أن الأديان السماوية جميعها بعيدة كل البعد عن الفكرة الإرهابية وما إليها. وعلى رأسها فإن الإسلام الذي جعل السلام تحية لمعتنقيه لا يمكن أن يقرّ شيئًا مما يسمى بالعمليات الإرهابية في المجتمع فضلا عن الويلات والرعب والعواقب الشنيعة التي تركتها أشكال العنف في المجتمعات.[8] إن ظاهرة الإرهاب ظاهرة غريبة في الأديان السماوية، وفي الإسلام على وجه الخصوص، والإسلام منه بريء، فالدين الإسلامي دين التسامح والتعايش السلمي بين الشعوب. فالإرهاب كما يؤكد الشاعر، ليس له دين لا إنسانية. إن الإسلام يكره التهديد باستخدام القوة غير المشروعة ضد الأبرياء لتحقيق الأهداف سياسية كانت أم غير سياسية. فالإسلام أولاً وأخيرًا يدعو إلى استقرار واستقامة الأمن الداخلي في كل صورة من صوره. الإسلام يدعو إلى الأمن الداخلي والخارجي، فإن المتأمل في تاريخ الدعوة الإسلامية منذ

بدايتها، يرى أنها قامت على العدل والإحسان والخير والحكمة والموعظة الحسنة والحوار مع الآخر بالتي هي أحسن.

ولقد روى لنا تاريخ صورا متنوعة تبين لنا ما للأدب بما فيه الخطابة من دور فعّال في دفع الناس إلى ما هو خير وحثهم على الفضائل، فعلى سبيل المثال تتجلى مبادئ التعايش السلمي والتواصل البناء الراقي في خطبة الخليفة أبي بكر الصديق رضي الله عنه التي ألقاها بعد البيعة بعد وفاة رسول الله صلى الله عليه وسلم عندما اختلف الناس فيمن يخلفه في سقيفة بني ساعدة، حيث إن الأنصار يريدون أن يكون الخليفة منهم، كما أن المهاجرين يرون أنهم خير من يستحق الخلافة مما أثار الخلاف والنزاع. فقام أبو بكر رضي الله عنه أخيرا في الناس وخاطبهم بخطبة حكيمة ينبغي أن يتخذها كل حاكم وداعية دستوراً. فبعد أن حمد الله وأثنى عليه بالذي هو أهله، قال:

أيها الناس، فإني قد وليت عليكم، ولست بخيركم، فإن أحسنت فأعينوني، وإن أسأت فقوموني. الصدق أمانة، والكذب خيانة، الضعيف فيكم قوي عندي حتى آخذ الحق له إن شاء الله، والقوي فيكم ضعيف عندي حتى آخذ الحق منه إن شاء الله. لا يدع قوم الجهاد في سبيل الله إلا ضربهم الله بالذل، ولا تشيع الفاحشة في قوم قط إلا عمهم الله بالبلاء. أطيعوني ما أطعت الله ورسوله. فإن عصيت الله ورسوله، فلا طاعة لي عليكم.[9]

ويتجلى في خطبة أبي بكر وتعبيراته شخصيته المتواضعة، وسياسته المرنة، وقوة فطنته، وسرعة البديهة وذكائه، وتلطفه في الكلام والحديث، تلك لغة السياسة التي تعلن للأجيال القادمة من بعده مبادئ التواصل السياسي والديني والاجتماعي التضامني الناضجة:[10]

وهذه المرونة تنطبق تماما مع قول الله تعالى: ﴿ادع إلى سبيل ربك بالحكمة والموعظة الحسنة وجادلهم بالتي هي أحسن إن ربك هو أعلم بمن

ضل عن سبيله وهو أعلم بالمهتدين﴾ (النحل: 152)، وعلى هذا المنهج دعا الهادي البشير صلى الله عليه وسلم إلى الإسلام تحت الأمن والسلام، ولم ينتشر الإسلام بالحرب ولا بالسيف ولا بالقهر ولا بالإجبار، ولا بأي أسلوب من أساليب القوة أو العنف، إن الإسلام يدعو إلى إحقاق الحق، وإزهاق الباطل، وكرامة الإنسان.

وفي البيتين الأخيرين يظهر الشاعر شعوره وآلامه نحو هذه الصنيعة الشنيعة وأعوانها من المخططين ومنفذيها ويدعو عليهم بالويلاب والهلاك لأجل الويلات والرعب والعواقب الشنيعة التي تركتها أشكال الإرهاب والعنف في المجتمعات. ذلك لأن الإرهاب الذي هو" الاستخدام غير القانوني للقوة أو العنف، أو التهديد بهما، من منظمة ثورة ضد الأفراد أو الممتلكات، مع نية إكراه الحكومات أو المجتمعات لتحقيق أغراض هي غالباً أيديولوجية"[11] ليس له مصلحة في المجتمع البشري. ولقد أثبتت أغلبية شعوب العالم حديثة الاستقلال أن رؤيتها السياسية واضحة جلية، وأن العوامل والقيم التي تحرك الشعوب في جميع أنحاء العالم في مجتمعنا الدولي الحديث واحدة في جوهرها لا خلاف عليها وهي الاعتراف بإنسانية الإنسان في المجتمع.[12]

ولقد تنبهت إدارة هيئة الإذاعة البريطانية (بي.بي.سي) إلى ما للكلمة من الخطورة، فأصدرت تذكيرا للعاملين فيها بتوخي الحذر الشديد عند استخدام كلمة (إرهابي)، مشددة على أن سوء استخدام الكلمة، قد يحول بين المستمعين وبين الفهم الصحيح للأحداث. وأكد مصدر في المكتب الصحافي في (بي.بي.سي) أن المذكرة الخاصة باستخدام لفظ (الإرهاب) و(إرهابي) ليست حديثة، وإنما بدأ العمل بها بعد تفجيرات يوليو (تموز) الماضي في العاصمة البريطانية وأن إعادة إصدارها الآن يهدف لتذكير العاملين بالاستخدام المتعارف عليه حسب دليل (بي.بي.سي)، وحسب الفقرة الخاصة باستخدام كلمة إرهابي في الدليل،

وعلى الصحافيين في الهيئة أن يعدوا التقارير الإخبارية الخاصة بالعمليات الإرهابية بدقة ومسؤولية، وأن استخدام مفردات اللغة، يجب ألا يتأثر بالعاطفة أو الحكم الشخصي، وذلك للحفاظ على المصداقية التي تتميز بها الهيئة."[13] فالعيش في بيئة يسودها السلام والأمن ضرورة من ضرورات الكرامة الإنسانية وتنمية المجتمع.

الدراسة الفنية للأبيات

- ### الشكل والمضمون

القاريء لشعر أبي بكر يلمس الرصانة في الوزن الشعري، وفي حسن اختيار الألفاظ والعبارات، وفي الوضوح الفكري، والسهولة الأدائية. يعتبر عن خواطره الأدبية بكل وضوح شكلاً ومضموناً مع الأسلوب الناجح. كانت ألفاظها بعيدة عن تفكير عميق، يرسلها إرسالاً بكل سهولة، وهو إلى ذلك يوردها بطريقة أدبية سهلة المأخذ، تلك الألفاظ والأسلوب الصادرة عن حسن الإختبار والعقل المفكر الهاديء الذي يتطلع إلى الحياة.

- ### الجانب العاطفي

تتجلى في الأبيات عاطفة الشاعر الصادقة في تعبيره عن قضايا عصرية وما يجري في المجتمع من الأزمات والأعمال الإرهابية عن طريق دفقات شعرية مكثفة ذات بعد إيحائي أحياناً، ونبرة خطابية في بعض الأحايين، لكن الشاعر في الحالتين يتجاوز تعبيره عن البعد الفردي إلى التعبير عن البعد الإنساني والديني. كما يتضح جلياً شعوره وفكرته ضد الإبادة والتنكيل، يقول الشاعر:

| س التي يُرْهقوها بفســـاد؟ | أيُّ شيء يا قومُ أغلى من النف |
| ثيل بالأبرياء لنيل المـــراد؟ | أيُّ دين دعا إلى العنف والتم |

• الصورة البلاغية

القارئ المدقق لأشعار عيسى ألبي أبي بكر يجدها تحتفل بالصور البلاغية الموافقة والخالية من التكلُّف الزائف، وعلى وجه المثال نجد الشاعر يتساءل متعجبًا ومستغربا في البنين السابقتين.

الاستفهام في البيتين فيه نوع من التصور يتحدى به السامع، إذ لا يوجد شيء أغلى من النفس، ولا دين من الأديان السماوية يشجع العنف والإرهاب وقتل الأبرياء، ففي الاستهامين الإنكار التوبيخي والتنبيه على ضلال[14] الإرهابيين والعنفيين، أي أن ما كانوا عليه لا ينبغي، وفي مثل هذا الاستفهام تنبيه اﻹرهابيين ومن في حكمهم حتى يرجعوا إلى نشر السلام والحوار السلمي.

خاتمة

ناقشت هذه الدراسة دور الشعر العربي النيجيري في الدعوة إلى التضامن والاندماج الوطني والعيش المشترك، وقد ساهم الشعراء في تحقيق نشر السلام والتنمية المستدامة وبناء المجتمع عن طريق التحلي بالتسامح الاجتماعي وإيجاد القدرة على احترام الاختلافات وأوجه التنوع. والقارىء لشعر عيسى ألبي يقف على طبيعة الإنسان في بغضه وكراهيته للحرب ونزوعه للسلام، فشاعرنا رجل اجتماعي يؤمن بالحياة المشتركة في الأمن والأمان، ويؤمن بأن الإنسان خُلق لكي يعيش في مجتمع يتفاعل وإياه تفاعلاً إنسانياً بعيداً عن شريعة الغاب، وبعيدا عن القلق والإضطراب. وهكذا نرى شاعرنا هو ابن الإنسانية يعمل في سبيل سعادة فردية واجتماعية يدعو إلى نبذ العنف والإرهاب، وقف موقف الهادي والمرشد والمصلح. وكان مبدؤه أن ما يحلّ سلمياً خير مما يحل حربياً، وأن العنف والعناد يقودان إلى الدمار، ويرى أن العنف لا يوّلد إلا العنف.

الهوامش والمراجع

1. الموسوعة العربية، **الجمهورية العربية السورية**: هيئة الموسوعة العربية،، 1998م ، 7/ 960-961.
2. عيسى ألبي أبو بكر، **السباعيات**، أوشن- نيجيريا، المركز النيجيري للبحوث العربية، 2008م، ص 65.
3. ينظر المعجم الوسيط، ج/2 ماد (عاش).
4. نعوم تشومسكي، **الإرهاب الدولي: الأسطورة والواقع**، نقلاً عن عرسان، علي عقلة، العنف والإرهاب، الموقف الأدبي، العدد 279، تموز 1994، ص 8، ص 8.
5. إريك، موريس، **الإرهاب: التهديد والرد عليه**. (ترجمة أحمد حمدي محمود)، القاهرة: الهيئة المصرية العامة للكتاب، 1991م ، ص 39.
6. انظر: داود محمد محمد، **اللغة والسياسة في عالم ما بعد 11 سبتمبر**. القاهرة: دار غريب ، 2003م ، ص 26.
7. سلطان، محمد خضير، أدب: "الإرهاب واللغة .. دلالات و وقائع". **جريدة الصبا**، الخميس 3 ربيع الأول 1428 هـ 22 اذار 2007 م العدد 1071.
8. السمّاك محمد، **الإرهاب والعنف السياسي**، بيروت، دار النفائس، 1992م، ص 3-5.
9. شلبي محمود، **حياة أبي بكر**، بيروت، دار الجيل، 1993م، ص 82.
10. عيسى كمال محمد، **كلمات في الأخلاق الإسلامية**، جدة: دار المجتمع للنشر والتوزيع، 1988م،. ص 27-29.
11. المرجع السابق، ص 960-961.
12. انظر: التهامي مختار، **الرأي العام والحرب النفسية**. القاهرة: دار المعارف، 1982م، ص 54.
13. ينظر: ((بي.بي.سي تؤكد على الحذر عند استخدام كلمة إرهابي))، **الشرق الأوسط**، الأربعاء 12 ذو الحجة 1426 هـ 11 يناير 2006 العدد 9906.
14. عبد المتعال الصعيدي، **بغية الإيضاح لتلخيص المفتاح في علوم البلاغة**، ج 2، القاهرة: مكتبة الآداب، 1991م، ص 44 – 46.

Chapter 19

Integration in Hamid Ibraheem al-Hijry's Ma'satul Hubb

Yunusa Muhammad Jamiu

مظاهر التآلف في قصة "مأساة الحب"
لحامد إبراهيم الهجري

يونس محمّد جامع

Abstract

The history of Arabic literature in Northern Nigeria is an ancient one. Being the earliest language of civilization in the region, Arabic has been and still is the language of communication and understanding among the heterogeneous ethnic groups in the region. Arabic which was introduced to the region through North African merchants gained wider spread through Islam as it was for decades the language of administration and interaction between people of different kingdoms in what is today West Africa. Arabic, however, suffered considerable neglect with the coming of the colonialists who supplanted it with their own languages and style of education. The language however regained its vibrancy in Nigeria with the independence and concerted efforts of the scholars who reinvigorated the learning of it using modern improved system of education. Written expressions in the language therefore become a source of integration and unity among the indigenous people of Northern Nigeria as contemporary writers employ the mechanism of literature to socialise readers of Arabic by emphasising areas of unity. This paper explores such endeavours as contained in *M'asaatulHubb* (The Tragedy of Love) written by Hamidu Ibrahim al-Hijri in which he projected Humanitarian feeling devoid of man-made acrimonious tendencies.

مقدمة

للغة العربية تاريخ عريق في شمال نيجيريا، كما أنّ لها أدوارا وإسهامات جبّارة في غرس التفاهم بين شعوب المنطقة. وبما أنّها أقدم لغات الثقافة تقييدًا –لا في شمال نيجيريا فحسب، بل حتى في القارة الأفريقية كلّها– فإنّ مكانتها في تكييف المواطنين تكييفًا ودّيًا يسوده أمن واتحاد لم تزل مرتفعة. ولقد اُستخدِمَت هذه اللغة لتسجيل الدواوين حتى في ممالك غير إسلامية،[1] وأصبحت لغة رسمية بعد الفتوحات الإسلامية التي شملت معظم أنحاء غرب أفريقيا. أما اليوم فإن المكانة التي تمتعت بها العربية زمانا أصبحت مهدَّدة على أيدي المستعمرين الذين قضوا على الدولة الإسلامية التي أسّسها عثمان بن فودي، ولكنّها قاومت التحديّات المتنوعة وتغلبت على العراقيل المتعددة وذلّلت العقبات التي نصبتها الاستعمارية إزاءها وارتدت جَمراتُها متوقدة بعد ما أوشكت أن تصير فحما، وعادت نارها متوهجة بعد أن كادت تصير رمادا وأصبح ضوءها يتلالأ بعد أن لم يبق منه إلّا بصيص.

تحمّل الكتّاب المعاصرون عبأ بثّ القيّم العالية التي تكمن في التعابير العربية وأجادوا في تناول موضوعات حديثة تُناسب المجتمع العصري، وصارت اللغة العربية بخدماتهم المضنية قافلةً للأحداث الحيّة وبؤرة يُنظَر منها إلى البيئة. تحرّرت المؤلفات العربية من التركيز على موضوعات دينية

وأصبحت الآن - كنظيراتها من اللغات الراقية - آلة للثقافة العالمية. والجدير بالذكر أنّ الشبان المثقفين ثقافة عربية هم الذين تزعموا هذا التطور وجعلوا من اللغة العربية أداة التآلف بين قبائل نيجيريا المختلفة. ومن طليعة هذا النضال حامد إبراهيم الهجري في قصته "مأساة الحبّ."

ستتناول هذه المقالة فاعليةَ اللغة العربية في توطيد الوئام بين شعوب الشمال النيجيري حسب محتوى "مأساة الحب" على الترتيب التالي: عرض وجيز عن كاتب القصة حامد إبراهيم الهجري، وملخص القصة "مأساة الحب"، وتحليلها لإبراز مظاهر التآلف بين الشعوب، ودراسة فنيّة للقصة، والخاتمة؛ وتتبنى المقالة في معالجة النقاط المخططة منهجي الاستقراء والتحليل.

حامد محمود إبراهيم

ولد حامد في أَبِغَوْرَوْ بحكومة محليّة إلورن الشرقية عام 1976م، وهذه القرية تبعد من إلورن عاصمة ولاية كوارا بحوالي خمسين كليومترا. تربى تحت رعاية والده الذي لقّنه القرآن ومبادئ العلوم الإسلامية، التحق بمدرسة دار العلوم بإلورن والتحق بعدها بدار الهجرة في مدينة كَنَوْ. أتمّ الدراسة الإعدادية والثانوية في دار الهجرة بكنو فيما بين 1993م و1998م. ارتحل إلى جمهورية تشاد عام 1999م حيث التحق بكلية العربية والإسلامية المنتسبة إلى جمعية الدعوة الإسلامية العربية بليبيا، ومنها حصل على الليسانس عام 2003م بتقدير ممتاز، ونال شهادة الدبلوم العالي والماجستير في كلية الدعوة الإسلامية ليبيا عام 2004م و2007م. وبعد رجوعه إلى الوطن عام 2007م خدم الوطن في ولاية غَوْمَيْ، وهو حاليًا محاضر في كلية أدم أَوْغِي للتربية بِأَرْغُنْغُ في ولاية كَبِّي.[2]

عرض لمحتويات القصة

يُتوقع أن تعكس قصة صورة تسلّط أضواء على البيئة التي منها نشأت ومن هذا الاتجاه فالقصة التي تحاول هذه الدراسة تحليلها ترجمة صادقة لمجتمعها. افتتحت القصة بحب حار بين ''أيُوكًا'' التي أمّها من مواليد ''أَبَادَوْ'' وعبد الله الذي مولده ''أيغَوْرُوْ''. القريتان متجاورتان متقاربتان، ليس هذا فحسب بل تربطهما آصرة القرابة، إلّا أنّ القرابة منبوذة إثر الحرب المحلّية التي دارت بين القريتين. والخلفية العدوانية هذه تهدد المحبّة بين الحبيبين من وجه ويهددها من وجه آخر إصرار ''فُنْلَايَوْ'' أمّ أيوكا التي تأبى زواج ابنته التي هي مسيحية بالوراثة من عبد الله الذي هو مسلم قح. ولما أيقنت الأم أنّ ابنتها مقبلة على حبّها كليًا دبّرت مكيدة كادت تقضي على حياة عبد الله إذ أوغرت صدور بعض الشباب وشنّوا عليه هجومًا في جنح ظلام ظلّ شجرة في ليلة مقمّرة وتركوه مكلوما بجروحًا.

عرضت القصة بيئة قروية من حيث سذاجتها، وألقت-كذلك- ضوءًا على عادات القرى من لعبة الأطفال تحت نور القمر، والصيد في الغابات والبواري. ولا يكون بعيدا إذا افتُرِضَ أنّ سخونة الجو في أيغورو هي ما ساق عبد الله إلى ''لاغوس'' في صحبة جار يزور القرية كل آخر سنة، وفيها التقى برجل ثري محسن تولّى رعايته وتربيته. وهذا الرجل يستحق أن يعتبر أباه الثاني لأنه لم ينثن عن عزمه في مساعدة عبد الله وتزويده بما يتطلبه لمواجهة الحياة مواجهة حسنة وذلك رغم الدسائس والوساوس التي تحاك حول شخصية الشاب من قِبَل زوجة الغني وأختها. خفتت لذعةُ مكيدة الزوجة ضد عبد الله بعد أن زال عنها العقم ورزقت ولدا ببركة دعاء الشاب وأرسله الزوج إلى الجامعة حيث درس القانون.

وحتى في الحرم الجامعي لم ينج من مصائب لأنه قد وقع فريسة هجوم على أيدي الطلاب الأشرار الذين يكوّنون جمعية سريّة ترهب الأبرياء

يخوّفونهم سدًّا لرغائبهم. والذي أوقعه في هذه الورطة هو أنه وجد نفسه في حبّ مرةً أخرى فجأةً وعنوةً لأنّ إحدى زميلاته في كلية القانون تكنّ له حبًّا جديًّا والفتاة "بوسَيْ" هذه شغوفة بعبد الله مميتة في حبّها له. ولما لاحظت أنّه غير خبير بمكائد الحبّ دبّرت حيلة تصطاده بها وطلبت إليه أن يزاملها في مراجعة الدروس وهنا وقع في أحبولتها ووقع بالتالي في حصن هؤلاء الأشرار الذين يحسدونه على ميل الفتاة إليه، فساموه سوء العذاب ولقنوه درسًا مريرًا.

وبعد أن أكمل الفتى دراسته في القانون وصار محاميا معترفا به محترما، زار قريته تلبية لنداء متكرر من قومه يطلبون إليه المشاركة في إصلاح الأوضاع التي قد فسدت في مجتمعهم لتتحسن الأحوال وتمتد الحضارة العصرية إلى القرية. لكن للأسف الشديد ما كاد يرى "أيوكا" من جديد حتى انقلبت غبطته حزنًا واشمئز قلبه من قذارتها وبداوتها، وآلمته للغاية هذه الهيئة التي عليها حبيبتُه الأولى ولم ير أحسن له إلّا الرجوع إلى "بوسي" المحامية المتحضرة واتخاذها زوجا وشريكة حياته، وقد نفذ هذا العزم وترك الحبيبة التعسة في القرية، وبذلك ماتت المحبّة وماتت "أيوكا" كمدًا آخر المطاف.

مظاهر التآلف في القصة

• وحدة البيئة والعقلية

من المتوقع أن تكون العلاقة بين بيئة الفنان وعقليته علاقة قوية كما رأينا في هذه القصة كما أشار شوقي ضيف،[3] وتناول الهجري للبيئة السائدة في قرية أيغورو تناولًا يبرز التوافق في بيئات البلدان المختلفة. يقول في تصوير سكان القرية:

حياتهم ساذجة سذاجة ثرواتهم، بسيطة في أكواخهم وتحت سقوفهم المبنية من أعواد الذرة والنخيل، كان كثير منهم يفترشون التراب ويغطون أجسامهم بالفضاء، يتخذون من الأشجار الضخمة وسائد، ومن الأصواف والأوبار لباسًا، ومن الغرابة أنّهم يعتقدون اعتقادًا جاسمًا بأن الحياة لديهم تنتهي، وأنّ هذه الأنهار التي تغتسل فيها قوافل صغيرة من الأوز والدجاج والمواعز والخراف حتى أطفالهم، والتي تملأ الفتيات جرارهن منها للشرب والطهي هي التي وصفها الله لهم بأنّها جنة تجري من تحتها الأنهار.[4]

أيغورو التي وصفها الهجري هي رمز لجميع القرى في شمال نيجيريا لأنّ كلّ ما يوجد في أيغورو هذه لا يختلف كثيرًا عن ما هو موجود في قرى أخرى ويدلّ هذا على وحدة الشعب الشمالي في تنظيمهم وحضارتهم بغض النظر عن اختلاف لغات القوم والتباين في الأديان. يكتشف هذه الوحدة في الطبيعة والعقلية كلّ من له إلمام بالقطر، وهذه القصة مرآة صادقة نرى بها ما لكلّ قرية من سذاجة.

• شريط الربط الجيراني والأسري

حبل آصرة القرابة متين جدًّا بين الشماليين، ويوضح هذا ما حال إليه أمر عبد الله بعد أن ضاقت عليه الأرض بما رحبت وخاف والداه على حياته إثر ما أذاقه منافسوه من ويلات وسقوه مرارة كادت تقضي عليه لما يرون من احتجازه بقبول من أيوكا ولما يناله من المحبّة من هذه الفتاة الحسناء. جاء أحد جيرانه المسمى سعد أثناء مروره بهذه الكدرات المتعبة وأخذه معه إلى لاغوس لعلّه يتنفس هناك ريحًا حرًّا طيّبًا. عرضت هذه الحادثة في الفقرة التالية:

في هذه الآونة الأخيرة التي تتوالى فيها الأحداث بقرية أيغورو، وتتزاحم المفاجآت من كلّ جانب، إذ رجع "سعد" أحد جيران

عبد الله، والذي اتخذ لاغوس مسكنًا، وقد قضى هناك أكثر من عشر سنوات لم تعرف الأسرة من أمره إلّا أنّه يأتيهم على رأس كلّ سنة في ديسمبر في عيد ميلاد المسيح، ويشتري لهم الخبز الطازج والكعك اللذيذ، كما يحمل دائما معه جهاز الشريط المتوسط، معه أشرطة موسيقية صاخبة خليعة، يجتمع حوله الصبيان والفتيان ليستمعوا إلى الأغاني الجديدة، وإن لم يفهموا منها شيئًا.[5]

وعادة تربية الأولاد نيابة عن والديهم الحقيقيين منتشرة في جميع أنحاء شمال نيجريا، والعادة آلة فعالة إيجابية لغرس المحبّة والألفة بين أفراد القطر بصرف النظر عن الاختلاف الدينيّ أو القبلي. قوي عري هذه العادة بين الشعوب المختلفة حتى نشأ بسببه مثل يورباوي القائل (تلد الولد أعين أربعة وتولى رعايته مئتا أعين)، ويعني هذا أنّ مسئولية إرشاد وتربية الناشئين واجبة كلّ أفراد المجتمع. وقد أنتج هذا ودًّا ومحبّةً بين الأمة في هذا الإقليم ذي قبائل متنوعة.

• التديّن وتأثيره في حياة القوم

إنّ عنصر الدين في شمال البلاد وطيد للغاية حتي أنّهم ليؤمنون إيمانًا يكاد يكون جازمًا أن ليس هناك شيء فوق طاقة الدعاء والرجاء. وتديّنهم هذا ذو حدين فيما بينهم؛ حينًا يلعب دورًا إيجابيًا، إذ معتنقو دين معيّن يتحابون بدون أيّ مبالاة بالاختلاف في الشعب، وأحيانًا أخرى يكون دوره سلبيًا لكنّ أدواره الإيجابية تبرز واضحًا كما حدث في شأن عبد الله وأبيه الثاني بلاغوس الذي رزق مولودا —من زوجته التي كانت عقيمًا—ببركة دعاء عبد الله لهما. وإنّ "فنلايو" (أم أيوك)، مثلًا، لا تنظر إلى أيّ تطور إلّا من وجهة نظر الدين كما أنّها لا تتصور أيّ شيء إلّا في صورة مسيحيتها وهي رمز لسلبية الدين، أمّا حتى هي رضيت أخيرًا وتركت وحيدتها تختار لنفسها لكن ليت رضاها أتت في أوان مناسبة!

• الأخوة الإنسانية

إنّ مما يوطد التآلف السلمي في أفراد المجتمع هي الأخوة العريقة بينهم، ومتى ظهر في أيّ شاب ملامح جدٍّ وهمّةٍ يتحمل أيّ محسن عبأ توجيهه، وهذا ما يتبدى فيما حدث لعبد الله بعد أن فوجئ بفراق أخيه الذي أتى به إلى لاغوس. والتالي ما جرى بينهما:

- ما الذي تفعل هنا يا ولد؟ إنه مكان مخيف لا يقف فيه إلّا المجرمون الطغاة، فهل أنت واحد منهم؟

- لا، لا، إنني غريب في هذه المدينة وقد دخلتها أمس، ثم خرجت مع أخي للعمل وأوقفتنا الشرطة، ففررنا منهم، ولم أعرف أين اتجه أخي، كما لا أعرف كيف أحصل عليه.

- من هو اخوك؟ وأين يسكن؟

- إسمه سعد، ولكن لا أعرف مكانه.

- أما قلت إنك معه بالأمس؟

- نعم! ولكن لم أحفظ عنوان المكان.

- هل تثق بي وتذهب معي لعلّ الله يلحقك بأخيك عن قريب؟

- لم أجد مخرجًا غيره، سأتوكّل على الله في الذهاب معكم.

ثم تمتم بقوله تعالى: رَبِّ إِنِّي لِمَا أَنزَلْتَ إِلَيَّ مِنْ خَيْرٍ فَقِيرٌ. ونام في بيت هذا الغني حتى الصباح.[6]

إنّ هذا الرجل الصالح لم يكن يعرف عبد الله مسبقًا لكنّ الأخوة الإنسانية والرحمة الكامنة فيه هي ما أدّى به إلى هذا التطوع في سبيل تحسين حال شاب وجد نفسه في ورطة عسيرة لا يتخلص منها إلّا أن يجد عونًا. الحصول على مثل هذه المساعدة صعب بمكان وأصعب منها الاطمئنان إلى

رجل غريب لكنّ الجوّ السائد في شمال نيجيريا جعل أحداثا مثل هذه شبه عادة، وتربية الأولاد على حسن الظن بالآخرين مما يقوي آصرة الودّ والرضى بين أفراد الشعب وهذا ما جعل هذا الشاب مطمئنًا إلى المساعدة التي أتت من رجل غريب.

دراسة فنيّة للقصة

إنّ العناصر الفنيّة التي يلزم تطبيقها في القصة كعمل أدبي كثيرة لكنّ هذا البحث يتناول ما من شأنه أن يساعد على وضوح البيئة المنتجة ويكون ذلك في الترتيب التالي.

• تصوير القصة لمجتمعها

إنّ القصة – كغيرها من قوالب الأعمال الإبداعية – وليدة العاطفة والشعور من أديب، ومعنى هذا أنّها ثمرة تجربة شعورية يرويها القاص في تعابير موحية مؤثرة، وينطبق على هذه القصة التي تتناولها هذه المقالة بالدراسة صفات عمل إبداعي مستهدف. ومن صفاتها أنّها ''ترجمان الشعوب إذ ترى فيها واقعها بجميع قضاياه ومواقفه وأوضاعه كما ترى فيها صورتها بجميع قسماتها وملامحها.''[7]

وكاتب القصة إذًا يحمّل على عاتقيه عبأ توعية الشعب نحو ما يحسّن التنظيم ويؤكد الأمن والوئام وذلك لأنّ حرصه كأديب هو:

> أن يصل بين نفسه وبين الناس، فهو لا يحس شيئًا إلّا أذاعه ولا يشعر بشيئ إلّا أعلنه، وهو إذا نظر في كتاب أو خرج للتروض، أو تحدث إلى الناس، فأثار شيء من هذا في نفسه خاطرًا من الخواطر، أو بعث في قلبه عاطفة من العواطف، أو حث عقله على الروية والتفكير، لم يسترح ولم يطمئن حتى يقيد هذا الرأي، أو تلك العاطفة أو ذلك الخاطر في دفتر أو على قطعة من القرطاس.[8]

ومعنى هذا كلّه أنّ القصة وثيقة حقيقية ومستند وطيد لأحداث في المجتمع لأنّ منشئ العمل الأدبي لم ينشئه عبثًا بل إنّه يؤدي رسالة ويخاطب القراء ولهذا "لا يوجد الأدباء في الأمة عبثًا، فهم لها هداة الطريق، وهم مرآتها الصافية النقية التي ينبغي أن تصور آلامها وآمالها ومواقفها وكلّ ما حلمت به في الماضي وتحلم به في الحاضر. وإنّ الأديب من أمته، ولها، يذيع أفكارها ومشاعرها وكلّ ما هزّها وأثر فيها من أحداث ظاهرة أو باطنة مستسرة."[9] والعمل العارض من أديب إذا استوفى النعوت المعروضة أعلاه يؤدي إلى تحقق "التعاطف بين البشر، ويكون الإنتاج الفني (من هذا النوع) خطوة تخطوها الإنسانية في ربط عواطفها، وتوحيد أمانيها، وتعميق التفاهم بين أبنائها..."[10] وأنّ القصة التي تتناولها هذه المقالة كُتبت بالعربية وهي تعالج مشاكل إجتماعية و بهذا أصبحت العربية كما قال مرتضى بدماس "آلة إصلاحية وذلك إذا حسن استخدامها"[11] كما استخدمها كاتب القصة.

هذا، وبالنظر الفاحص في القصة يُكتشَف أنّ الكاتب حاول محاولة جديّة في استخدام فنّه للتآلف بين شعبه الشمالي. إنّ تدقيق النظر في العناصر الآتية يُظهر هذا بوضوح:

- **الشخصية**

إنّ اختياره للشخصيات وطريقة تناولهم في القصة رائع بحيث إنّه أعطى كلًّا من الرجال والنساء أدوارهم اللائقة بهم، وإن كان معظم شخصياته ثابتة حتى أيوكا وعبد الله، وقد أحسن في اختيارهم وفي حركاتهم طول القصة وقد لعب كلٌّ أدوارًا ساعدت على سير الأحداث وإبراز الرسالة التي قصد إليها الكاتب.

- **الصراع**

تبنى الكاتب الصراع بين الدين والحبّ إذ إنّ محور الأحداث هو عبد الله المسلم الذي يطلب يد أيوكا للزواج وهذا أمر عادي، وربما يتبادر إلى

الأذهان أنّ الحروب المحليّة التي حدثت بين أيغورو وأبادو ولم تبرد حرارتها تمامًا بعد هي التي تجعل الأم تقف موقفًا مضادًّا لكنّها صرحت أنّها تمقت هذا الأمر مقتًا لا لأيّ شيء سوى الفارق الدينيّ بين أسرتي الحبيبين، ولهذا تقول: ''وماذا أقول لأبيك إذا التقينا لو تزوّجتِ بهذا الرجل الذي لا يدين ديننا ولا يصلي صلاتنا، إنّ أباك مسيحيّ قحّ إيمانًا وعملًا، إنّني لست راضية بعلاقتك مع عبد الله، لم يعجبني في شيء...''12

لكنّ الحبيبين لا يريان مبررا لتحكيم الدين وسيطرته في شأنهما إذا كان يحول بينهما والسعادة، ولذا يقول عبد الله: ''أما تزال أمّك تنوي التفريق بيننا؟ وكأنّها لا تعرف معنى الحبّ الحقيقيّ الذي يحمله قلبانا، إنّها لا تدرك مدى الخطورة في هذا الأمر، الحبّ لا يعرف الدين ولا العُرف ولا العِرق، إنّه فوق كلّ شيء...''13

ومرة أخرى رجحت كفة الحبّ على كفة الشعور الدينيّ لما حاولت جَوَّكيْ–أخت زوجة الرجل الغني–أن تستأثر قلب عبد الله وهي لا تدري أنّه قد وهب قلبه لفتاة أخرى ألا وهي أيوكا التي تسكن في القرية. ولما رأت جوكي الفشل عيانًا وأنّ إله الحب لا يختارها لمحبة عبد الله إذ قد فازت به غيرها مسبقا لجأت إلى مكيدة كادت أن تقضي بها على مروءته لولا أنّ ربّ المنزل أدرك توًّا أنّ الحادثة من كيد النساء، وبعد أن استتب الأمر ألحقه ذلك الرجل بالجامعة حيث درس القانون. وكأنّه خُلِقَ لمكابدة الشدائد لما يعرضه النسوة له من المحبّة لأنّه حتى في الجامعة وجد نفسه في مصيبة جديدة لما ينج منها لولا التدخل الإلهي وذلك لأنّ ''بوسي'' زميلته في الكلية والقسم تُكنّ له محبّة فوق التصوير.

زار المحامي قريته على نداء من قومه بعد أن أكمل الدراسة وأصبحت حاجة قومه ماسة إلى إصلاح الوضع وجلب الحضارة العصرية إلى القرية، استدعاه مجتمعه وكلفوه بتخطيط يؤدي بقريتهم إلى الترقي. وأثناء هذه الزيارة

رأى أيوكا التي تحتفظ بحبّها إياه رغم الصعوبات التي عانتها وحتى حين زُفَّتْ بها إلى رجل من دينها المسيحيّ لم تنشّ عن حبّها الأول. وإن كان الحبّ تغلب أخيرًا على الدين لأنّ فنلايو رضيت ما اختارته ابنتنه وتنزلت عن إصرارها على أن تتزوج أيوكا من مسيحيّ إنقاذًا لوحيدته التي قد أذابها الحزن والكآبة وعلاها الشحوب والنحافة، وهنا وقع صراع آخر قضى على هذا الحبّ الذي عبده كلٌّ من المحبين وهو أنّ الهوة بينهما الآن قد أصبحت عميقة جدًّا من حيث المنزلة الاجتماعية والثقافة، كل هذا لم يسمح لعبد الله أن يرضى بأيوكا شريكة الحياة ولم يجد بدًّا من الرجوع إلى "بوسي" المحامية المسيحية وهي التي انتصرت بالزواج من هذا الشاب الذكي. إنّ وقوع هذه الصدمة على أيوكا لم يكن خفيفا وقد أقعدها الفراش مريضة ولم تبرحه حتى ماتت أخيرًا كمدًا ضحية الحبّ.

• الحبكة

حبكة القصة هي سلسلة الحوادث التي تجري فيها، مرتبطة عادة بربط السببية[14] ومعنى هذا هو أن يكون للطريقة التي بها تناول القاص الشخصيات والحوادث والصور ارتباطٌ بدون أيّ إخلالٍ في عمليته. وتبعًا لهذا يجب عليه أن يكون عمله منسقًا رائعًا حتى لا يملّ القارئ القراءة ويترك قصته في وسط القراءة. وقد حاول هذا الكاتب وأجاد، إنه يحبب القصة إلى القراء من البداية إلى النهاية، نظرًا إلى أسلوب عرضه وطريقة تصويره للأفكار بالإضافة إلى تلوين القصة بالثقافة المحلية التي تشوّق القارئ وتجعله يشعر كأنّه واحد من أفراد القرية التي يقرأ عنها، ومن ذلك قوله: "الولد الذي سأل أبويه: لماذا لم تسعدا؟ فإنّه الآن غارق فيها سيرى كيف تسهل الأمور وتخضع الظروف، والذي يسأل والده: لماذا لا تجيد الطهي؟ يريد أن يسمع قصة طلاق أمّه. ألم تعلم يا أخي الصغير بأنّ الدجاج تتصبب عرقًا لولا أرياشها، هنا ليس سهلًا، والصعود ليس ميسورًا."[15]

وهذا مثلٌ محليٌّ متداول بين شعوب مختلفة في نيجيريا، والعثور على مثله في المكتوبات العربية يزيدها إقبالًا من الناس. والمثل إرشاد للناشئين الذين لا يرون مبررًا لفقر والديهم ويعتقدون أنّ مرجع فقرهم عدم الكياسة وحسن التدبير، وإنّ الأيّام ستبدي للشباب خطأ نظرهم كما سيكتشفون أنّ الغنى لا يتوقف على الكياسة وحسن التدبير بل على التوفيق من الله. والمثل الثاني يوضح أنّ أيّ ولد أبدى عدم رضاه بدسم أعدّه أبوه لعدم اللذة التي يتوقعها يسمع قصة ما من سببه طلق أبوه أمّه أي إذا لم يحترم ولد تضحيّات الوالد في تنشئته وتوجيهه ولا يقدّر مجهودات الأب سوف يسمع حكاية كريهة من الوالد تكشف له العناء التي تجشمه في سبيل نجاحه. ويقول في مكان آخر: "أرأيتم، إذا اصطاد الولد سمكًا يأكله وحده، وإذا قتل أرنبًا يستأثر بملذاته، أما إذا تحصل على جاموس كبير فإنه يأتي به إلى أبويه، نحن لا نمنع ولدا أن يلعب مع المجذوم، إذا أيقن أن يعيش في الغابة وحده."[16]

وأمثال هذه التعبيرات متوفرة في القصة، وهذا من طبيعته يجعلها أكثر لصوقًا بقلب القارئ لأن ذلك يجعله يشعر كأنّه بين قومه في شعبه الخاص وأنّ الحوادث في القصة تجري في مجتمعه.

هذا، وإنّ كاتب هذه القصة سخر كل ما في وسعه في طيّات الحبكة وخرج عمله مرآة اجتماعية تعكس ما يجري في مجتمعه واستطاع بها أن يحيطنا علما بما يهدي إلى أن يعيش أفراد المجتمع عيشة وئامٍ ومحبّةٍ، وبذلك استحق صفة الأديب الناجح وعمله سجل اجتماعي كما قال شوقي ضيف: "وينبغي أن نلاحظ أن من يدرسون الأدب دراسة اجتماعية لا يريدون أن يتبينوا فيه انعكاسات المجتمع فحسب، فتلك بديهية، إنما يريدون أن يتبينوا ما في بيئة الأديب من ظواهر اجتماعية..."[17]

• تعليق

حاول كاتب القصة في غرس الحب بين المجتمع لما أوصت به قصته من اجتناب الأراذل من التصرفات التي تثير الحقد والبغض بين الشعب، إلّا أنّه يُلاحَظ عليه أنّه رجح كفة الرجل على كفة المرأة ولذلك تضحي أيوكا بكلّ ما لديها –حتى بدينها– لتفوز بالزواج من عبد الله ولم تنجح حتى ماتت كمدًا. وكذلك صبرت بوسي طويلا حتى نالت الإقبال من عبد الله أخيرًا. لكن ربّما لا يكون هذا غريبًا إلى المستوى الذي يراه هذا الباحث لأنّ هذا الموقف إزاء النساء عالميّ لأنّها تتصرف وراء الصف حتى في الأمم التي تدّعي أنّها راقية وأنها تمنح حريّة للنساء تساوي ما للرجال.

ويبدو أنّ الكاتب يتعصب للرجال إلى حد يكاد يكون متجاوزًا إذ لم يأت من أية امرأة في القصة تحركات موجهة نحو تحسين المجتمع، إلّا ما حدث من قبل بوسي التي أصرت على مصاحبة عبد الله في الحرم الجامعي مع ما قاست من الصعوبات والتخويف بل والتعذيب لكنّها تحمّلت كل ذلك لغرضٍ وفازت بطلبها أخيرًا.

وقد يعدّ هذا التعصب للذكر من ملامح الوضع قي شمال نيجيريا وأن النساء في الإقليم ليست لهن حرية التصرفات وإلّا لمْ تعرضهن القصة عرضًا أحسن؟ ذلك لأنّ كلّا من فنلايو، وربة المنزل زوجة الرجل الغني، وجوكي، لم تتصرف تصرفًا إيجابيًّا! الشاذة الوحيدة في هذا الصدد هي خادمة البيت التي أفشت بسرٍّ أسرّت به جوكي قبل تشويه عبد الله بتهمة كاذبة. نعم! خففت القصة من الجوّ الساخن الذي يسود العلاقة الوديّة بين الناشئين في الشمال النيجري ويؤدي هذا حقًّا إلى تحسين التآلف بين أفراد الإقليم.

ثمّ إنّه يلاحظ على الكاتب أنّه ربما يحيّر القراء بمن هو بطل القصة الحقيقي. صحيح أنّ عبد الله تجشم شدائد وكابد الصعوبات وحوله تتمحور

الأحداث لكن كيف تموت أيوكا لأجل حبّها لعبد الله ويبقى هو في بحبوحة الحياة؟ وزيادة على ذلك وإنّ القصة مأسوية، وأيوكا هي التي ماتت حزينة لأنها فشلت في بغيتها، إذًا أليست هي البطلة الحقيقية؟

الخاتمة

قد حاولت هذه المقالة أن تلقي ضوءًا على إسهامات الأدب النيجيري المكتوب باللغة العربية في توطيد المحبّة بين الشعب الشمالي بدون النظر إلى اختلافات لغوية أو غيرها. يُستظْهَرُ هذا في القصة حيث المحور الأكبر هو توحيد صفوف الأمّة والنداء إلى ما يساعد على النموّ ويطوّر الحركات التقدمية، وكذا ناشد إلى عدم التشدد الديني الذي يؤدي إلى خصومة ويفرّق المجتمع. وهذه الخطوة التي خطاها كاتب القصة جديدة للغاية وهي من التيّارات الحديثة التي تعومها اللغة العربية في نيجيريا حاليًا. وقد استطاع الكاتب أن يلعب الدور المتوقع من الأديب كما قال شوقي ضيف: "وواجب الأديب حقًّا أن يعيش المشاكل التي تقلق عصره صادرًا في آثاره عن الطبقة التي ينتمي إليها ونفسيتها وكلّ ما يجري فيها من تناقضات وصراعات."[18] وأدبه، بهذه المشاركة والمعايشة وتفسيره للوضع في شعبه، أدبٌ اجتماعي "لأنّ الأدب في حقيقته، ليس إلّا تفسيرٌ للحياة."[19]

الهوامش والمراجع

1. غلادنث، شيخو أحمد، **حركة اللغة العربية في نيجيريا**، الطبعة الثانية، ص-21 25.
2. Jamiu Muhammad Yunusa, Contemporary Arabic Novelist and Social Responsibility: A peep into al-hijiri's al-sayyid al-raees. *Journal of Islamic Studies and Culture*, USA: American Research Institute of Policy Development, V 2, No 1, 2014, p 13.
3. شوقي ضيف، **البحث الأدبي**، مصر، دائرة المعارف، الطبعة الثانية، 1976م، ص 122.

4. حامد محمود إبراهيم الهجري، المرجع السابق،ص 8-9.
5. المرجع نفسه، ص 43.
6. المرجع نفسه، ص 54- 55.
7. شوقي ضيف، **في النقد الأدبي**، القاهرة، دار المعارف، الطبعة التاسعة، ص 223.
8. طه حسين، **أديب**، **مصر**، دار المعارف، 1962م، ص 7.
9. شوقي ضيف، المرجع السابق، ص 191.
10. علي نائبي سويد، كيف **نتذوّق الأدب العربي**،نيجيريا، دار العربية، 1986م، ص 12.
11. مرتضى بدماص، **فاعلية اللغة العربية في نيجيريا**،إجبو أودي، نيجيريا، مطبعة شَيْبِأُوْتِيمَا، الطبعة الثانية، 2014م، ص 8.
12. حامد محمود إبراهيم الهجري، المرجع السابق، ص 15.
13. المرجع نفسه، ص 21.
14. محمد يوسف نجم، **فن القصة**، بيروت، دار بيروت، الطبعة الثالثة،1959م، ص 63.
15. حامد محمود إبراهيم الهجري، المرجع السابق، ص 51.
16. المرجع نفسه، ص 25.
17. شوقي ضيف، **البحث الأدبي**،مصر، دار المعارف، الطبعة الثانية، 1976م، ص 101.
18. المرجع نفسه، ص 102.
19. محمد يوسف نجم، المرجع السابق، ص 64.

Notes on Contributors

- Professor Olu Obafemi teaches in the Department of English, University of Ilorin, Ilorin.
- Dr Abdullahi Salihu Abubakar teaches in the Department of English, University of Ilorin, Ilorin.
- Dr Abdulrazaq Mohammed Katibi teaches in the Department of Languages and Literary Studies, Kwara State University, Malete
- Dr Aliyu Okuta Ahmed teaches in the Department of Languages and Literary Studies, Kwara State University, Malete.
- Dr Hakeem Ọláwálé teaches in the Department of Linguistics and African Languages, Kwara State University, Malete.
- Dr Oluwatomi Adeoti teaches in the Department of English, Kwara State University, Malete.
- Dr Moshood Zakariyah teaches in the Department of English, Kwara State University, Malete.
- Kayode Afolayan teaches in the Department of English, University of Ilorin, Ilorin
- Muhammad Mushin Ibrahim teaches in the Department of Theatre and Performing Arts, Bayero University Kano, Kano.
- Kehinde Akano teaches in the Department of English, Kwara State University, Malete
- Abibah Zaka is a postgraduate student in the Department of English, University of Lagos, Lagos.
- Giwa Garuba teaches in the School of Basic and Remedial Studies, Kwara state College of Education, Ilorin.
- Sarat Adenike Salihu teaches in the Department of English, University of Ilorin, Ilorin
- Sani Abubakar teaches in the Department of English and Literary Studies, Bayero University Kano, Kano.

- Hasheem Abdullahi Tanko teaches at Binyaminu Usman Polytechnic Hadejia, Jigawa State.
- Olushola Ayodeji Akanmode teaches in the University Wide Course Unit, Landmark University, Omu Aran.
- Dr Rabi Abdulsalam Ibrahim teaches in the Department of English and Literary Studies, Bayero University Kano, Kano.
- Dr. Abubakar Othman and Dr. Razinat Mohammed teach in the Department of English, University of Maiduguri, Maiduguri.
- Jubril Abdullahi and Habeeb Adebayo Salaudeen are Postgraduate Students in the Department of Theatre and Performing Arts, Bayero University Kano, Kano
- Anne Omotayo Alaiyemola teaches in the University Wide Courses Directorate, Landmark University, Omu-Aran.
- Dr. Tajudeen Yusuf teaches in the Department of Languages and Literary Studies, Kwara State University, Malete.
- Yunusa Muhammad Jamiu teaches in the Department of Languages and Literary Studies, Kwara State University, Malete.

Index

Abdalla Uba Adamu, 88
Abdul-Azeez Muhammad Salman al-Yāqūtī, 27, 31, 32, 36, 37, 38, 40, 41
Abdullahi Abubakar, 17
Abdulsalami Abubakar, 72
Abomey-Kalavi University, Republic of Benin, 32
Abubakar Gimba, 4, 5, 111, 113, 114, 124, 129, 141, 205
Abuja, 4, 217
Academic and Non-Fiction Authors Association of Nigeria (ANFAAN), 9
Adam al-Ilori, Shaykh, 33, 34, 174
Adamawa, 39
Aderemi Bamikunle, 5
Àfọ̀njá Ààrẹ-Ọ̀nà-Kakaǹfò, 50
Afrobeat, 57, 61
Agbojulogun, 17
Ahmadu Bello, Sir, ix, 2, 5, 36, 150, 220, 228
Ahmadu Bello University, 5, 150, 220, 228
Ahmed Maiwada, 5, 208
Aisha Zakary, 5
Alhaji Sulu Gambari, 107
Aliyu Kamal, xiv, 127, 128, 137, 139, 208
   Hausa Girl of, 127–137
   Hausaland of, 141–148
Almajiri/Almajirai, 29, 30, 118, 120, 121, 123, 184, 190, 191, 192, 193, 194, 195

American films, 87, 90
Aminu Kano, 2
Anti-graft, 21, 105
Arewa Consultative Forum (ACF), 28
Association of Nigerian Authors (ANA), 4, 5
Audee T. Giwa, 5
Auwalu Yusufu Hamza, 183, 184
Awards, 3
   BET, 61
   Channel O Music Video, 61
   Headies, 61
   KORA, 61
   MOBO, 61
   MTV Africa Music, 61
   MTV Europe Music, 61
   World Music, 61
Awolowo, Chief, 2, 125

Baobab tree, 149
Bawa Ruling House of Ilorin, 53
Bayero University, Kano, xi, 1, 5, 142, 175, 269, 270
Beijing, 215
Benue, 60, 214
Bernth Lindfors, 3
BET Award, 61
Biafra, 73
Binta Salma Mohammed, 5
Birnin Kebbi, 111
Boko Haram, 14
Bollywood films, 87, 88, 89, 90, 93, 97, 98
British protectorate, 27

Charles Bodunde, 5, 80
China, 215
Chinua Achebe, 6, 112, 131, 138, 172, 174, 201
Christopher Okigbo, 71
City University, 184
Co-existence, xiii, 54, 55, 65, 111, 167, 169, 236, 243
Crispin Oduobuk, 5
Cultural diversity, 175
Cultural values, 188, 190, 194, 217, 229, 236, 239

Dadakuada, 5, 101, 102
Dandali, 5, 8
Danladi, 28, 30, 41
Dan Mairaya, 172
Daura, 143, 201
Dele Giwa, 72
Denja Abdullahi, 5
Dramatic heatre, xiii, 12, 23
Dramatic theatre, 11, 13
Dzukogi, B. M., 5, 208

Egalitarianism, 16
Eid-el-Fitri, 49
Emirs, 31, 37, 45, 47, 49, 51, 52, 53, 107

Federal Radio Corporation of Nigeria (FRCN), 4
Film adaptations, 88–98. *See also* Hindi films adapted into Hausa
Film industries, 85, 86, 88, 89, 93, 94, 96, 97, 98. *See also* Bollywood films, Hollywood films, Kannywood films, Nollywood films

Filmmakers, 87, 89, 93
Films, 85, 86, 87, 88, 89, 90, 91, 92, 93, 94, 96, 97, 98
  American, 87, 90
  Bollywood, 87, 88, 89, 90, 92, 93, 97, 98
  Hausa video, 135
  Hindi, 88, 89, 90, 91, 92
  Hollywood, 87, 88, 92, 93, 94, 96
  Indian, 89, 90, 93
  Kannywood, 85, 88, 89, 90, 92, 93, 94, 96, 97, 98
  Korean, 88
  Nollywood, 92, 94, 98
Funk, 57

Gabriel Okara, 172
Ghana-Must-Go, 6

Hadiza Amapa, 5
Halima Sekula, 5
Hamid Ibraheem al-Hijry, xiv, 253
Haruna Ishola, 172
Hausa Television Drama, 9
Hauwa Kassam, 5
Headies Awards, 61
Helon Habila, 4, 5, 208
Highlife, 57
Hindi films, 88, 89, 90, 91, 92
Hindi films adapted into Hausa, 88–98
Hip-hop, 57, 61
Hip-hop Award. *See* Awards, Headies
Hollywood films, 87, 88, 93, 94, 96
Human Rights, Universal Declaration of, 215

Ibadan, 25, 84, 107, 109, 110, 125,

138, 175, 176, 177, 178, 179, 180, 182, 211
Ibrahim Babangida, 72
Ibrahim Malumfashi, 5
Ibrahim Sheme, 5
Ilorin, ix, x, xiii, 1, 5, 24, 25, 31, 32, 34, 40, 41, 43, 44, 45, 46, 47, 48, 49, 50, 51, 52, 53, 54, 100, 103, 107, 146, 181, 241, 242, 243, 269
   Emirate of, 44–46
   Emirs of, 31, 45, 47, 48, 49, 51, 52, 53, 54, 107
   traditional songs of, 46–54
Indian films, 89, 90, 93
Integration
   cultural, 179–180
   Hamid Ibraheem al-Hijry's Ma'satul Hubb on, 253–267
   national, 171–175
   prose and drama play for, 174
   regional, 177–178
   social, 178–179
   traditional songs for, 43–54
Isiaka Aliagan, 5
Ismail Garba, 5
Issa Alabi Abubakar, 243

Jaigbade Alao, ix, 47, 53, 55, 103
Jeremy Bentham, 12
Jihad, 111, 143, 146
John Pepper Clark, 71
Jos riot, 111
Juju, 57

Kaduna uprising, 111
Kannywood, x
Kannywood films, 85, 88, 89, 90, 92, 93, 94, 96, 97, 98

Kano, xi, 1, 4, 5, 32, 88, 91, 94, 141, 142, 143, 145, 146, 150, 175, 176, 180, 181, 184, 269, 270
Ken Saro Wiwa, 73
King Korar, 145
King Lamba, 144, 145
Kogi, 151
KORA Award, 61
Korean films, 88
Kwara, ix, x, xi, xiii, 1, 31, 32, 34, 44, 45, 102, 107, 108, 269, 270
Kwara State University, xi, xiii, 1, 269, 270

Libyan University, 34
Literary Society of Nigeria (LSN), 9
Lizi Ashimole, 5
Lokoja, 4

Maiduguri, 4, 270
Makurdi, 4
Mamman Vatsa, 5, 72
Maria Ajima, 5
Masud Abdulkadir, 5
Military regimes, 72, 73, 75, 78, 79, 82
Minna, 4
MOBO Award, 61
Mohammadu Buhari, 72
Moshood Abiola, 72
MTV Africa Music Awards, 61
MTV Europe Music Award, 61
Mujahideen, 119, 121
Murja Iro, 5

Nana Embaga, 5
Nasarawa, 32, 39

Nasarawa State University, 32
National integration, 171–175
National Tribune, 72
National Youth Service Corps (NYSC), 32
Nereus Tadi, 5
NGO 2Face Idibia Reach-out Foundation, 61
Niger Delta, 73, 108
Niyi Osundare, 71, 72
Nollywood films, 4, 94, 98
Northernism, xiii, 27, 28, 31, 34, 40, 41
Northern Nigeria Development Company (NNDC), 28
Northern Nigerian Literature, xi, 1, 27, 197, 203, 207
  woman in, 197–212
Northern Nigerian Publishing Company, 3, 25
Northern People's Congress (NPC), 28
Northern Protectorate, 2

Ọba Aliyu, 53
Odoh Diego Okenyodo, 5
Odolaye Aremu, xiv, 99, 100, 101, 102, 103, 104, 105, 109
  songs of exorcism, 99–110
Okunland, 151, 152, 153, 154, 169, 238
  women's roles in, 153–156, 165–169. See also traditional weddings
Oliver De Coque, 172
Olu Obafemi, xiii, 1, 4, 14, 84, 110, 113, 174, 269
Oral literature, 52, 68, 112, 128, 132, 138
Oral tradition, x, 43, 127, 128, 130

Oyo, 175
Oyo kingdom, 151

Plateau, ix, 39, 60
Premier of Northern Nigeria, 36
Press freedom, 72

Radio Kaduna, 9
Ramadan, 31, 48
Rap, 57
Rasheed Oniyangi, 5
R&B, 57
Readers' Association of Nigeria (RAN), 9
Reggae, 61
Republic of Benin, 33, 34, 40
Rights of expression, 72
River Niger, 151
Rock, 57

Samaru Writers' Club, 4
Sanni Abacha, 72
Sardauna of Sokoto, 36
Sokoto, x, 4, 30, 45, 49, 54, 119, 150, 217
Sokoto Caliphate, 30, 45, 217
Songs of exorcism, 99–110
Southern Protectorate, 2
Structural Adjustment Program (SAP), 77
Sunday Ododo, 5

Tarawih, 48
Terrorism, xiv, 108, 207, 243
  war against, 243–251
Traditional music, 101
Traditional songs, xiii, 43–54. See also wedding songs
Traditional weddings, 47, 152, 154–163, 165, 166, 169

Tsenongo, 5
Tunde Olusunle, 5

University of Ibadan, 176, 178
Usman Dan Fodio, 143, 217
Utilitarianism, 12, 13, 15, 16, 25, 131

Victoria Kankara, 5

Wakilin Agwatashi, 39
Wakilin Lantang, 39
War Against Indiscipline (WAI), 78
War against terrorism in Issa Alabi Abubakar's Assubaa'iyyat, 243–251
Wedding songs, 156, 156–164. *See also* traditional songs
Wole Soyinka, 6, 28, 41, 71, 73, 80, 83, 84, 113, 172, 173, 174, 182
Woman in Northern Nigerian literature, 197–212
Women, Convention on the Elimination of all forms of Discrimination against, (CEDAW), 215
Women empowerment in Northern Nigeria, 213–227
Women's roles in Okunland, 153–156, 165–169. *See also* traditional weddings
World Music Award, 61

Yahaya Dangana, 4
Yakubu Nasidi, 5
Yeats, W. B., 12
Yusuf Adamu, 5

Zakat, 148

Zamfara State, 32
Zaria, 5, 25, 138, 139, 143, 150, 212, 220, 227, 228
Zaynab Alkali, 3, 4, 129, 141, 195, 203, 205, 212

www.ingramcontent.com/pod-product-compliance
Lightning Source LLC
Chambersburg PA
CBHW061708300426
44115CB00014B/2599